ETHICS FOR DIGITAL JOURNALISTS

The rapid growth of online media has led to new complications in journalism ethics and practice. While traditional ethical principles may not fundamentally change when information is disseminated online, applying them across platforms has become more challenging as new kinds of interactions develop between journalists and audiences.

In *Ethics for Digital Journalists*, Lawrie Zion and David Craig draw together the international expertise and experience of journalists and scholars who have all been part of the process of shaping best practices in digital journalism. Drawing on contemporary events and controversies like the Boston Marathon bombing and the Arab Spring, the authors examine emerging best practices in everything from transparency and verification to aggregation, collaboration, live blogging, tweeting, and the challenges of digital narratives. At a time when questions of ethics and practice are challenged and subject to intense debate, this book is designed to provide students and practitioners with the insights and skills to realize their potential as professionals.

Lawrie Zion is an Associate Professor of Journalism at La Trobe University in Melbourne, Australia, and editor-in-chief of the online magazine *upstart*. He has worked as a broadcaster with the Australian Broadcasting Corporation and as a film journalist for a range of print publications. He wrote and researched the 2007 documentary *The Sounds of Aus*, which tells the story of the Australian accent.

David Craig is a Professor of Journalism and Associate Dean at the University of Oklahoma in the United States. A former newspaper copy editor, he is the author of *Excellence in Online Journalism: Exploring Current Practices in an Evolving Environment* and *The Ethics of the Story: Using Narrative Techniques Responsibly in Journalism*.

ETHICS FOR DIGITAL JOURNALISTS

Emerging Best Practices

Edited by Lawrie Zion and David Craig

Routledge
Taylor & Francis Group

NEW YORK AND LONDON

First published 2015
by Routledge
711 Third Avenue, New York, NY 10017

and by Routledge
2 Park Square, Milton Park, Abingdon, Oxon OX14 4RN

Routledge is an imprint of the Taylor & Francis Group, an informa business

Library of Congress Cataloging-in-Publication Data
Ethics for digital journalists : emerging best practices / edited by Lawrie Zion
    and David Craig.
        pages cm
    Includes bibliographical references and index.
    1. Journalistic ethics. 2. Journalism—History—21st century. I. Zion,
Lawrie, editor. II. Craig, David, 1960– editor.
    PN4756.E815 2014
    174'.907—dc23
    2014012433

ISBN: 978-0-415-85884-7 (hbk)
ISBN: 978-0-415-85885-4 (pbk)
ISBN: 978-0-203-70256-7 (ebk)

Typeset in Bembo
by Apex CoVantage, LLC

CONTENTS

FIGURES

PREFACE

A headline on a blog post says a lot about what we hope this book will do for journalism students and journalists. As we were editing chapters from our contributors, Steve Buttry, then digital transformation editor for Digital First Media, was writing this: "Journalism ethics conversation needs one more thing: Detailed situational advice." Current discussions about ethical principles, he said, need to be accompanied by in-depth guidance on how to put them into practice. This book offers that kind of advice by media scholars from seven countries, all of them with a foot in digital and social media themselves and an understanding of the issues reshaping journalism.

The frame for the discussion is the idea of best practices. All of us writing are well aware that what's best is hotly debated in digital media—and that it will look different in different parts of the world and will continue to evolve over time. But talking about best practices can help to foster journalism that is of excellent quality and welcomes the contributions of both professionals and public. In Chapter 1, Lawrie Zion lays a foundation by examining the concept of best practices and how it relates to the development of digital journalism.

The book also connects best practices to ethics. In Chapter 2, David Craig looks at how three ethical perspectives—duty, virtue, and care—are relevant to the daily work of digital journalism. The chapter shows how these perspectives are connected with both scholarly thinking and the ways journalists and journalism organizations pursue excellent work. These frameworks of ethics provide a basis for readers to think about the issues raised in the rest of the book. In the final chapter of the introductory section of the book, Chapter 3, Ansgard Heinrich places discussion of best practices in the context of the global network of information flow that provides new opportunities for excellent journalism but presents significant challenges, as well.

The rest of the book examines best practices across a wide range of issues relevant to the daily work of digital journalists. In Chapter 4, Stephen J. A. Ward shows how transparency—a hot issue in digital journalism and an important value—is sometimes embraced without sufficient consideration about what it actually contributes in relation to other ethical principles. In Chapter 5, Alfred Hermida suggests several approaches to the sticky challenges of verifying information when it is flowing constantly in the digital network through social media users and others.

Juliette De Maeyer writes in Chapter 6 about best practices in linking, one of the fundamental features of digital presentation. Fiona Martin looks at aggregation—one of the most controversial areas in digital journalism—in Chapter 7 and offers detailed advice about doing "curatorial journalism" ethically. Chapter 8 (Neil Thurman) and Chapter 9 (Jonathan Hewett) discuss the evolving practices of live blogging and tweeting. In Chapter 10, Tim Currie discusses the ethics of what happens when things don't go right and mistakes have to be corrected.

Chapters 11 and 12 focus on elements of engagement with citizens. Lily Canter navigates the ethics of collaboration, and David Domingo focuses on fostering constructive engagement through online comments. In Chapter 13, Kelly Fincham examines best practices for navigating the ambiguous borders between the public and private self on social media.

Multimedia, a key dimension of online storytelling, is the subject of Chapter 14. Mindy McAdams looks at best practices in several areas including interactivity, animation, and navigation. In Chapter 15, Paul Bradshaw discusses another continually evolving area, data journalism, around a number of issues including accuracy, context, and privacy.

Each chapter in this book is designed to encourage discussion and application. Each one closes with a case study of "best practices in action" related to the chapter topic and a series of discussion questions. The focus on discussion underlines the fact that everyone reading this has a stake in thinking about what the best means in the open, collaborative environment of digital journalism.

Lawrie Zion
Melbourne, Australia

David Craig
Norman, Oklahoma, USA

ACKNOWLEDGMENTS

The authors would like to acknowledge the International Symposium for Online Journalism in Austin, Texas, which provided a forum for the paper presented by Lawrie Zion that was the genesis of this book in April 2012.

We would also like to acknowledge the wonderful support this project has received from Erica Wetter, who commissioned the book, and from her colleague Simon Jacobs at Routledge in New York, who have guided the book through all of its stages.

Thanks too to our colleagues at La Trobe University in Melbourne, Australia, and the University of Oklahoma in Norman for providing supportive environments for this book to evolve through conversations with our students and colleagues.

And we'd also like to express our appreciation to the 13 other contributors from seven countries whose chapters follow in the pages ahead.

1

WHY BEST PRACTICES?

Lawrie Zion

LA TROBE UNIVERSITY, MELBOURNE, AUSTRALIA

This book is about how journalists and journalism can realize their potential at a time of enormous change. It is a contribution to developing debates about the crisis of journalism—a crisis not just of business models or technologies, but also one of ethics. But the book also aims to point forward by examining how journalism might actually be improved by the changes that are transforming it as a profession and a practice. Amid the chaos stemming from both the collapse of the traditional business model for print journalism and the explosion of digital media, many practitioners are addressing questions about how journalism's mission to inform, enlighten, and entertain might be renewed in more open and collaborative ways.

This project, which features contributions from 15 academics and journalists from seven countries, is itself designed to be an example of this collaboration. It begins with an examination of the utility of the concept of "best practices" as a framing device for the application of ethical principles and for dealing with the practical challenges that have arisen in the wake of changes to journalism practice. It also discusses how the process of exploring emerging best practices might make journalism more open and accountable.

The book will explore themes of emerging best practices as they relate to network journalism sphere, transparency, verification, links and attribution, aggregation and curation, live blogging and tweeting, corrections and unpublishing, collaboration, moderation and audience participation, the private and public self on social media, and the challenges of multimedia storytelling and data journalism.

It will examine these topics by illuminating some of the new kinds of relationships being forged between individuals and organizations producing media and their audiences, and providing case studies that illustrate how emerging best practices in digital journalism can enhance the application of ethical principles and lead to better journalism.

Best Practices

> Question: Is it true, as one respondent confidently asserted, "If it's fact-checked, it's not a blog," and is this an existential or a definitional question? The issue is an important one because so many in the blogosphere insist that blogs have (and are entitled to) their own rules of the road. Subject for discussion: Why have earlier attempts at standardizing the world of blogs and social media notoriously failed? Is it, at long last, possible to identify best practices for using the tools and techniques of digital journalism?
>
> (Navasky and Lerner 2010, 42)

The term "best practices" has emerged relatively recently in discussions about journalism. But its origins can be traced back almost a century to Frederick Taylor's 1911 book *The Principles of Scientific Management* (Taylor 1911) where he stated that "among the various methods and implements used in each element of each trade there is always one method and one implement which is quicker and better than any of the rest" (quoted in King 2007). This came to be called "one best way" (King 2007).

While the private sector and management provide one trajectory for the history of the term, another origin for "best practice" comes from the very different area of agricultural extension where research-based innovations in the United States were promoted at the county and state level early in the 20th century (King 2007; McKeon 1998).

The term has since gained currency in a broad range of professional fields including law, medicine, management, education, information technology, immigration, public policy, and in the nongovernmental organization (NGO) sphere (McKeon 1998; Bendixsen and de Guchteneire 2003) and continues to be used widely in diverse contexts (King 2007). UNESCO's International Migration program, which ran its own best practices project to realize its goal of promoting human rights for migrants, defines best practices as "successful initiatives which have a demonstrable and tangible impact on improving people's quality of life." Best practice activities, it is suggested, have the potential for replication, can lead to other ideas, and can inspire policy development and initiatives elsewhere (UNESCO 2014). Other "best practices" definitions include "a set of guidelines, ethics or ideas that represent the most efficient or prudent course of action" (Investopedia 2013) and "an industry accepted way of doing something that works" (itSMF Australia 2013).

This book is based in part on the assumption that the speed of changes in journalism practice and the emergence of new kinds of journalism in the digital sphere necessitate new approaches to exploring and developing standards and guidelines within the media sphere, and that some of the approaches to this, to be discussed below, show a promising start.

But first it's useful to note how the issue of adopting best practices has been approached in another area. Writing about education, Denise McKeon (1998) suggests three approaches to strengthening the efficacy of best practices. The first of these, she argues, is to develop an exploratory framework:

> The one-size fits all approach to best practice does not usually work in medicine or law, and it is not likely to work in education, either. Therefore, what is more likely to work in education (as in medicine or law) is a more generative approach to the concept of best practice—with teachers asking questions, exploring the research, making educated guesses about the models that are most likely to fill the bill, trying those models, and observing the effect those models have on their classes and their practice.
>
> (498)

Second, McKeon advocates ensuring collaboration between researchers and practitioners.

> Could a collaborative research and development system be constructed in education? Could it include teachers as colleagues and partners in the research and development enterprise? Could it permit both formal research and practical inquiry (research conducted by practitioners to help them understand their contexts, practices, and students)? There is evidence to suggest that it could.
>
> (499)

Her final consideration in strengthening best practices in education is the importance of the dissemination or diffusion function. "Once there is some agreement about what constitutes best practice, how does that knowledge make its way to the people who need it most?" This is a particularly pertinent issue in the case of digital media, with so much now being published outside of the traditional professional domain of journalism.

Critiques of best practices also point to some of the challenges and limitations inherent in any attempt to develop useful outcomes. A 2007 policy brief focusing on best practice approaches by the Network for International Policies and Cooperation in Education and Training stressed that best practices

> are not fruits just waiting to be plucked. They need to be re-potted, grafted, and reworked for different soil conditions. . . . Our authors acknowledge that there is potentially good practice or best practice, but these can't just be borrowed and mainstreamed. Or if there is borrowing, there needs to be an awareness of the culture, "chemistry", history, and political economy of the education system that produced the innovation, as well as a recognition

of the learning and adapting that has to take place, if these practices are to be effectively embedded in a new context. This is not just a requirement for a handful of policy-makers but for education communities more generally.

(Network for International Policies and Cooperation in Education and Training 2007)

Best Practices in Digital Journalism

How might these considerations apply in the context of the media? A new set of problems arising simultaneously due to rapid technological developments and the emergence of new practices in everything from blogging to user-generated content, verification, correcting errors, and hyperlinking has created confusion, and in some cases, exasperation on a wide scale. Take linking for instance, which is the subject of Chapter 6. It's one thing to affirm the need to acknowledge sources, but how might this best be done using hyperlinks? What kinds of information require linking? What should you link to? Traditional ethics codes remain an important foundation for thinking about journalism, but can be hard to apply in emerging terrain.

Linking is just one of many best practice issues to be explored in this book. That the term "best practices" has turned up only relatively recently in discussions about journalism might be in part because of factors associated with the professional identity of journalists (including some resistance to being seen as "professionals"). As Ivor Shapiro suggests:

the lack of a widely recognized framework for assessing quality or excellence in journalism amounts to a fog of aspiration whose origins presumably lie in journalism's historically feisty culture, which is largely hostile to corporate or institutional concepts such as "quality assurance" or even "best practices."

(Shapiro 2010, 145)

Codes of ethics, Shapiro argues, "have been accepted, sometimes reluctantly, as a bulwark against abuses or against perceived threats to credibility, but words like "standards" raise the specter of journalism becoming a "profession"—a term associated, for some, with government-imposed collective self-regulation and with diminished individual autonomy and innovation." By contrast to doctors, lawyers, engineers and other professionals, "journalists, scholars of journalism, and others with interest in the field lack a common evaluative lexicon. This hermeneutic gap cannot but make a difference to quality in practice" (Shapiro 2010, 145).

But this is changing as journalists and scholars have continued to wrestle with the challenges of a rapidly evolving mediascape. The term "best practices" has been used—apparently at least partly coincidentally—in a number of recent initiatives involving the application of ethical principles online, as well as in discussions of how to optimize the capacities of technological innovations.

In a study I undertook for a paper presented at the 2012 International Symposium on Online Journalism (Zion 2012a) which is the genesis of this book, I examined a number of best practice initiatives undertaken by media organizations, including the American University's Center for Media & Social Impact formerly known as the Center for Social Media. One of the conclusions of its report "Scan and Analysis of Best Practices in Digital Journalism in and Outside U.S. Public Broadcasting" was that "Although the nature of technology, audiences, and journalism itself continues to change, recent reports . . . begin to suggest a set of emerging best practices, principles, and norms that can guide how public broadcasting outlets and producers adapt to the digital landscape." The term "best practices," it points out, is "more than a buzz phrase":

> In any professional sector or industry, researchers commonly identify a set of activities, principles, themes, norms, or routines that appear to aid industry members in meeting common challenges or achieving shared goals. Best practices are intended to be generalizable across organizations and settings, though the decision to adopt any recommended activity will depend on the needs, resources, and goals of a particular organization.
>
> (Aufderheide et al. 2009)

Another Center for Media & Social Impact report, "Copyright, Free Speech, and the Public's Right Know: How Journalists Think About Fair Use," found that journalists are facing ever-greater challenges to applying the doctrine of fair use in daily life, in part because of confusions associated with the growth of digital media. "Social media, video, and user-generated content pose new challenges and unfamiliar choices. Online aggregators, bloggers and citizen journalists copy original material and further destabilize business models" (Aufderheide and Jaszi 2012).

The report concluded that

> until journalists establish their own best practices in fair use, journalists and their institutions and gatekeepers will continue to be haunted by fear, letting unfounded risk-management calculations substitute for a clear understanding of what is normal and appropriate in employment of fair use. As new opportunities develop with the evolution of digital culture, the very mission of journalism is at stake.

Another organization that has been proactively developing best practices initiatives in response to the evolution of digital media is the Canadian Association of Journalists. In 2010 it published "The Ethics of Unpublishing" report, which offered guidelines on the issues of correcting online content and handling public requests to "unpublish" material (English, Currie, and Link 2010).

This is significant because the capacity to "unpublish"—that is, to remove material from a website—is something that was not possible in the print era, and traditional ethical codes don't really equip publishers with guidance about circumstances in which it might be considered ethical to unpublish. Further complicating the issue is that while it's technically simple for an editor or blogger to erase content from a specific site, this does not eliminate the many echoes that may exist all over the web on search engines, blogs, and news sites (Fisher 2010).

This report's recommendations, to be discussed further in Tim Currie's chapter, were underpinned by three key unpublishing principles that became the basis of a subsequent report on best practices in digital accuracy and correction, which began with the suggestion that while the principles outlined in its unpublishing report all reinforce normative ethical practices, they also raise some "relatively new issues." These are:

- Is there a difference between corrections and updates to digital content in a 24/7 publishing cycle?
- When digital content requires an update, amendment or correction, should changes be made to in the article text and the content republished, or . . .
- Does transparency demand that corrections note are appended to tell audiences when content has been updated/amended/corrected?
- Should corrective notes explicitly acknowledge the changes made to content?
- Are varied measures of corrective action required, depending on the nature of the error?
- How do news organizations ensure consistency across publishing platforms as information is updated, amended and corrected?

(English 2011)

This is just one example of how new technological advances lead to discussions of best practices in journalism. In my 2012 study I found that the best practice initiatives I had analyzed shared most of the following characteristics. They:

- Identified emerging situations—in each instance the case studies are attempted to address moving targets.
- Shared findings—the guidelines, and in all cases here, the rationale behind them, are accessible by the public.
- Foster collaboration—none of these projects could have been realized solely through the expertise of a single group.
- Suggested rather than prescribed—problems were addressed and discussed rather than solved.
- Consulted—all of these projects used expertise and engagement with communities to develop guidelines.

- Enhanced media literacy—the reports were designed to provide guidelines to journalists and other content producers that will improve interactions with their users/audiences.
- Regenerated—the case studies connected back to the practices linked to tradition by exploring emerging practices.

(Zion 2012a)

We can also see here how the approaches of the Center for Media & Social Impact and the Canadian Association of Journalists are in keeping with McKeon's suggestion that "best practices" can best be realized if they are envisaged as generative, collaborative, and broadly diffused and disseminated. In this respect they are different from many codes of practice or ethics that are intended for members of specific organizations.

Another noteworthy development is the newly established Tow Center for Digital Journalism's $2 million research initiative "to study best practices in digital reporting." Announcing the initiative in 2012, Center Director Emily Bell explained:

> We are focusing on funding research projects which relate to the transparency of public information and its intersection with journalism, research into what might broadly be termed data journalism, and the third area of "impact" or, more simply put, what works and what doesn't.
>
> (Bell 2012)

The discussion about what works and what doesn't has also been developing elsewhere. Iyer (2010), for instance, suggests that the decline of print means that a best practice culture is more likely to evolve in an online environment:

> Best practice has a good reason to exist under normal circumstances, outside of the journalism of prize-winning efforts. It does not need the incentive of accolades to prevail. But it does need some groundwork: it can only survive within an organizational culture of excellence.... [Websites] ... are benefiting from increased competition. It is quite likely that best practice definitions will emerge from them.
>
> (Iyer 2010, 31)

It's not simply a matter of competition. An array of niche websites discussing the changing journalism landscape is constantly engaged with discussions about best practice issues. These include PBS Mediashift, 10,000 Words, Reportr.net, Nieman Journalism Lab, and Poynter.

In late 2012 the Tow Center released "Post-Industrial Journalism: Adapting to the Present," which discusses the skills, structures, and systems now needed to provide the best chance of creating good journalism (Anderson, Bell, and Shirky 2012). The report emphasizes five core beliefs:

- Journalism matters.
- Good journalism has always been subsidized.
- The internet wrecks advertising subsidy.
- Restructuring is, therefore, a forced move.
- *There are many opportunities for doing good work in new ways.* (Emphasis in the original.) Here, the authors argue that "If you believe that journalism matters, and that there is no solution to the crisis, then the only way to get the journalism we need in the current environment is to take advantage of new possibilities." They go on to suggest that "the most exciting and transformative aspect of the current news environment is taking advantage of new forms of collaboration, new analytic tools and sources of data, and new ways of communicating what matters to the public."

The report concludes: "The past 15 years have seen an explosion of new tools and techniques, and, more importantly, new assumptions and expectations, and these changes have wrecked the old clarity."

This wrecked clarity extends to journalism ethics in two main respects. First, new kinds of journalism practice spawned by technological innovation often aren't covered by traditional codes. It is one thing to acknowledge the traditional ethical imperative of correcting errors; quite another to gauge how this might be achieved across of a range of digital practices.

The other ethical conundrum stems from the increasing volume of journalistic content being produced and disseminated by people who do not identify as journalists and whose practices often take place outside of the kinds of institutional and professional milieus within which codes of ethics were developed. As Stephen Ward argues elsewhere: "a once-dominant traditional ethics, constructed for professional journalism a century ago, are being questioned. Journalism ethics is a field where old and new values clash" (Ward 2011b). In his book *Ethics and the Media* (2011a), he suggests that the changes go to the core of media ethics:

> The challenge runs deeper than debates about one or another principle, such as objectivity. The challenge is greater than specific problems, such as how newsrooms can verify content from citizens. The revolution requires us to rethink assumptions. What can ethics *mean* for a profession that must provide instant news and analysis; where everyone with a modem is a publisher?
> (p. 208)

Ward is not alone in emphasizing the significance of this development. As Jay Rosen put it to a group of Australian journalism educators at Sydney University: "What we need to do is completely explode the question of ethics, so that it includes new actors like bloggers and citizen journalists" (Rosen 2010). For Rosen, ethics are "the practices that lead to trust on the platforms where users actually are. That's what we should care about. How can we find them, and refine them and teach them to people?" (Rosen 2010).

One premise of this book is that the development of best practices initiatives could facilitate different ways of thinking about ethics in the senses that Rosen and Ward identify above. The pursuit of best practices in digital media is conceptually related to three emphases in ethical thought—duty, virtue, and care—that will be discussed in more detail in the next chapter by this book's co-editor, David Craig. These concepts provide ways to frame discussions of best practices that connect both with scholarship in media ethics and the reality of how journalists and news organizations have discussed and pursued excellence. The concepts, while rooted in a long history of ethics scholarship, are relevant to the transforming world of digital media in which both professionals and public play a key role.

One issue with the term "best practices" is the potential for conceptual confusion. Could it be that this is just another way of saying "ethics"? To quote Ward again: "Ethics is sometimes identified with an inflexible set of rules and self-righteous moralizing. It is said that rules are rules—an action is either right or wrong. It either breaks a rule or it doesn't. This view over-simplifies ethical thinking" (Ward 2012).

But perhaps one advantage of "best practices" is that it circumvents this potential misconception. Tonally, the term "best practices" is normative without seeming too prescriptive. And perhaps this open-endedness of the term is not a bad thing. The web is crawling with sites claiming to provide lists of "best practices" that don't necessarily imply ethical behavior or ethical content—the term can relate to questions of efficiency, expediency, and commercial considerations of market share—see, for instance, Facebook's best practice guide for journalists (Lavrusik and Cameron 2011), or "6 Best Practices for Modern SEO" (Everhart 2011), which, like many other posts on the popular site Mashable, points users to what are claimed to be the most effective ways to enhance their visibility online.

Yet the content of these posts exploring best practices in the nonethical sense of the term isn't necessarily incompatible with the quest to enhance ethical practice. Indeed, perhaps the blurring of the different connotations of the term "best practices" could help synergize elements of ethics and efficiency. For bloggers and other content producers who are not professional journalists, the term "best practices" may be more tangible than "ethics," but by following "best practice" principles, all kinds of practitioners also contribute to more ethical outcomes. Think of a blogger publishing material about how best to attribute sources. Won't she be more effective in sharing her views with a broader audience if she understands which keywords to embed in her URL, or what hashtag to include with her tweet about the article, or what tags will enhance searchability?

This isn't a call to dumb down ethics, but rather to open them up and broaden the discussion about realizing the potential of digital media at a time when most people publishing content online have no training in or professional experience of mainstream journalism. Writing about ethics codes and privacy in the digital media age, Ginny Whitehouse concludes that "citizen journalists, bloggers, and even those making comments on mainstream news pages do not have the same expectation to follow journalism ethics codes" (Whitehouse 2010, 324). But, she argues, if these standards can be embedded into journalism practice, "then expectations about privacy and nonmainstream digital forums might be strengthened" (p. 324).

Even established journalists must grapple with the fact that traditional codes often lag behind media practices, especially when content is produced outside of the institutional norms, processes, and structures of traditional media. Therefore, notions of "ethics" become difficult to operationalize without ongoing explorations of emerging best practices. This book is an attempt to contribute to those explorations.

Building such a framework of thinking requires us to recognize what kinds of initiatives are pointing forward through their approaches to both technology and ethics. In other words, how can these practices be put into action? The case study that follows provides one possible example.

Best Practices in Action: *The Conversation*

The Conversation (http://theconversation.edu/au) is an Australian-based publication that examines issues in the news by harnessing academic expertise. It is also an interesting incubator of emerging best practices in digital media. Since launching in March 2011 it has built a readership of 1.5 million unique visitors a month in Australia alone with a subsequent reach through Creative Commons republications of 5 million unique page views (The Conversation 2014); 87 percent of all articles are republished elsewhere, with 8,000 websites having republished the site's content. (The Conversation 2014). And many of the 10,000 academics registered with the site (including this author) have found new audiences for their ideas and analysis—around 80 percent of the readership are nonacademics.

For its first two years, it was wholly based in Australia. But since mid-2013 a UK edition of the site has also been operating at http://theconversation.com/uk. In both countries, The Conversation is a not-for-profit that is mostly funded by partner universities, and so, unlike many digital publications, does not rely on advertising or paid subscribers.

The site has been designed to facilitate public discourse and provide a means of extending and measuring the impact of academics in the public sphere. In so doing, it has also made its mark in developing best practices for online journalism not only for its readers, but also for its editors and writers, says co-founder, Executive Director and Editor Andrew Jaspan, who previously edited the Melbourne daily the *Age* and several British newspapers (Zion 2012b).

The Conversation's charter (The Conversation 2011b) sets out how it aims to fulfill its mission:

- Give experts a **greater voice** in shaping scientific, cultural and intellectual agendas by providing a trusted platform that values and promotes new thinking and evidence-based research.
- **Unlock the knowledge** and expertise of researchers and academics to provide the public with clarity and insight into society's biggest problems.
- Create an **open site for people around the world** to share best practices and collaborate on developing smart, sustainable solutions.
- Provide a **fact-based and editorially-independent** forum, free of commercial or political bias.
- Ensure the site's **integrity** by only obtaining non-partisan sponsorship from education, government and private partners. Any advertising will be relevant and non-obtrusive.
- Ensure **quality, diverse and intelligible content** reaches the widest possible audience by employing experienced editors to curate the site.
- Support and foster **academic freedom** to conduct research, teach, write and publish.
- Work with our academic, business and government partners and our advisory board to ensure we are operating for the **public good**.

To facilitate these aims, *The Conversation* has developed "author dashboards" for contributors that provide details of the impact of articles by recording a range of metrics including the numbers of readers each article receives, where they're from, comments, "likes" on Facebook and tweets on Twitter, and republications through its Creative Commons license.

While many academics already have established media profiles, *The Conversation* also nurtures experts who have yet to contribute to newspapers or websites. "We started with saying a lot of academics either don't enjoy engagement with the media or they are shy or some of them just need the experience and help," says Jaspan (Zion 2012b). The site employs professional editors who work with contributors to ensure that their material can be understood by a general audience.

Technological innovations also help the site to realize its mission. All authors write on a specially developed collaborative writing platform which is designed to enhance transparency and trust. Contributors must register to demonstrate that they have credentials in a particular area. "We only allow people to write in the area that they know about, and we want the reader to know that that person really has deep expertise," Jaspan explains (Zion 2012b). Contributors must also fill out a disclosure statement "because we need to know who is funding them," says Jaspan, who adds that sometimes the perception of conflict of interest can be best dealt with just by being open about a relationship or connection, while, conversely, hiding the fact that you're affiliated to something can diminish trust.

Another notable feature of the site is its community standards (The Conversation 2011a), which were designed to enhance the quality of discussion for not only its readers, but also its writers and editors. These standards were developed after examining best practices in sites such as ProPublica, Nieman Journalism Lab, *The Guardian*, NPR, and Newser. As Jaspan explains:

> If you want to actually rebuild trust you need to demonstrate how you're doing that. Make sure you know who people are, the provenance of that person, the funding of that person, what they actually know about it. Make sure that you can actually deal with complaints properly, and make sure you have proper process in place to have people engage with the authors.
>
> (Zion 2012b)

Discussion Questions

1. How does *The Conversation* present a new approach to technology and ethics?
2. What best practice innovations has it developed that are specific to a digital environment?
3. Which of these might be applicable in other digital publications?
4. How does it provide for new kinds of collaborations between journalists, academics, audiences, and communities?
5. Overall, how could *The Conversation* be seen to ethically strengthen journalism in the digital era?

Acknowledgment

The author would like to acknowledge that this chapter is based in part on the paper he presented at the 2012 International Symposium for Online Journalism in Austin, Texas.

References

Anderson, C. W., Emily Bell, and Clay Shirky. 2012. *Post Industrial Journalism: Adapting to the Present.* Columbia University 2012. Accessed January 8, 2013. http://towcenter.org/research/post-industrial-journalism/

Aufderheide, Patricia, Jessica Clark, Matthew B. Nisbet, Katie Donnelly, and Carin Dessauer. 2009. *Scan and Analysis of Best Practices in Digital Journalism in and outside U.S. Public Broadcasting.* Center for Media & Social Impact 2009. Accessed July 8, 2012. www.cmsimpact.org/future-public-media/documents/white-papers/scan-and-analysis-best-practices-digital-journalism-and-o

Aufderheide, Patricia, and Peter Jaszi. 2012. *Copyright, Free Speech, and the Public's Right to Know: How Journalists Think about Fair Use.* Center for Media & Social Impact,

February 2012. Accessed February 2, 2012. www.cmsimpact.org/fair-use/best-practices/copyright-free-speech-and-publics-right-know-how-journalists-think-about-fai

Bell, Emily. 2012. *Emily Bell: How a New Research Effort Will Help Newsrooms Determine What's Next.* Knight Foundation, April 30, 2012. Accessed May 17, 2012. www.knightfoundation.org/blogs/knightblog/2012/4/30/emily-bell-how-new-research-effort-will-help-newsrooms-determine-whats-next/

Bendixsen, Synnøve, and Paul de Guchteneire. 2003. "Best Practices in Immigration Services Planning." *Journal of Policy Management and Analysis* 22(4):677–82.

English, Kathy. 2011. *Best Practices in Digital Accuracy and Correction.* Canadian Association of Journalists 2011. Accessed December 2, 2011. www.caj.ca/?p=1866

English, Kathy, Tim Currie, and Rod Link. 2010. *Ethics of Unpublishing.* Canadian Association of Journalists, October 2010. Accessed March 5, 2012. www.caj.ca/?p=1135

Everhart, Erin. 2011. *6 Best Practices for Modern SEO.* November 9, 2011. Accessed March 11, 2012. http://mashable.com/2011/11/08/seo-best-practices/

Fisher, Marc. 2010. *Is It Ever Ok to Unpublish a Story?* April 27, 2010. Accessed March 4, 2012. http://blog.washingtonpost.com/story-lab/2010/04/is_it_ever_ok_to_unpublish_a_s.html

Investopedia. 2013. *Best Practices.* Accessed May 12, 2013. www.investopedia.com/terms/b/best_practices.asp

itSMF Australia. 2013. *About Best Practice.* Accessed March 5, 2013. www.itsmf.org.au/best-practice/about-best-practice/

Iyer, Padma. 2010. "Commentary: The Intellectual Component in Best Practices of Journalism." *Asia Pacific Media Educator* (20):23–32.

King, Kenneth. 2007. *Engaging with Best Practice: History and Current Priorities.* January 10, 2007. Accessed May 29, 2013. www.norrag.org/es/publications/boletin-norrag/online-version/best-practice-in-education-and-training-hype-or-hope/detail/engaging-with-best-practice-history-and-current-priorities.html

Lavrusik, Vadim, and Betsy Cameron. 2011. *Study: How People Are Engaging Journalists on Facebook & Best Practices.* Facebook, July 13, 2011. Accessed December 13, 2011. www.facebook.com/notes/facebook-journalists/study-how-people-are-engaging-journalists-on-facebook-best-practices/245775148767840

McKeon, Denise. 1998. "Best Practices—Hype or Hope?" *TESOL Quarterly* no. 32(3): 493–501. doi:10.2307/3588119

Navasky, Victor, and Evan Lerner. 2010. *Magazines and Their Websites: A Columbia Journalism Review Survey and Report.* Columbia University. Accessed March 11, 2012. http://cjrarchive.org/img/posts/CJR_Mag_Web_Report.pdf

Network for International Policies and Cooperation in Education and Training. 2007. *NN39 Policy Brief.* NORRAG, January 10, 2007. Accessed June 5, 2013. www.norrag.org/es/publications/boletin-norrag/online-version/best-practice-in-education-and-training-hype-or-hope/detail/nn39-policy-brief-best-practice.html

Rosen, Jay. 2010. Jay Rosen discussion with Australian journalism educators. Sydney, August 12.

Shapiro, Ivor. 2010. "Evaluating Journalism: Towards an Assessment Framework for the Practice of Journalism." *Journalism Practice* no. 4 (2):143–62. doi:10.1080/17512780903306571

Taylor, Frederick Winslow. 1911. *The Principles of Scientific Management.* New York and London: Harper & Brothers.

The Conversation. 2011a. *The Conversation: Community Standards: The 10 Rules.* Accessed December 11, 2011. http://theconversation.edu.au/community_standards

The Conversation. 2011b. *The Conversation: Our Charter.* Accessed March 20, 2014. https://theconversation.com/au/our_charter

The Conversation. 2014. *A Look behind the Numbers on Our 3-year Anniversary.* Accessed March 20, 2014. https://theconversation.com/a-look-behind-the-numbers-on-our-3-year-anniversary-24633

UNESCO. 2014. *Best Practices in International Migration.* UNESCO. Accessed March 9, 2014. www.unesco.org/new/en/social-and-human-sciences/themes/international-migration/priorities/human-rights-of-migrants/best-practices-in-international-migration/

Ward, Stephen J. A. 2011a. *Ethics and the Media: An Introduction.* New York: Cambridge University Press.

Ward, Stephen J. A. 2011b. *5 Principles for Teaching Journalism Ethics in the Digital Age.* February 15, 2011. Accessed December 12, 2011. www.pbs.org/mediashift/2011/02/5-principles-for-teaching-journalism-ethics-in-the-digital-age046.html

Ward, Stephen J. A. 2010. *Ethics in a Nutshell.* University of Wisconsin 2010. Accessed March 11, 2012. http://ethics.journalism.wisc.edu/resources/ethics-in-a-nutshell/

Whitehouse, Ginny. 2010. "Newsgathering and Privacy: Expanding Ethics Codes to Reflect Change in the Digital Media Age." *Journal of Mass Media Ethics* no. 25 (4): 310–27. doi:10.1080/08900523.2010.512827

Zion, Lawrie. 2012a. " 'Best Practices' in the Journalism Ethics Frame: A Comparative Study." *#ISOJ Journal (The official journal of the International Symposium on Online Journalism)* 2(2):71–99.

Zion, Lawrie. 2012b. *A Conversation about* The Conversation, August 22, 2012b. Accessed March 2, 2014. www.upstart.net.au/bestpractices/2012/08/22/conversation/

2

JOURNALISM ETHICS AND BEST PRACTICES

David Craig

UNIVERSITY OF OKLAHOMA, USA

The pursuit of best practices in digital media can be related to three major emphases in ethical thought: duty, virtue, and care. All of these have histories stretching back to ancient times, but they remain relevant to 21st-century journalism. These concepts provide three ways to frame discussion of best practices that connect with what scholars who study media ethics have been saying before and after the development of digital media. The concepts also connect with the reality of how journalists and news organizations have discussed and pursued excellence. This chapter will examine all three concepts by providing an overview connected to scholarly discussion and professional application.

In the digital media era, duties such as being transparent and being accountable are more obviously relevant, but other responsibilities such as seeking truth and minimizing harm remain relevant and are sometimes in tension with each other. Virtue-based approaches provide an important alternative for digital journalists in thinking about best practices and the ethics supporting them. Although virtue ethics points to similar priorities such as transparency and honesty, it goes beyond rules to connect with people's character and habits of life and to draw attention to other priorities in the digital era such as humility. More broadly, attention to virtue ethics can help motivate the continued development of excellence in journalism. Care-based ethics is particularly relevant to the interactive aspect of digital media in which people have an unprecedented opportunity to connect and relate to one another and to build community, an opportunity that has seldom realized its potential.

Duty: Best Practices and Ethical Principles

Duty-based ethics focuses on principles or standards for conduct. In this view, pursuing best practices means identifying and articulating ethical responsibilities.

This section will provide a brief overview of this approach based on both ethics scholarship and the professional discussion and work of journalists and journalism organizations.

Historical Context

A duty-based approach is known in ethics scholarship as deontological ethics. This branch of ethical thought has held a key place in the history of ethics in various forms. This section is not intended to provide an exhaustive overview of deontological ethics, only to provide a basic frame of understanding. (For more detailed discussions, see Christians et al. 2012; Denise Peterfreund, and White 1998; Patterson and Wilkins 2014.)

In philosophical ethics, Immanuel Kant's work in the 18th century placed duty as central in the decisions of reasoning human beings. Kant argued that humans' ability to reason enables us to understand what our duties are and that our freedom enables us to act on our knowledge. The same ability to reason calls for us to treat all other humans with respect (Plaisance 2009, 8–9). For Kant, the key test of ethical action is whether the principle we are following could be applied to everyone, or universalized. He cites the example of lying. If we consider the ethics of making a false promise, we can test by asking ourselves whether we would support the notion that "'Everyone may make a deceitful promise when he finds himself in a difficulty from which he cannot otherwise extricate himself.'" We would quickly conclude that we would not want this to become the norm for everyone (Kant 1998, 158).

Deontological ethics carried into the 20th century through the work of others including W.D. Ross, who is known for his statement of what he called "prima facie duties." These include fidelity, reparation, gratitude, justice, beneficence, self-improvement, and nonmaleficence (avoiding harm). More than one of these duties may be relevant to a situation, and it is necessary to examine circumstances carefully to decide which carries the most weight (Ross 1998, 279–80). His recognition that people often have to weigh multiple responsibilities in their decisions is important not only in general daily life but also in professional work (Patterson and Wilkins 2014, 13).

Aside from philosophers' discussions of duty, perspectives of duty based in religious traditions provide frameworks of responsibility that guide many people in their decisions. In religious ethics, notions of duty are often prominent—for example, in the Jewish and Christian traditions (e.g., Ten Commandments) and in Islam in directives for conduct in the Quran.

Duty in Media Ethics Study

Duty-based ethics also occupies a central place in academic work in media ethics. In media ethics textbooks, duty-based perspectives such as Kant's and Ross's have received a lot of attention. (See, for example, Christians et al. 2012; Patterson et al. 2014.) Scholars in media ethics have done an increasingly sophisticated job of explaining deontological approaches and their implications for journalism. For example, Patrick Plaisance studied Kant's concept of transparency and concluded:

> Kant's notion of "duty" to others here is really a core principle in the jour-
> nalistic mission to "serve the public." This notion of "duty" also is reflected
> in increasing efforts by journalists and news organizations to respond to calls
> for greater accountability in what they do.
> (Plaisance 2007, 204; for applications of Ross see Meyers 2003, 2011)

Pursuing what are truly best practices may mean going beyond what duty calls for—what ethics scholars call supererogatory action (Harris 2007). But ethical duties set a bar for conduct that points the way to the best.

Connection to Professional Discussion and Work of Journalists

In relation to the work of journalists and professional discussion of their responsibil-ities, ethical duties are stated or implied in a number of places including ethics codes, professional training sessions, and informal discussions such as social media posts.

Ethics Codes and Formal Guidelines for Practice

Codes essentially express statements of duty as perceived by professional groups or news organizations. For example, the Society of Professional Journalists code spells out four broad principles: seek truth and report it, act independently, minimize harm, and be accountable, with more specific obligations under each (SPJ 2013). The Aus-tralian Media Alliance Code of Ethics commits members to honesty, fairness, inde-pendence, and respect for the rights of others (Media Entertainment & Arts Alliance 2013). These statements convey expectations of what the best practice will look like.

With developments in digital journalism including social media, some recent professional meetings—such as a symposium sponsored by the Poynter Institute for Media Studies in fall 2012—have focused on whether and how guidelines for practice should change with the evolution of digital media. In a book that fol-lowed the symposium, Kelly McBride and Tom Rosenstiel spelled out a revised set of ethical principles that replaced the three previously used at Poynter. One principle, "Seek truth and report it as fully as possible," remained and was called "the first among equals." "Act independently" was replaced by "Be transparent" with the argument that independence is still important but that legitimate jour-nalism can be done from a point of view. "Minimize harm" was replaced by "Engage community as an end, rather than as a means" with the argument that minimizing harm is part of journalists' obligation to a community they serve (McBride and Rosenstiel 2014, 2–5).

This shift reflects increasing attention among journalists, especially in the online realm, to transparency (though, as Stephen Ward's chapter notes, transparency can become a "magic" concept (Pollitt and Hupe 2011)—popular, easily invoked, but not always used thoughtfully—and needs to be carefully weighed with other ethical norms). Likewise, community—sometimes a buzzword or a commercially motivated value—is getting increasing attention with the capacity of online and social media to foster communities of interest around topics of all kinds. For digital journalists, it will be important in the continued development of best practices to consider how these duties can be carried out, how they should be weighed against one another, and where the challenges lie. For example, how can journalists be transparent about the process of their reporting via social media while reporting truthfully to the fullest extent possible—when the truthfulness of information reported as a story develops may not be fully established? How can they do this kind of reporting while minimizing harm to their communities from information that turns out to be false?

In developing best practices guidelines that articulate duties, is also important in the 21st-century media environment of global reach to draw in nonprofessionals—members of the community who have a stake in good journalism. Ward and Wasserman have argued for an "open ethics" in which members of the public contribute to discussion of ethical principles. In their view, in a world in which citizens have the tools to do and talk about journalism, it is imperative they be welcomed in discussions of media ethics—as intended users of ethical guidelines, meaningful participants in ethical decisions, and contributors to determination and revision of ethical content (Ward and Wasserman 2010). That is a challenging expectation for journalists, but one that is important to the future value and health of media ethics. (The case study at the end of this chapter looks at how NPR engaged the public in developing its new ethics guidelines.)

Professional Training in News Organizations and Industry Groups

Best practices are also at the center of workshops conducted within news organizations and corporate groups as well as sessions at conferences held by journalism professional organizations such as the Online News Association. For example, Steve Buttry, former digital transformation editor for the US media company Digital First Media, has taught in numerous settings on digital storytelling, live blogging, and other topics. One workshop in October 2013 focused on "Better Journalism through Engagement." Among the topics he, Mandy Jenkins, and Ivan Lajara covered was advice on uses of Facebook including asking questions to invite conversation (Buttry 2013). Although effective engagement also advances business interests, it is consistent with the duty of fostering community—something noted in the new Poynter Institute guidelines but also reflected in philosophies including communitarian thought (Christians, Ferré, and Fackler 1993)—as well as the responsibility to seek truth, which can be advanced through public engagement.

Members of the Online News Association also do an excellent job of providing training on best practices through sessions at the organization's annual conference. In 2013 these included storytelling with data, information visualization in mobile and breaking news, and exploration of new story formats (ONA 2013b). One session focused entirely on ethical questions including whether all content should be posted permanently and how to work with user-generated content (Storify 2013). Although again ethical duties were not always explicitly in the forefront, a concern about seeking and reporting truth—a high value in professional statements of duty as well as philosophical underpinnings—is implied across discussions of how to work with and present information in various formats and from a variety of possible sources.

Informal Discussions of Ethical Responsibilities

Other communication about best practices happens daily via social media, blogs, journalism publications, and other online venues that draw in journalists as well as members of the public and others interested in journalism. For example, erroneous reporting on Twitter has prompted comments and follow-up blog posts on verification of information during and after breaking stories. After the shootings at the Navy Yard in Washington, D.C., in September 2013, a post on the Poynter Institute website noted mistakes in media coverage including erroneous reports by NBC and CBS identifying the shooter that led "online detectives" to point people to the man's LinkedIn page and a photo supposedly of him (Beaujon 2013). An editor for *The Huffington Post* wrote about the mistakes, as well, which it called "depressingly familiar" after mistakes in coverage of the Boston Marathon bombings and school shootings in Newtown, Connecticut (Mirkinson 2013). *The Huffington Post* posting resulted in 876 comments. Though some focused on gun issues, some media criticism also appeared—including a comment from someone identified as 19MadMonk62: "there's just too many people trying to nail down the story 'in real time' for there to be any true objective sifting out of the apparent facts. Too many tweets ruin the soup." These kinds of posts and comments may refer only vaguely or indirectly to duties, if at all, but they imply concern about the duty to tell the truth—as suggested in the commenter's reference to sifting out facts.

Some of this online discussion, particularly in professional venues such as Poynter, engages fellow professionals more than it does members of the public. But interaction through websites with broader audiences and through social media at least offers the opportunity for discussion of journalistic responsibilities that is more open to the public.

Discussions of digital media ethics that state or imply ethical duties are valuable if for no other reason than they can provide journalists clear considerations on which to anchor decision-making. Approaching ethics based on duty has its limitations. Simply prescribing duties as rules to follow does not guarantee a change in behavior. It also does not ensure clarity in decision-making since important duties—such as truth telling and minimizing harm—often come into conflict. For example, posting a graphic image of an accident might cause pain to the family of the accident victim. Beyond that, stated duties in ethics codes or newsroom policies can go unseen and ignored unless managers and individual journalists choose to draw attention to them. Still, these frameworks can sharpen and clarify discussion of what best practices mean in digital ethics.

Virtue: Best Practices and Ethical People

This perspective turns the focus from moral rules that may foster ethical conduct to people who do excellent work and the personal qualities or virtues that drive their conduct. In this view, pursuing best practices means living a life and doing work that models excellence. Virtue ethics does not provide as clear a path to ethical decision-making, but it is important as a driving force behind pursuit of best practices.

Historical Context

Virtue-based approaches to ethics have ancient roots in Aristotle. For him, living the best human life meant acting consistently over time in keeping with virtues such as courage and justice. In contrast with duty-based approaches, virtue ethics centers on qualities of character people live out rather than rules or principles they follow. As Aristotle put it, virtues develop when we exercise them. "[W]e become just by doing just acts, temperate by doing temperate acts, brave by doing brave acts" (Aristotle 1998, 31). Living out virtues means taking a path of conduct that represents a mean between extremes—for example, being courageous means acting in a middle ground between cowardice and overconfidence (Aristotle 1998, 33–34).

A number of contemporary philosophers continue to work within the virtue tradition. As the next section details, one of them, Alasdair MacIntyre, has been particularly influential in scholarship about journalism.

Virtue in Media Ethics Study

Virtue-based ethics, like deontological ethics, has been an important focus of contemporary writing in professional ethics. Notre Dame philosopher Alasdair

MacIntyre's work has been influential, particularly his idea of a practice. He defines a practice this way:

> By a "practice" I am going to mean any coherent and complex form of socially established cooperative human activity through which goods internal to that form of activity are realized in the course of trying to achieve those standards of excellence which are appropriate to, and partially definitive of, that form of activity, with the result that human powers to achieve excellence, and human conceptions of the ends and goods involved, are systematically extended.
>
> (MacIntyre 2007, 187)

Although MacIntyre does not limit his definition to professions, it is relevant to journalism as well as other fields—particularly in a time of change and development. In his framework, members of a practice, acting with virtue, pursue standards of excellence leading to the achievement of certain "internal goods." For journalism, these goods can include knowledge and inquiry (Borden 2007), as well as fostering of community (Craig 2011). As these goods are achieved, the very meaning of excellence in the practice can be reshaped (Lambeth 1992). This process is challenged, in MacIntyre's view, by the fact that practices function in institutions, where "external goods" such as profit and status act as powerful forces that can undermine excellence.

A number of media scholars (Aucoin 2005; Borden 2007; Craig 2011; Lambeth 1992; Zion 2012) have applied MacIntyre's perspective to journalism. Focusing on online journalism, I have argued that journalists pursuing standards of excellence online—speed and accuracy with depth in breaking news, comprehensiveness in content, open-endedness in story development, and centrality of conversation—can help to transform the nature of excellent journalism. In this view, journalists modeling "best practices" are redefining the potential of journalism. This redefinition is evident, for example, in the expanded capacity to visualize complex data, thanks to new technological tools and creative uses of them, and in the ability to develop stories through a wider range of public expertise, thanks to journalists' use of the capabilities of social media and online comments. (For more discussion of the state of data journalism, see Paul Bradshaw's chapter. For more discussion of online comments and audience engagement, see the chapter by David Domingo.)

In relation to digital media, some virtues become more obviously important than in previous modes of journalism. Transparency, discussed above as a duty, is also a virtue and is important to the ethical life of journalists working in the constant open network of information flow. Likewise, humility is important because engaging with information and opinions from the public means thinking and working in a way that welcomes and respects these contributions (while remaining appropriately critical) and doesn't view them as a threat to one's authority (Craig 2011).

Ties to Psychology

Media scholar Patrick Plaisance has recently called for using scholarship in moral psychology and virtue science to study people who are exemplars of ethical practice in journalism. Plaisance proposed a five-component model—including people's narratives about themselves, their personalities, how they internalize morality, "moral ecology" (the influence of a work environment) (Huff, Barnard, and Frey 2008, 284–316), and their moral skills and knowledge (Plaisance 2011, 96–113). This is another approach that connects with the idea of best practices—in this case, building from study of what people actually do rather than from ethical theory about what they ought to do. This kind of study can lead to insight about what drives digital journalists who strive for moral excellence in their work.

Connection to Professional Discussion and Work of Journalists

In relation to the work of journalists and professional discussion of their responsibilities, a virtue approach is implied in professional awards and in mentoring that goes on in newsrooms and news companies. It is also important in recent best practices initiatives and important to consider in the development of future ones.

Professional Awards

Awards such as the Pulitzer Prizes and Online News Association awards in the United States and the Walkley Awards in Australia recognize excellence in professional work (Pulitzer 2013a; ONA 2013a; The Walkley Foundation 2013). The fact that they focus on individuals and groups who have done outstanding work draws attention to exemplars of excellence in practice. Although an excellent product does not in itself demonstrate virtue in a person, the nature of the work can suggest insights about virtues that might be drivers behind excellent work. For example, reporters Lisa Song, Elizabeth McGowan, and David Hasemyer of the online publication InsideClimate News won the 2013 Pulitzer Prize for, as the award citation put it, "their rigorous reports on flawed regulation of the nation's oil pipelines, focusing on potential ecological dangers posed by diluted bitumen (or 'dilbit'), a controversial form of oil" (Pulitzer 2013b). Executive Editor Susan White's nomination letter said Song, supported by the other two reporters, spent 15 months reporting almost entirely on pipeline safety and dilbit. The reporting for a three-part series on a spill in Michigan plus follow-up stories (Pulitzer 2013c) involved, among other things, extensive interviews, use of federal documents, and data analysis (Pulitzer 2013d). The nature of the reporting suggests virtues of perseverance and courage because these would almost surely be necessary to report in depth on this controversial topic.

Mentoring in Newsrooms and News Companies

Informal or formal mentoring activities also imply a focus on virtue because they enable younger or less experienced journalists to learn from what Aristotle would call the practical wisdom of their more seasoned colleagues. Formal mentoring is difficult to keep up in an environment of economic pressure (connected with what MacIntyre would call the external good of profit) and constant, tight deadlines in the digital environment. But mentoring enables newer journalists to observe the exercise of virtues—in person and online—such as transparency in communication and perseverance in reporting.

Development of Recent Best Practices Initiatives

Lawrie Zion's chapter points to characteristics that have been mostly common in recent best practices initiatives such as the Canadian Association of Journalists' development of guidelines on "The Ethics of Unpublishing" (English, Currie, and Link 2010), discussed in more detail in Tim Currie's chapter. One of these characteristics is, as Zion puts it, to consult—using "expertise and engagement with communities to develop guidelines." Truly consulting with communities is in keeping with the virtue of hospitality that Ward and Wasserman cite as an important aspect of open discourse about ethics. "The virtue of *hospitality* would require media to open up ethical discourse to the widest possible range of voices, including voices that contradict media ethics orthodoxy" (Ward and Wasserman 2010). They argue further that another virtue, sincerity, would call for media to incorporate dissenting voices in more than a token manner that keeps control over discourse about media ethics (Ward and Wasserman 2010). Both of these virtues are important to the future development of best practices initiatives because digital journalists are immersed in a network that requires them to engage meaningfully with members of the public who have their own voices in the network and a stake in the impact of public discussion. One of the biggest challenges facing digital journalists going forward will be to consider best practices in ways that truly draw on both professional traditions and public thinking.

Care: Best Practices and Mutual Concern

A third ethical perspective that can provide insight about best practices is centered on care for others. It raises issues that overlap with considerations of duty, such as minimizing harm, and virtue, such as hospitality. But care-based ethics highlights a concern that underlies real interaction in digital space.

Historical Context

Broadly speaking, ethics that focus on care are rooted in both ancient traditions in religion and recent scholarship, particularly in feminist ethics. In religiously based ethics, caring for others is both a duty and a way of life that flows from beliefs. In Jewish and Christian teaching, love for one's neighbor should be at the core of one's life. In the Christian New Testament tradition, *agape*, a Greek word for self-giving love, is modeled by Jesus and is to be displayed by his followers (Craig and Ferré 2006). Yao has noted that the idea of *jen* in Confucian teaching has a great deal in common with agape in that both involve care for others as one would exercise for oneself, though *jen* is connected more strongly to family affection (Yao 1996). Yao notes more broadly that religions, despite their great differences, share a common concern for altruism. In all faiths, the reality does not always live up to this expectation, but the ideal is strong (Craig and Ferré 2006).

Contemporary feminist scholarship has, from a different perspective, emphasized care. Carol Gilligan, one of the major figures in this scholarship, articulated an ethic of care based on psychological studies of women's conceptions of morality—though she emphasized that this ethic is not relevant only to women (Craig 2003). The meaning of this perspective is evident in this statement about one of her interviewees: "Her world is a world of relationships and psychological truths where an awareness of the connection between people gives rise to a recognition of responsibility for one another, a perception of the need for response" (Gilligan 1982, 30). Commenting on another interviewee, she writes: "The ideal of care is thus an activity of relationship, of seeing and responding to need, taking care of the world by sustaining the web of connection so that no one is left alone" (Gilligan 1982, 62). Gilligan wrote these statements before the public was using the Internet, but they have important implications in a world with the potential for constant connection.

Care in Media Ethics Study

Media scholars have related care-based ethics perspectives to journalism. A series of 2006 articles in the *Journal of Mass Media Ethics*, growing out of a conference focused on ethics of care and media ethics, presented perspectives on care drawing on a wide range of sources including feminist ethics (Steiner and Okrusch 2006; Vanacker and Breslin 2006) and religious ethics (Craig and Ferré 2006). The focus of these discussions was not on ethical practice in the digital sphere, but the relevance of care becomes more obvious when engagement in and building of communities online becomes a central element of the work of many journalists and news organizations. Fiona Martin discusses the ethics of care in her chapter in this book on aggregation and curation. She notes that the notion of reciprocity (also discussed in Ward 2010, 130–31) is central to care-based ethics and, in turn, "Reciprocity is a critical concept for networked media."

Reciprocity also relates to the idea of mutuality that Clifford Christians and colleagues argue as a norm in the practice of journalism in a communitarian ethical perspective. This perspective, based on the idea that people's identities are fundamentally grounded in their relationships to each other, calls for mutual concern in society to be a motivator in the priorities and work of journalists (Christians, Ferré, and Fackler 1993). In this view, best practices in digital media involve a true and lasting commitment to engagement with others.

Connection to Professional Discussion and Work of Journalists

Interaction in True Communities

The kind of real, sustained engagement that builds community in digital space has proved more elusive for journalists than what the power and availability of the technological tools to communicate might suggest. Journalists, like others, have social media at their disposal, and they also have space for comment on stories as well as, sometimes, forums created on news sites to foster discussion. However, discussion that is sustained, constructive, and truly reflective of care for the participants is difficult to establish. Still, some bright spots have appeared. David Domingo's chapter on audience participation and comments notes research (Graham 2013) that found *The Guardian* to be relatively effective in fostering constructive public debate in comments, with "diversity of points of view in 23% of the threads analyzed and 40% of the comments engaged in a conversation with others." An example of community-building on social media is investigative news organization ProPublica's Patient Harm Community (Facebook 2013). ProPublica created this Facebook group to connect victims of medical harm and others who care about the issue (Allen, Marshall, and Victor 2012). The group had more than 2,000 members by March 2014 and active discussion continuing around an important topic of medical and human concern.

Despite some successes, digital journalists have a great deal to work on in identifying practices that connect and engage with people in caring ways. Josh Stearns—a journalist, organizer, and community strategist who worked for Free Press—argued eloquently in a PBS MediaShift post for initiatives to truly engage and develop community capacity in media ethics so that practices of the public as well as journalists can be advanced (Stearns 2013). This is in line with the open ethics that Ward and Wasserman argue for (Ward and Wasserman 2010), and at its best it could foster more caring interactions among both journalists and the public.

The ethical perspectives based on duty, virtue, and care are all relevant to carrying out best practices in digital journalism. The following case study examines how one organization developed ethical guidelines that express duties but also connect with the concerns of these other perspectives.

Best Practices in Action: Development of NPR's Ethics Handbook

NPR built a reputation for excellence starting in the 1970s as National Public Radio, offering its US listeners a depth of treatment of issues well beyond the norm of American broadcast journalism. In recent years, it has extended its reach to online.

In late 2010, Vivian Schiller, then CEO and president of NPR, enlisted Bob Steele, who trained and advised journalists on ethics for nearly 20 years on faculty of the Poynter Institute for Media Studies, to help in re-examining its ethics code in the wake of NPR's firing of analyst Juan Williams for remarks he made about Muslims on a Fox News program (Steele 2013). Managers had first assembled the code in 2003 from previous ethical guidance circulated in the organization (NPR 2013a).

Steele recommended creating a task force including people from inside and outside NPR. He also recommended including citizens—by having a couple of them on the task force as well as having conversations with groups at NPR stations. He said the task force ended up being composed of about six NPR journalists, a nonjournalist in NPR, four or five journalists from other news organizations, and two members of the public. Focus groups with citizens took place at NPR member stations in three cities. Steele said the conversations included about 50 to 75 people who were given the code ahead of time and came to discuss its strengths and weaknesses.

NPR adopted Steele's recommendation that the organization consider moving from a code to a statement of principles with a separate handbook of application. Based on his work with SPJ and other organizations, he was concerned that codes "tend to lead to rigidity and to rule-following rather than strong ethical decision-making and application of principles and wrestling with competing principles."

After the NPR board decided to implement the handbook, workshops with hundreds of NPR journalists provided additional input. The primary creators of the handbook itself within NPR were Mark Memmott and Matt Thompson.

Steele said the members of the public on the task force provided a perspective of news consumers and of citizens in a democracy. They also asked questions about clarity of language. One of them asked questions about how employees of NPR could be trained and put the material to use. Citizens in the focus groups offered thoughts on matters including whether the range of ethical issues was "properly addressed" and whether the language was appropriately assertive. Task force members received either transcripts or audio from the focus groups and, in some cases, cited specifics of what citizens said. Steele said the comments influenced what was presented to NPR leadership in recommending the change from a code to the principles and handbook.

Steele said the process-oriented approach used at the Poynter Institute affected his work with NPR. "I'm a big, big believer in the skills of ethical decision-making.

I don't think that we are born with that skill. I think we develop it—in the same way we're not born as writers; we develop that." Steele said this belief shaped both how he facilitated the work at NPR and his emphasis on having more than just a code of ethics. Principles, he said, provide the "moral compass" but specific protocols are needed to make decisions "because we are almost always struggling with competing principles."

The final product included these guiding principles: accuracy, fairness, completeness, honesty, independence, impartiality, transparency, accountability, respect, and excellence (NPR 2013b). The handbook provides more specific points, questions, and case studies to help with application of the principles.

Stu Seidel, NPR managing editor for standards and practice, said this about the impact of the handbook: "By bringing together in one place NPR's professional guidelines and policies, the handbook has simply made it easier for NPR journalists to connect with that guidance, prompting more conversations about best practices and the underlying thinking behind those policies" (Seidel 2013). As for any other intended users: "The handbook was put together as a tool for NPR and its journalists and to provide our audience with an opportunity to see the guiding principles behind NPR's journalism. If there are beneficiaries beyond that, terrific!"

Discussion Questions

1. How do the NPR guiding principles and ethics handbook reflect a duty-based approach to ethics?
2. How is the ethical perspective of virtue reflected in the guiding principle and handbook discussion about excellence?
3. How is the ethical perspective of care reflected in the guiding principle and handbook discussion about respect?
4. How can the process used to develop the NPR materials provide a model for development of other best practices initiatives?
5. How and to what extent do this process and the intent behind it reflect the "open ethics" approach described by Ward and Wasserman?

References

Allen, Marshall, and Daniel Victor. 2012. "Join ProPublica's Patient Harm Community." ProPublica, May 21, 2012. Accessed November 13, 2013. www.propublica.org/getinvolved/item/join-propublicas-patient-harm-community

Aristotle. 1998. "Moral Character." In *Great Traditions in Ethics,* 9th ed., edited by Theodore C. Denise, Sheldon P. Peterfreund, and Nicholas White, 23–39. Belmont, CA: Wadsworth, from *Nicomachean Ethics,* translated by William D. Ross. Originally published in *The Works of Aristotle,* Vol. IX, edited by William D. Ross (Oxford: Clarendon Press, 1925).

Aucoin, James. 2005. *The Evolution of American Investigative Journalism*. Columbia: University of Missouri Press.

Beaujon, Andrew. 2013. "The Media's Mistakes in Covering Navy Yard Shooting." *Poynter*, September 16, 2013. www.poynter.org/latest-news/mediawire/223726/the-medias-mistakes-in-covering-navy-yard-shooting/

Borden, Sandra L. 2007. *Journalism as Practice: MacIntyre, Virtue Ethics and the Press*. Burlington, VT: Ashgate.

Buttry, Steve. 2013. "Slides and Links for New England Workshops." *The Buttry Diary*, October 14, 2013. http://stevebuttry.wordpress.com/2013/10/14/slides-and-links-for-new-england-workshops/

Christians, Clifford G., John P. Ferré, and P. Mark Fackler. 1993. *Good News: Social Ethics and the Press*. New York: Oxford University Press.

Christians, Clifford G., Mark Fackler, Kathy B. Richardson, Peggy J. Kreshel, and Robert H. Woods. 2012. *Media Ethics: Cases and Moral Reasoning*. 9th ed. Boston: Allyn & Bacon.

Craig, David A. 2003. "The Promise and Peril of Anecdotes in News Coverage: An Ethical Analysis." *Journalism & Mass Communication Quarterly* 80:802–17.

Craig, David A. 2011. *Excellence in Online Journalism: Exploring Current Practices in an Evolving Environment*. Los Angeles: Sage.

Craig, David A., and John P. Ferré. 2006. "Agape as an Ethic of Care for Journalism." *Journal of Mass Media Ethics* 21:123–40.

Denise, Theodore C., Sheldon P. Peterfreund, and Nicholas White. 1998. *Great Traditions in Ethics*. Belmont, CA: Wadsworth.

English, Kathy, Tim Currie, and Rod Link. 2010. "Ethics of Unpublishing." *Canadian Association of Journalists*, October 27, 2010. Accessed November 26, 2013. www.caj.ca/?p=1135

Facebook. 2013. "ProPublica Patient Harm Community." Accessed November 13, 2013. www.facebook.com/groups/patientharm/

Gilligan, Carol. 1982. *In a Different Voice: Psychological Theory and Women's Development*. Cambridge, MA: Harvard University Press.

Graham, Todd. 2013. "Talking Back, But Is Anyone Listening? Journalism and Comment Fields." In *Rethinking Journalism: Trust and Participation in a Transformed New Landscape*, edited by Chris Peters and Marcel Broersma, 114–27. London: Routledge.

Harris, Charles E. 2007. *Applying Moral Theories*. 5th ed. Belmont, CA: Wadsworth.

Huff, Chuck, Laura Barnard, and William Frey. 2008. "Good Computing: A Pedagogically Focused Model of Virtue in the Practice of Computing (part 2)." *Journal of Information, Communication and Ethics in Society* 6:284–316.

Kant, Immanuel. 1998. "Duty and Reason." In *Great Traditions in Ethics*, edited by Theodore C. Denise, Sheldon P. Peterfreund, and Nicholas White, 149–65. Belmont, CA: Wadsworth, from *Fundamental Principles of the Metaphysic of Morals*, translated by Thomas K. Abbott. Originally published in *Kant's Critique of Practical Reason and Other Works on the Theory of Ethics* (London: Longmans, Green, 1898).

Lambeth, Edmund B. 1992. *Committed Journalism: An Ethics for the Profession*. Bloomington: Indiana University Press.

MacIntyre, Alasdair. 2007. *After Virtue: A Study in Moral Theory*. Notre Dame, IN: University of Notre Dame Press.

McBride, Kelly, and Tom Rosenstiel, eds. 2014. *The New Ethics of Journalism: Principles for the 21st Century*. Los Angeles: Sage.

Media Entertainment & Arts Alliance. 2013. "Journalists' Code of Ethics." Accessed November 17, 2013. www.alliance.org.au/code-of-ethics.html

Meyers, Christopher. 2003. "Appreciating WD Ross: On Duties and Consequences." *Journal of Mass Media Ethics* 18:81–97.

Meyers, Christopher. 2011. "Reappreciating WD Ross: Naturalizing Prima Facie Duties and a Proposed Method." *Journal of Mass Media Ethics* 26:316–31.

Mirkinson, Jack. 2013. "Navy Shooting Coverage Mistakes Feel Depressingly Familiar." *The Huffington Post*, September 16, 2013. www.huffingtonpost.com/2013/09/16/navy-shooting-coverage-media_n_3934816.html

NPR. 2013a. "NPR Ethics Handbook." Accessed November 17, 2013. http://ethics.npr.org/wp-content/uploads/2012/05/NPR-Ethics-Handbook-5.2.2012-Final-Edition.pdf

NPR. 2013b. "NPR Guiding Principles." Accessed November 17, 2013. http://ethics.npr.org/wp-content/uploads/2012/02/NPR-Guiding-Principles-2.22.2012-Final-Edition.pdf

ONA. 2013a. "Online Journalism Awards." Accessed November 17, 2013. http://journalists.org/awards/

ONA. 2013b. "ONA13 Program Schedule." Accessed November 17, 2013. http://ona13.journalists.org/sessions/

Patterson, Philip, and Lee Wilkins. 2014. *Media Ethics: Issues & Cases.* 8th ed. New York: McGraw-Hill.

Plaisance, Patrick L. 2007. "Transparency: An Assessment of the Kantian Roots of a Key Element in Media Ethics Practice." *Journal of Mass Media Ethics* 22(2&3):187–207.

Plaisance, Patrick L. 2009. *Media Ethics: Key Principles for Responsible Practice.* Thousand Oaks, CA: Sage.

Plaisance, Patrick L. 2011. "Moral Agency in Media: Toward a Model to Explore Key Components of Ethical Practice." *Journal of Mass Media Ethics* 26:96–113.

Pollitt, Christopher, and Peter Hupe. 2011. "Talking about Government: The Role of Magic Concepts." *Public Management Review* 13:641–58.

Pulitzer. 2013a. "The Pulitzer Prizes." Accessed November 17, 2013. www.pulitzer.org/

Pulitzer. 2013b. "The 2013 Pulitzer Prize Winners: National Reporting." Accessed November 22, 2013. www.pulitzer.org/citation/2013-National-Reporting

Pulitzer. 2013c. "The 2013 Pulitzer Prize Winners: National Reporting." Accessed November 22, 2013. www.pulitzer.org/works/2013-National-Reporting

Pulitzer. 2013d. "InsideClimate News." Accessed November 22, 2013. www.pulitzer.org/files/2013/national-reporting/insideclimatenewsentryletter.pdf

Ross, William D. 1998. "Prima Facie Duty." In *Great Traditions in Ethics,* 9th ed., edited by Theodore C. Denise, Sheldon P. Peterfreund, and Nicholas White, 276–87. Belmont, CA: Wadsworth. Originally published in *The Right and the Good* (New York: Oxford University Press, 1930).

Seidel, Stuart. 2013. Email message to author, November 8, 2013.

SPJ. 2013. "SPJ Code of Ethics." Accessed November 17, 2013. www.spj.org/ethicscode.asp

Stearns, Josh. 2013. "Considering Ethics for Anyone Who Commits Acts of Journalism." *MediaShift*, November 19, 2013. www.pbs.org/mediashift/2013/11/considering-ethics-for-anyone-who-commits-acts-of-journalism/

Steele, Robert. 2013. Skype interview by author, October 3, 2013.

Steiner, Linda, and Chad M. Okrusch. 2006. "Care as a Virtue for Journalists." *Journal of Mass Media Ethics* 21:102–22.

Storify. 2013. "Online Ethics." Accessed November 17, 2013. http://storify.com/slilwall/online-ethics

The Walkley Foundation. 2013. "The Walkley Awards for Excellence in Journalism." Accessed November 17, 2013. www.walkleys.com/walkley-awards

Vanacker, Bastiaan, and John Breslin. 2006. "Ethics of Care: More Than Just Another Tool to Bash the Media?" *Journal of Mass Media Ethics* 21:196–214.

Ward, Stephen J. A. 2010. *Global Journalism Ethics.* Montreal: McGill-Queen's University Press.

Ward, Stephen J. A., and Herman Wasserman. 2010. "Towards an Open Ethics: Implications of New Media Platforms for Global Ethics Discourse." *Journal of Mass Media Ethics* 25:275–92.

Yao, Xinzhong. 1996. *Confucianism and Christianity: A Comparative Study of Jen and Agape.* Brighton, UK: Sussex Academic.

Zion, Lawrie. 2012. "Best Practices in the Journalism Ethics Frame: A Comparative Study." Paper presented at the International Symposium on Online Journalism, Austin, TX, April 2012.

3

BEST PRACTICES IN THE NETWORK JOURNALISM SPHERE

Ansgard Heinrich

UNIVERSITY OF GRONINGEN, THE NETHERLANDS

Journalism is a gateway to learn about the world. And in an increasingly globalized sphere, the responsibility of journalists to enhance our knowledge about the world and provide context appears to become ever more important. Scholars concerned with globalization (e.g., Appadurai 1990; Beck 2000, 2005) have explained that in the networked era, social, cultural, economic, and financial matters are interconnected across borders. But how can journalists make sense of this interconnected world? Digital technologies provide greater access and allow journalists to connect to virtually anyone anywhere. Yet journalists still have to learn how to use these technologies to enhance their reporting. This ultimately leads to ethical considerations. What makes journalism ethical in a globalized world? Can we identify best ethical practices when reporting from afar? And how can digital tools help to cover news in the global sphere?

This chapter first discusses the new global landscape of journalism in the digital, networked age. It then focuses on the ethical implications of the network journalism sphere. After examining the challenges of foreign reporting in this environment, it offers suggestions for best practices in global journalism. This is followed by an exploration of the difficulties of navigating between global norms and local differences in ethics. A case study looks at the role of one international journalism organization in contributing to best practices.

Journalism in the Global Sphere

The digital age has radically changed the landscape in which journalists work. Technological innovations from satellite communication to the Internet enabled instantaneous communication across distance and fostered the digitization particularly of Western societies. Along with digitization has come globalization: "the worldwide spread, over both time and space, of a number of new ideas, institutions, culturally defined ways of doing things, and technologies" (Straubhaar 2007, 81). Taken together, this erosion of temporal and spatial distances has led to an increase in global information flows. One of the first indicators of these processes was the development of 24/7 news channels that consider themselves global in reach. CNNI, BBC World, or more recently, Al Jazeera International and the Chinese CCTV NEWS, for example, not only aim to cover *news* across the globe. They also cater to *audiences* across the globe.

Yet, where satellite technology enabled this first wave of media globalization, the emergence of the Internet in the 1990s took this evolution of a global news media sphere to a new level. With the drop in production costs, a myriad of bloggers, citizen journalists, small news organizations, and alternative news outlets emerged, distributing their news and views online and offline, locally and globally. Journalists working for large-scale news organizations are not the only ones reporting events that attract attention across the globe. Information about the Arab Spring, the global Occupy movement, or the anti-government protests in the Ukraine can be accessed through traditional media platforms as well as via new media platforms, and it is spread by journalists, bloggers, and social media users.

There has been a fundamental shift, especially in Western societies, in communication structures from a closed system to a more open system of information gathering, production, and distribution. Sociologist Manuel Castells discussed this shift in his seminal works about the "network society" (1996). When he developed the paradigm of the network society, his main concern was to outline how social structures have changed in the networked age. He explained in detail how the digital networks of the information age diminish physical borders and enable new forms of social interaction across space. And what Castells asserts for social structures can be adapted to the gathering, production, and dissemination of (news) information.

The paradigm of "network journalism" (Heinrich 2011) outlines this shift. It explains how information exchange is now organized within a complex network of global information nodes. Digital networks are the structural patterns of information exchange and they support a revised organization of information gathering, production, and distribution. Within an interconnected system of information nodes, journalistic organizations are just some network nodes among many. The individual tweeter spreading the word about the situation in Egypt, the Al Jazeera correspondent, the CNNI reporter, or bloggers who see themselves as activists all constitute information nodes and move within a *shared information space*. These nodes might differ in size and reach, some of them might be known to more users than others, but they all can potentially inform users *across* the globe. They can also all *build* or *extend* connections to other nodes via digital paths. Here, the paradigm of network journalism outlines new opportunities for information provision. It sketches the evolution of an interactive sphere that, at least in theory, fosters a greater level of interaction and exchange. Connection, interaction, and collaboration are the markers of this shift.

This shift, however, poses great pressure on journalism as it challenges the traditional ways journalism is practiced. Whom do you allow into your information network? Under what circumstances is it acceptable to use social media sources and work together with activist bloggers? Which platforms do you use to distribute information? What are the tools to assist you in gathering information? And all of these questions carry an ethical dimension. As journalistic outlets have become global in reach, they are also attributed with "global impact" (Ward 2011, 248; see also Ward 2010) on news consumers. What journalists cover and how they cover news can potentially frame public perceptions of any given event. What is more: "with global reach comes global responsibilities" (Ward 2011, 247). These global responsibilities are the core of the discussion when reflecting on ethics in relation to journalism in the global sphere.

Ethical Implications of Global Network Journalism

The global reach, particularly of Western media outlets, and the new access opportunities demand that journalists think carefully about ethics as they report about the world and engage with others in their information networks. Think about the role that is traditionally assigned to journalism in the West. Journalists have been described as sense-makers, watchdogs, and as the Fourth Estate. Their work is seen as crucial to monitoring the actions of political leaders and to explaining conflicts or wars. But journalists have tended to reflect on these issues within national (or even regional) frameworks. What is important for *my* readers, viewers, or listeners in *one* country? What are the effects a news story has on one *specific* country? This nationally inward looking focus of news reporting, however, does not do justice to a world (1) where events in one corner of the world might affect the other; (2) where news stories produced by one outlet are not restricted in access to "local," i.e., national audiences; and (3) in which many voices roam through the spheres of a digitally connected world that might provide an alternative take on a news story.

There is more than one way to interpret the uprisings in Egypt; understanding the Occupy movement is inherently complex; and how a Tibetan blogger might assess the conflict with China could significantly differ from Chinese state-media reports or the accounts of Chinese bloggers. Rather, journalists now increasingly have to consider a "global outlook" on news, as Peter Berglez (2008, 847) proposes. A "global outlook," for him, "seeks to understand and explain how economic, political, social and ecological practices, processes and problems in different parts of the world affect each other, are interlocked, or share commonalities." The events in the Ukraine can be seen through different frames—for example, a Russian perspective, a European, or a North American one.

According to Stephen Ward, journalists "should see themselves as agents of a global public sphere. The goal of their collective actions is a well-informed, diverse, and tolerant global 'info-sphere' that challenges the distortions of tyrants, the abuse of human rights, and the manipulation of information by special interests" (2005, 16). And a "global info-sphere" asks for coverage that acknowledges different perspectives. National perspectives, therefore, have not been diminished by globalization. However, a "global info-sphere" contributes to an *increased visibility* of different perspectives.

The idea of a "global outlook" connects to what Ward terms a "globally responsible journalism." Journalists, he explains, "owe credible journalism to all potential readers of a global public sphere. Loyalty to humanity trumps other loyalties, where they conflict" (2011, 258). Rather than having specific national audience segments in mind, the global journalist considers the global impact of a news story and reports for a "global citizen." How do others view the conflict between Tibet and China? What are the political interests of different sides? And who is affected by a conflict and how? Journalists carry the responsibility to widen their scope in reporting, to contextualize news, and to ensure that stories are told from a variety of angles.

It is exactly at this point where one can identify the opportunities of rethinking journalistic practice in light of the "network journalism" paradigm. When we think of the journalistic sphere as a series of interconnected information nodes, we can begin to rethink the possibilities a shared, global information sphere has to offer. And today's information structures do support a journalism that integrates more voices through reaching out to a multitude of information nodes. Making these connections and reaching out can help to make journalism more "globally responsible."

Yet, is it possible to globalize best practices and to reach common agreement on how global issues *should* be covered? If one adapts McNair's idea (2012) that the networked age is the "age of ascendant global democracy," then digitization might be seen to amplify and extend democratization across the globe. This increase in democratization fits the idea of a "globally responsible journalism." In an era of global democratization trends, demanding that journalists "see themselves as agents of a global public sphere" (Ward 2005, 16) to serve a global public rests on the idea that one can identify common grounds as to *how* to produce journalism. This does not mean that every journalist is the same. Journalists are still individuals, influenced by their own social upbringing. However, what appears to be needed is the awareness of a "global plurality" (Ward 2011, 247)—with news coverage reflecting this.

For Ward, this is a question of a "cosmopolitan" attitude: "We need a cosmopolitan media that reports issues in a way that reflects this global plurality of views and helps groups understand each other better" (Ward 2011, 247). Aiming for a "global outlook" in news through seizing the opportunities of digital access is one way to achieve this. Optimizing digital technologies can help to build network journalism, allowing for greater participation and contextualization.

But is this what is actually happening? The reality of current news practice—despite all the talk about globalization, global audiences, and global news outlooks—suggests that this ideal is not being fully realized. Constable (2007), for example, explains in her article "The Demise of the Foreign Correspondent" that many newspapers have dramatically reduced the number of their foreign desks and they have not found suitable replacements to make up for the lack of presence on the ground. What is more, as Curran and Witschge outline, "communication about public affairs has not been properly 'globalized' " (2010, 103). Rather, our "[U]nderstanding of the world is still filtered through a national prism" (2010, 103). After all, the above stated ideas that could potentially guide journalistic practices do clash with traditional notions of journalistic practice. This clash might be most visible in traditional foreign reporting.

Foreign Reporting and the Quest for a Globally Responsible Journalism

Foreign reporting is an area of journalistic practice that, already by definition, crosses borders. However, the ways in which foreign reporting is traditionally practiced do not necessarily take into consideration a "global outlook." As I have outlined elsewhere (Heinrich 2012), traditional foreign reporting concepts are strongly tied to the 19th-century idea of the nation state when media were assigned a crucial role in nation building processes. Packaging news for national audiences does help to create what Anderson (1983) called "imagined communities" and interpretation frameworks for stories mainly draw upon "national" or "domestic" frameworks (Berglez 2008).

Sourcing practices at journalistic organizations illustrate the point. As literature on sourcing suggests, organizational routines and imperatives do have an impact on news gathering processes, and journalists tend to consult standard sets of sources. To deal with time and resource limitations while ensuring credibility (e.g., Gans 1979; Shoemaker and Reese 1996), journalists concentrate on official or elite sources. Reporters are not always on the scene and need to make strategic choices about whom to contact (Sigal 1973). Economic and social factors or issues of proximity contribute to a packaging of foreign news in "domestic" frames to make it understandable and "relevant" for home audiences (Galtung and Ruge 1965). In addition, foreign reporting practices are expensive operations with just a few players having dominated the field of international news provision for decades (Hamilton and Jenner 2004).

These reflections on traditional sourcing practices correspond with the often-raised criticism against mainstream media that alternative views frequently go unheard. But this way of practicing foreign reporting demands re-evaluation all the more with the shift towards reporting both *within* a global sphere (as news stories are accessed by global audiences) and *about* a global sphere (as news access is granted to more spots on earth and with more sources at hand), particularly in light of the ideal of a "globally responsible journalism." Journalists reporting on the global stage today have to take into account that the impact of their journalism could be global in scope; and therefore that acting responsibly when reporting means being responsible not only for a national, but also for a global audience.

Sourcing practices that concentrate on elite (Western) sources and framing practices that highlight story angles of national or domestic interest collide with these ideas. Here, the sphere of network journalism allows journalists to act in a more "globally responsible" manner. The information provided via blogs, Twitter feeds, YouTube videos, or Facebook pages can contribute to a more diverse global news map, and mitigate the risk of overreliance on elite sources that might favor existing power structures (McNair 2003). To put it in the language of the network journalism paradigm, each node might provide different insights, help to contextualize events, and add further perspectives (Archetti 2008; Hafez 2009). This enhances the opportunities to find a broader range of stories and to add angles to the narratives provided in everyday news practice.

But what do journalistic organizations actually need to produce and promote a globally responsible journalism and how can digital technology assist? The following section spells out two suggestions to foster best practices in global reporting and outlines some accompanying challenges.

Suggestions for Best Practices in Reporting on the Global Stage

To meet the ideals of a "globally responsible journalism" in the network era, this section focuses on two suggestions: careful sourcing through social media and blogs, and collaborating with international journalism training organizations. Both of these take advantage of the possibilities of digital technologies, but both have limitations.

1. Use Social Media and Blogs to Seek Sources That Provide Alternative Voices, but Engage with These Sources Carefully and Critically

Nontraditional digital sources provide a potentially rich source of information. Using, identifying, and citing alternate voices through social media and blogs is a first step in widening perspectives on news stories. A second step is building and nurturing collaboration while turning these new links into continuous connections; that is, making them *part* of the network.

The practices at the BBC user-generated content hub are a prime example of this. The BBC has established a database of contacts and goes back to these when news breaks to secure on-the-ground sources across the world. Nurturing these contacts can help to create a continuous awareness of a range of perspectives on any given story. The hub represents best practices by supplementing the perspectives of BBC journalists and critically evaluating the content from social media and other sources. The hub also provides an example of the kind of organization and collaboration needed in news organizations to responsibly use user-generated content by building on the very idea of digital networks and the sphere of network journalism.

The strength of digital *networks* is their *global nodal structure*. Because each node in the network—whether a traditional reporter, blogger, or social media user—is connected to other nodes via a multitude of strings, users can follow these strings to learn more about individual nodes. One journalist who has worked through the nodes of social media networks effectively is Andy Carvin, formerly of NPR. Carvin used sophisticated social media sourcing practices to report the Arab Spring. He used his Twitter network to verify information and accounts linking to traditional news media, collaborating with bloggers, or drawing upon information from NGOs (Heinrich 2012; Hermida, Lewis, and Zamith 2012).

Journalists working with social media and blogs, however, face several important challenges. First, for small news organizations and independent journalists, the responsibility of verifying social media posts—and doing so without experts on a region—creates particular risks of receiving and spreading false information. Budget cuts at some organizations make the situation even worse. Even in news outlets where there are staffers like Carvin to focus on social media, engaging and verifying is not only time-consuming, but money needs to be assigned for social media staff. However, it is essential that staff is assigned to create and nurture these networks, as greater collaboration with actors from outside the traditional sourcing circle can help to secure access to information on the ground in various places on earth. In addition, greater collaboration *within* newsrooms (i.e., teamwork and labor division) helps to embed more voices.

A second challenge is that it is easy to manipulate digitally distributed information. The intentional spread of false information has become big business in the world of secret services and authoritarian regimes. Scholars like Morozov (2009), Mintz (2012), and van Niekerk and Maharaj (2013) elaborate extensively on these online dangers. The Syrian Electronic Army, a group of pro-Assad hackers that targets opposition groups or Western websites through various forms of cyberattacks, is just one example. Tackling these issues requires journalists who know how to identify when information is being falsified or manipulated. In addition, reporting about issues of censorship and creating awareness among a global public might help fight restrictions imposed on citizens in repressive countries. For example, when the Egyptian government under Mubarak shut down the country's Internet network in January 2011 at the start of the Egyptian uprisings, this became a major global news story. And while the cameras of the world pointed towards Egypt, services such as speak2tweet enabled people to call an international phone number and leave voice messages. An audio file of the message then appeared in the speak2tweet Twitter feed. The fact that the shutdown became a major global news story might have not only helped speak2tweet to gain international recognition, but international reporting on the Internet shutdown might have also added to the pressure on the regime to loosen the communication restrictions imposed on Egyptian citizens.

The decision on how to reference sources accessed in repressive countries presents a third challenge, apart from whether the information has been manipulated. These sources might be put in danger when their names appear in news reports. Besides using common sense, one way that journalists could help to avoid endangering sources is to contact them via direct messaging on Twitter or YouTube (when these platforms are even available). But this is no guarantee of safety if everything is being monitored. Contacting sources before publishing material might also lead to extra information. However, knowledge about surveillance methods in respective countries should be gathered first. Working with IT specialists who have expertise in sophisticated surveillance techniques might be crucial here to identify safe ways to contact information sources without compromising their safety.

A fourth challenge to carrying out best practices in use of social media and blogs is language barriers. These have always been an issue for journalists, but they are more evident with greater access to more nodes that are spreading information globally. While one might aim to ensure that these voices receive attention, the speed of information spread also makes the dangers of misunderstanding more serious. If journalists are restricted to English, this can lead to distorted pictures of often complex situations. One way to overcome these barriers is collaboration with translators or with journalists who not only know these regions, but speak the local language and can help to sift through social media content. Services like Google Translate might also assist here, but the service is at this point not trustworthy enough to ensure accurate, reliable translations.

2. Collaborate with International Journalism Organizations for Training, Advice, and Connections

Several journalism organizations in various parts of the world have trainers and advisors with first-hand knowledge of the regions and countries they serve. Established organizations such as the International Center for Journalists (ICFJ) and the Dart Center for Journalism & Trauma are concerned with a globally responsible journalism (for more about Dart, see the case study at the end of this chapter). And in the digital era, the potential importance of their work increases. They can serve as gateways to reliable contacts and can help to build connections among professional journalists, activists, bloggers, or citizen reporters.

ICFJ, for example, works with both citizen journalists and professional news organizations. Its International Journalists' Network (IJNet) provides training material, expert advice, and information on new media innovations. Other centers and projects that provide best practice guides on ethical reporting or further journalism education include the Center for Global Communication Studies (with a specific focus on education and training in comparative media law and policy) and the Institute for War & Peace Reporting (with a specific focus on strengthening local journalism in conflict and crisis zones to enhance their voices globally). Journalists in search of contacts in the Middle East, North Africa, or Iran might also consider the digital platform Aswat. The portal provides resources, dialogue, and perspectives from the region and gives activists and reformers a voice (*Aswat* means "voices" in Arabic)—all this while striving towards making governments more transparent and responsive to citizens. News providers can profit from the knowledge of organizations such as ICFJ or Aswat—and from their expertise in countries that often go under the radar of news operations.

These organizations help to foster best practices among journalists globally through their training and advice. In addition, they are themselves nodes in the global information sphere, whether by providing outlets for others to communicate—as with the Aswat portal for bloggers—or posting their resources and training opportunities. Their international expertise can help enhance a globally responsible journalism and within a digital era, their contact network with a variety of information sources on the ground can serve as a gateway for journalistic organizations to build new and continuous links with professional and alternative sources across the globe.

The difficulties of working with international journalism organizations stem mainly from their often limited capacity, especially when it comes to training journalists in person. Some countries and regions of the world will necessarily have less access, or none, to programs in their locations. This limitation points more broadly to the reality of uneven access to digital media tools, a huge challenge to realizing the potential of digital journalism globally.

These organizations are also not immune from political controversy. And the perspective they provide will always be limited by the cultural backgrounds of the people doing the training. Still, they have the potential to help journalists in many places to do their work more professionally and critically.

Common Ground and Differences in Global Ethics

An important issue to revisit in conclusion is the place of global standards of journalism ethics. Past discussions have seen attempts to create global codes of ethics, yet they all have been critiqued for their top-down approach, dictating to journalists across countries what they should or should not do (for a summary of such attempts and their critiques, see Wasserman 2011). Instead of paying attention to national specifics, these codes tended to ignore difference. They tried to apply the same rules and regulations to all journalists across the globe despite national specifics, not taking into account occupational realities or cultural specifics.

At the same time, studies comparing codes from various countries and regions have found differences but also significant common ground, particularly on the importance of telling the truth (Hafez 2002). On various philosophical bases, scholars including Christians (1997) and Ward (2011) have argued for a common commitment to humanity as a priority in communication ethics. The debate over the possibility of moral universals and what they should be, versus the reality of local differences, is a large one that can only be touched upon here. But it is a global reality that the common concerns we have as human beings coexist with differences of ethical thinking and priorities in different cultures. This coexistence of common ground and difference plays out in the work of journalists across the world.

A necessary precondition to weighing these two realities is to *understand* global and digital practices in which debates of ethics come up. With this in mind, I propose a bottom-up approach towards global journalism ethics. A crucial first step is to acknowledge difference through developing awareness of how journalism is practiced across the globe. Given that we are brought up in specific localities, journalism education needs to shape awareness of these differences while providing knowledge about the interconnected global networks that shape our lives and the lives of others—even for those who are *excluded*. This approach is global in scope, but it starts in the *locality* of classrooms across the world. This includes discussing the issue of Western-centric models of journalism. More cross-national comparisons of journalistic practices are necessary to sharpen awareness that there is not a "one-size-fits-all" journalistic practice.

This emphasis on understanding of differences in journalism practice does not eliminate the relevance of looking at decisions through the lens of specific, ethical perspectives such as the three discussed by David Craig in the previous chapter. The ethical frameworks of duty, virtue, and care can help to foster more careful thinking about decisions in a variety of settings. For example, the duty of minimizing harm is relevant to considering the impact of false social media messages wherever they may appear. But a careful understanding of local differences may help journalists to understand in more detail what the impact of those messages is likely to be.

Whatever the local differences in culture and journalistic practice, graduates need to know how to use digital technologies to source global perspectives on stories. They need to understand how journalism is changing and what the options as well as the challenges are when aiming towards a globally responsible journalism practice.

DART CENTER FOR JOURNALISM & TRAUMA
A PROJECT OF COLUMBIA JOURNALISM SCHOOL · Search term or keyword · **SEARCH** · FOLLOW US

GATEWAYS FOR ▼ · PROGRAMS ▼ · GLOBAL ▼ · About · Contact

Trauma Training in Mongolia: A Look Inside

Dart Centre Asia Pacific spoke to media trainer Lisa Gardner about Mongolia' pollution problem and preparing local journalists to investigate the story in Ulaanbaatar, the world's second-most polluted city, where the poor air quality accounts for 25 percent of deaths.

Read more

RELATED:

Self-Care Amid Disaster · Self Care Tips for News Media

Courtesy Lisa Gardner

Smog rises from the ger districts on the outskirts of Ulaanbaatar, Mongolia.

TIPS & TOOLS

Disaster
Homicide
Self-Care
Sexual Violence
Suicide
Veterans

PUBLICATIONS

OTHER LANGUAGES

JOIN THE DART NETWORK

Figure 3.1 The Dart Center website (dartcenter.org)

Best Practices in Action: The Dart Center for Journalism & Trauma

The activities of the Dart Center for Journalism & Trauma present a good example of a capacity building project that aims to provide resources on best ethical reporting practices for journalists. The project of the Columbia University Graduate School of Journalism has specialized in issues of violence, conflict, and tragedy and aims to promote ethical reporting through education. The center is global in scope. Many of its resources are dedicated to topics of best practices when covering events that have global relevance such as wars, terrorist attacks, or traumatic disasters such as natural catastrophes—all topics that are prominent on international news agendas—and they provide advice on how to ensure balanced and fair global reporting. Dart provides journalism educators with a range of materials that can be used in classrooms.

The Center runs regional hubs in Europe and Asia Pacific where, as its homepage states, its staff "promote discussion, develop training, and exchange specialist knowledge on the most challenging of media issues." These aims are at the heart of promoting a globally responsible journalism. And the hubs created by Dart can serve as important connection nodes for journalistic organizations in search of trained and knowledgeable stringers on the ground.

The Dart Center promotes globally responsible journalism in a number of ways. For example, it provides "a wide range of quick tips, deep background and training and support programs to help journalists cover bad news better" (Dart

Center for Journalism & Trauma 2014). Offering workshops or seminars for journalists and editors is just one part of this. The website is also a rich resource of information on *how* to cover these events and what challenges journalists might face in the field. The Center provides guidebooks, fact sheets, and DVDs that offer guidelines for more effective coverage of disasters and terrorism and that give advice on how to interview victims of an attack. Other fact sheets provide information about how news is framed. These sheets raise awareness about how important it is to provide contextual background and information and reflect on the impact of journalistic coverage on shaping consumers' perceptions and opinions of events. Another tip sheet gives advice on best practices for using digital tools in the event of breaking news of a major disaster—among them acting quickly, thinking visually, and pacing yourself (Tomlin 2013).

Discussion Questions

1. Pick one of the fact/tip sheets provided on the website of the Dart Center (http://dartcenter.org/). How do these relate to the idea of a "globally responsible journalism"?
2. Look at one of the international journalism organizations listed in the section on suggestions for best practices. How do their missions and recommendations enhance global network journalism? How might they contribute to global best practices?
3. Can you find an example from current journalistic practice to discuss opportunities and challenges that emerged through the use of social media as a reporting tool in covering a global media event?
4. Choose an international news topic and check how many different sources major news media outlets in your home country cite. How do you assess their sourcing practices in light of the discussions raised in this chapter?

References

Anderson, Benedict R. 1983. *Imagined Communities: Reflections on the Origin and Spread of Nationalism*. London: Verso.

Appadurai, Arjun. 1990. "Disjuncture and Difference in the Global Cultural Economy." *Theory, Culture & Society* 7:295–310.

Archetti, Cristina. 2008. "News Coverage of 9/11 and the Demise of the Media Flows, Globalization and Localization Hypotheses." *International Communication Gazette* 70(6): 463–86.

Beck, Ulrich. 2000. *What Is Globalization?* Malden, MA: Polity Press.

Beck, Ulrich. 2005. *Power in the Global Age*. Cambridge and Malden, MA: Polity Press.

Berglez, Peter. 2008. "What Is Global Journalism?" *Journalism Studies* 9(6):845–58.

Castells, Manuel. 1996. *The Rise of the Network Society*. Oxford: Blackwell.

Christians, Clifford G. 1997. "The Ethics of Being in a Communications Context." In *Communication Ethics and Universal Values*, edited by Clifford Christians and Michael Traber, 3–23. Thousand Oaks, CA: Sage.

Constable, Pamela. 2007. "The Demise of the Foreign Correspondent." *The Washington Post*, February 18, 2007. Accessed February 3, 2014. www.washingtonpost.com/wp-dyn/content/article/2007/02/16/AR2007021601713_pf.html

Curran, James, and Tamara Witschge. 2010. "Liberal Dreams and the Internet." In *New Media, Old News*, edited by Natalie Fenton, 102–18. London: Sage.

Dart Center for Journalism & Trauma. 2014. Section "Gateways for Journalists." Accessed February 20, 2014. http://dartcenter.org/gateway/journalists

Galtung, Johan, and Mari Holmboe Ruge. 1965. "The Structure of Foreign News." *Journal of Peace Research* 2(1):64–90.

Gans, Herbert J. 1979. *Deciding What's News*. New York: Pantheon Books.

Hafez, Kai. 2002. "Journalism Ethics Revisited: A Comparison of Ethics Codes in Europe, North Africa, the Middle East, and Muslim Asia." *Political Communication* 19(2):225–50.

Hafez, Kai. 2009. "Let's Improve 'Global Journalism'!" *Journalism* 10(3):329–31.

Hamilton, John M., and Eric Jenner. 2004. "Redefining Foreign Correspondence." *Journalism* 5(3):301–21.

Heinrich, Ansgard. 2011. *Network Journalism: Journalistic Practice in Interactive Spheres*. New York and London: Routledge.

Heinrich, Ansgard. 2012. "Foreign Reporting in the Sphere of Network Journalism." *Journalism Practice* 6(5–6):766–75.

Hermida, Alfred, Seth C. Lewis, and Rodrigo Zamith. 2012. "Sourcing the Arab Spring: A Case Study of Andy Carvin's Sources during the Tunisian and Egyptian Revolutions." Paper presented at the International Symposium on Online Journalism, Austin, TX, April 2012. Journalistsresource.org. Accessed December 8, 2013. http://journalistsresource.org/wp-content/uploads/2013/01/Hermida.pdf

McNair, Brian. 2003. *An Introduction to Political Communication*. 3rd ed. London: Routledge.

McNair, Brian. 2012. "Wikileaks, Journalism and the Consequences of Chaos." *Media International Australia* 144:77–86.

Mintz, Anne P., ed. 2012. *Web of Deceit: Misinformation and Manipulation in the Age of Social Media*. Medford, NJ: Information Today.

Morozov, Evgeny. 2009. "Iran: Downside to the 'Twitter Revolution.'" *Dissent* 56(4):10–14.

Shoemaker, Pamela J., and Stephen D. Reese. 1996. *Mediating the Message: Theories of Influences on Mass Media Content*. New York: Longman.

Sigal, Leon V. 1973. *Reporters and Officials: The Organization and Politics of Newsmaking*. Lexington, MA: D.C. Heath and Company.

Straubhaar, Joseph D. 2007. *World Television: From Global to Local*. Los Angeles and London: Sage.

Tomlin, Robyn. 2013. "Disaster Coverage: Digital Tips for News Organizations." Dart Center for Journalism & Trauma, June 17, 2013. Accessed February 20, 2014. http://dartcenter.org/content/disaster-coverage-as-it-applies-to-digital-world#.UrHxxI2Jab9

Van Niekerk, Brett, and Manoj Maharaj. 2013. "Social Media and Information Conflict." *International Journal of Communication* 7:1162–84.

Ward, Stephen J. A. 2005. "Philosophical Foundations for Global Journalism Ethics." *Journal of Mass Media Ethics* 1:3–21.

Ward, Stephen J. A. 2010. *Global Journalism Ethics*. Montreal: McGill-Queen's University Press.

Ward, Stephen J. A. 2011. *Ethics and the Media: An Introduction*. Cambridge: Cambridge University Press.

Wasserman, Herman. 2011. "Towards a Global Journalism Ethics via Local Narratives. South African Perspectives." *Journalism Studies* 12(6):791–803.

Link List: International Journalism Organizations

Aswat www.aswat.com
Center for Global Communication Studies (CGCS) www.global.asc.upenn.edu/index.html
Dart Center for Journalism & Trauma http://dartcenter.org
International Center for Journalists (ICFJ) www.icfj.org
ICFJ: International Journalists' Network (IJNet) Ijnet.org
Institute for War & Peace Reporting http://iwpr.net/

4

THE MAGICAL CONCEPT OF TRANSPARENCY

Stephen J. A. Ward

UNIVERSITY OF OREGON, USA

Transparency, according to optimistic accounts, is the answer to bad government, official wrongdoing, and the arrogant power of corporations and news media. Let the "sunshine" of transparency enter the public domain and watch these evil forces retreat.

Transparency is a "god" of political and institutional ethics.

The British Academy has said that transparency has attained a "quasi-religious significance in debate over governance and institutional design." The term is more often "preached than practiced, more often invoked than defined, and indeed might ironically be said to be mystic in essence, at least to some extent" (Heald 2006, 60).

Journalists who reject objectivity commonly say: "I am biased but at least I am honest and transparent. I tell people where I am coming from." Journalists who practice new forms of journalism, such as nonprofit journalism, use transparency to justify their close relations with funders. Textbooks and codes of ethics increasingly make transparency a principle of good practice. In *The New Ethics of Journalism*, McBride and Rosenstiel argue that transparency is now more basic than the principle of independence (McBride and Rosenstiel 2013, 1–6).

This chapter asks: What is transparency's place in journalism ethics, relative to other values? It rejects the enthusiast's simplistic faith in transparency, without rejecting transparency *tout court*. I argue that transparency is neither an all-powerful god nor a minor deity. Transparency belongs to a group of core values that must be weighed when making editorial decisions. Transparency by itself is not sufficient for responsible journalism. Practitioners should honor a web of values. Transparency is only one of the gods in the pantheon of journalism ethics.

I begin with the meaning of transparency and its intellectual history. I assess the sufficiency of transparency as a norm for public agencies and practices. Then I turn to the place of transparency in the practice of journalism.

The Insufficiency of Transparency

Roots of Transparency

Transparency is a late 16th-century term that derives from the medieval Latin word *transparere*, from *trans* ("through") and *parere* ("appear"). Literally, it means to "shine through."

The original meaning referred to materials that allow light to pass through so that objects behind can be distinctly seen, such as the transparency of ice. By the 18th century, we extended the term to social practices and public institutions (Fung, Graham, and Weil 2007).

For this chapter, the form of transparency in focus is access to information about government, institutions, corporations, and professional practices. Transparency is about being able to "look into" these agencies and see how they operate.

The idea of public accountability is as old as Western society. In ancient Athenian democracy, auditors monitored the use of public funds and the incomes of military generals. Early standards of accountability in Western government are found in England's Magna Carta of 1215, which required that the King not raise taxes before consulting his barons. In recent times, a movement toward transparency began in the 20th century as the public grew wary of the increasing influence of corporations and government in their lives. In the early 1900s, an era of professionalization led to codes of ethics and ombudsmen. Later, new global institutions, such as the International Monetary Fund, insisted that countries which received assistance be transparent about how they spent the funding. By mid-century, leaders of social movements called for accountability from almost every form of institution—universities, sports organizations, and news media. Laws allowed public access to government records.

The intellectual roots of transparency go back to the ideal of "publicity" in the 18th-century public sphere, especially in England and America, where reformers sought to make government more responsible to the public. Reformers demanded that government explain decisions and publish parliamentary discussions and laws. Jürgen Habermas, in his study of the European public sphere, showed that the demand for publicity occurred as citizens questioned absolute power (Habermas 1989).

The English philosopher Jeremy Bentham provided one of the first theories of publicity. Bentham argued that all persons have a right to information about government actions. He saw publicity as providing information to a public that sits as an informal tribunal, passing judgment on government. It is a court of public opinion. (For a good discussion of Bentham's ideas on publicity and transparency, see Baume and Papadopoulous 2013.) Bentham gave several reasons for publicity: (1) it protects the public by exposing and punishing bad conduct; (2) although originating in distrust, it increases public confidence in government; (3)

it supports honorable officials by showing that they work in proper ways; (4) it informs government of the wishes of the people; and (5) it generates discussion that can lead to better policy (Bentham 1983, 37–39).

Bentham's reasons for publicity are repeated today as reasons for transparency.

Conceptual Insufficiency

Bentham never regarded publicity as a cure for the ills of society. He rightly regarded publicity as a necessary but not sufficient condition for good government. Insufficiency does not mean that publicity or transparency is not important. To arrive at a correct notion of the value of transparency, we need to examine its two insufficiencies: conceptual and empirical insufficiency.

The conceptual problem is that transparency is gregarious. It will associate with almost any concept. Transparency is used improperly as a synonym for democracy, accountability, responsibility, honesty, frankness, and lack of pretense. Important distinctions collapse.

For example, it is important to *not* equate democratic practice with transparent practice. The latter are, at best, a subset of the former. Transparent actions can be non-democratic, and non-transparent practices can be democratic. Democracies endorse values other than transparency. Democracy, for example, needs non-transparent practices that protect privacy. Also, there is a place for confidential practices, such as discussions between lawyers and clients, private voting booths, and collective bargaining behind closed doors. Society needs transparent and non-transparent processes.

It is important to *not* equate transparency with responsibility. Being responsible means considering the impact of one's actions on others, following norms, correcting errors. What responsibility means differs according to one's situation and social role. Whatever its meaning, responsibility is not transparency, which shows whether someone acted responsibly.

Transparency encourages responsible conduct by exposing misconduct. But it can conflict with responsibilities. A social worker investigating abuse of children has a responsibility to *not* make public the identities of suspects in her case file. A priest would be irresponsible to make public the information provided during confession. A teacher would be irresponsible if she made public the marks of a student, or the marks of her entire class. In being non-transparent, the teacher, priest, and social worker are not undemocratic. They are being responsible.

Also, transparency should *not* be equated with publicity or accountability. Daniel Naurin notes that transparency refers to information that is accessible, ready for viewing by citizens who are willing and able to seek it (Naurin 2006). Publicity is more demanding. It is the effective dissemination of such information, bringing it to the notice of the public, and indicating how the information should spark action. Transparency makes publicity possible. Yet, the bridge from transparency to publicity may not be crossed for many reasons, for example, lack of media coverage, citizen apathy toward public engagement, or unwillingness to invest time in publicity.

Similar points block the equating of transparency with accountability. Accountability adds to responsibility the idea of "answering" for one's actions to someone, and the possibility of sanctions. Who I am accountable to, and to what extent, is determined by pre-defined responsibilities, not by demands for transparency. Informational transparency often assumes the full accountability of officials to all citizens, equally. But few people are accountable in this way. As director of an academic institution paid in part by public taxes, I have a general accountability to the public. I am accountable in more specific (and direct) ways to my supervisor, the Dean, to center employees, and to university administrators. My specific accountabilities may come into tension with a general demand for transparency. I am accountable to the university for following rules on privacy regarding information on students. I am accountable to my supervisor on how I handle an internal personnel dispute. To be informationally transparent in these situations—to reveal private information, or details of a personnel dispute—would be irresponsible.

Moreover, we make a conceptual mistake if we consider transparency as a stand-alone principle. We misunderstand moral reasoning. Ethics in general and the ethics of practices in particular operate by applying a web of norms to situations to determine best practice. The norms often conflict, so we have to weigh and balance them. As we will see, journalism ethics balances many values, from transparency and truth-seeking to minimizing harm. There is no absolute hierarchy of values with transparency at the top.

To summarize, transparency is related to responsibility, accountability, and publicity. But we have to define those relations carefully. To be related is not to be equal (or synonymous) in meaning. The range of actions that are responsible and accountable is larger than the range of transparent actions. Some transparent actions are correct exercises in responsibility and accountability, while other transparent actions are irresponsible and clash with accountability.

Our analysis leads to the view that transparency should not simply "replace" different and more basic concepts, such as responsibility. Ethics is based on the bedrock notions of responsibility and accountability, not transparency. Transparency arguments presume that certain agencies and persons have pre-determined responsibilities and accountabilities, for example, serving the public. Take away responsibilities and accountabilities and there is no basis for demanding transparency. Only after we have determined our responsibilities and aims can we meaningfully discuss the demands of transparency.

One result of using normative concepts without care is that we start to think these concepts have a magic to resolve difficult problems. Pollitt and Hupe have created a list of "magic concepts." The list includes transparency along with governance, networks, innovation, and participation (Pollitt and Hupe 2011). Magic concepts are popular because they are broad (apply to many things), are easy to invoke, are in fashion, and ignore tensions with other values. They are attractive because it is difficult to be against them. The trouble with magic words is that they are used glibly. They short-circuit reflection and clear thinking. Yet transparency doesn't have to be a magic word. We just need to define carefully its meaning and role in ethics.

Empirical Insufficiency

When norms become magic, they raise unrealistic expectations.

One response is to show how terms like transparency are empirically insufficient. That is, we make an empirical mistake if we think that transparent mechanisms are causally sufficient to ensure good governance in institutions. Our expectations of transparency are unrealistic. An antidote to magical thinking is to remind ourselves of the various ways in which transparency may fail to ensure good public conduct. Here are some:

Loopholes, Blame Avoidance, and Institutional Culture

In an agency of any reasonable complexity, there will be people who can find loopholes in any transparency process. Despite sanctions, employees get around rules and take advantage of any vagueness in transparency language. Officials are given discretion is interpreting rules for conflicts of interest or, for instance, what constitutes legitimate travel expenses. Discretion can cover questionable conduct.

Even when accused of misconduct, the accused may adopt an effective blame avoidance strategy. They may: fight vigorously every claim; dispute every fact; make counter-allegations and claim discrimination; seek support from a union; and exhaust every legal and appeal procedure. Some administrators may become wary of rigorously enforcing transparency measures. Or the culture of the institution may be an "old boys' network" where a public façade of transparency hides a desire to protect one's own and deal internally with problems. Such agencies may make the process of obtaining information so byzantine and time-consuming that it discourages queries.

Limits to Naming and Shaming

Expectations for transparency are based on a belief in the efficacy of "naming and shaming" violators. Naming and shaming works because it (a) touches our moral conscience, or (b) threatens our desire to be socially respected, or (c) threatens our self-interest by leading to sanctions and by damaging job prospects. Unfortunately, there are many situations where (a) to (c) have limited force. The person in question may lack a moral conscience, care little for his or her reputation, or be able to protect his or her self-interest. For instance, a political leader or multinational corporation may be so powerful and independent that they are unmoved by public criticism. They can hire a battery of lawyers to harass critics and launch a campaign to win the battle in the court of public opinion. The effectiveness of transparency depends, to a great degree, on the balance of power in a society.

Negative Consequences

Transparency is often seen as a threat to agencies and companies, prompting regrettable responses. Officials may develop better forms of deception and better ways to "cover one's trail." Officials may stop using written correspondence to conduct business, and resort to telephone and face-to-face conversations. The official record of governance, then, is incomplete and misleading.

Constant surveillance through transparent mechanisms may cause honest officials to speak and act cautiously when frank talk and bold actions are needed. It may lead to an obsession with rule following rather than creative problem solving and risk taking. Heald points to a feeling of "suffocation" in organizations from the necessity to account for everything (Heald 2006).

Transparency is misguided when it demands that agencies hold most (or all) discussions in public, under the glare of the media. This changes the dynamic of communication, and not always for the better. There *is* a reason why crucial stages in collective bargaining or attempts to reach international agreements are not carried out entirely in public in real time. Discussions in public may encourage public posturing and "winning the news cycle." Spokespersons may over-simplify issues, follow opinion polls, or cave in to "outrage" from lobby groups when they seek compromise. Leaders who advance firm positions in public appear decisive and strong. It also makes it difficult to reach reasonable agreements.

Questionable Assumptions

Arguments for strong transparency usually take an overly optimistic view of Bentham's court of public opinion: transparency improves trust in institutions. Does it? Always? Polls have charted a decline of public trust in institutions at the same time that transparency mechanisms and media coverage of corruption have increased. Is this a correlation or a causal relationship? Despite the debate, the point remains that we cannot assume that transparency has an unqualified positive impact on public trust.

Also, our philosophy of transparency should not assume that making information public will necessarily improve the court of public opinion. Transparency provides materials for informed discussion and reform of public policy. But we are never sure that making data public will lead to fair deliberation and better policy. This is because the positive force of publicity depends on the virtue of the agency that provides access to the data. It also depends on the virtue of the person who accessed the data and disseminates it for publicity; and, it depends on the virtue of deliberating citizens.

We cannot assume that those who circulate information are motivated by pure intentions. Advocacy groups, individuals with political agendas, and others circulate information that is incomplete or biased. Information can be used to falsely accuse a political opponent of corruption. Environmental groups may "reinterpret" for the public a study on the safety of nuclear reactors. We live in a public sphere where transparency can assist worthy citizens or manipulators. Even if information is circulated in an accurate manner, public discussion may fall short of deliberation. The discussion may be marred by partisan and intolerant voices.

Transparency in Journalism

Applied to journalism, transparency allows citizens to look into the internal workings of newsrooms, viewing their operations, decisions, and conduct. Transparency includes the following sorts of information:

1. *Methods of editorial production:*
   - Ethical basis of editorial judgments: Why a story was chosen; why a certain image was used; ethical standards followed by the publication and its approach to journalism, e.g., objective, advocational, or political; ways for the public to question a story or to seek correction.
   - Evidence: Reliability of facts and research done; noting of any uncertainties; vetting for accuracy; handling of citizen materials and data from social media.
   - Sources: Amount of original reporting; what material borrowed from other media; status of experts; the variety of voices; anonymous sources and sources not mentioned in story.
   - Editorial partners: Who they are; their reliability; their qualifications and journalistic standards; what they contributed.

2. *Influencing factors:*
   - Conflicts of interest: Personal, political, and financial relationships between journalists and the sources and subjects of their stories; process for handling conflicts of interest.
   - Funders: What donors supported the journalism; funding policies; "strings" attached to funding; differences between advertorial and editorial copy.

Transparency and accountability methods have grown rapidly since the birth of online media. They add to existing methods such as letters to the editor, corrections, press councils, and newsroom ombudsmen. Online methods include: "about" pages on websites, highlighting corrections and apologies online, and maintaining a record of changes; explanatory "boxes" for controversial decisions; links to codes of ethics, press councils, and ways for the public to question stories; editorial notes at top or bottom of stories explaining a reporter's relation to a source in the story (or some other matter); links to background knowledge, experts, and other journalistic treatments of the same story; links to original documents, raw interview notes, unedited interview tape, and video of an entire news conference; editorial policies on external partners, citizen images or text, online forums with editors, reporters, or ombudsmen; placing reader comments and questions alongside the online story; regular publication of in-house evaluations of compliance with standards; facts about ownership and readership.

Given this plurality of methods, we should expect differences in how journalists implement transparency. An informal scan of news media suggests interesting differences that warrant research. For example, there is the difference between transparency as an explicit principle in a newsroom's code of ethics and transparency as "implied" by other norms. The code for the Society of Professional Journalists (SPJ) does not make transparency one of its four principles (SPJ 2013). However "Be Accountable" is among the four principles. Some norms that fall under the principles encourage transparency. Under "Seek Truth and Report It," we find the norm: "Identify sources whenever feasible. The public is entitled to as much information as possible on sources' reliability." Similarly, transparency is not a principle in the code for the main American broadcast association, the Radio Television Digital News Association (RTDNA 2013). However, under its accountability principle, the RTDNA states: "Explain journalistic processes to the public, especially when practices spark questions or controversy."

The BBC makes transparency one of its chief editorial values: "We will be transparent about the nature and provenance of the content we offer online" (BBC 2013). The Canadian Association of Journalists names transparency as a principle. It focuses on deceptive practices. Journalists should, as much as possible, identify themselves and identify sources (CAJ 2013).

Online, the same variety of approaches prevails. Many popular sites, such as *The Huffington Post* or Slate.com, do not provide readers with a code of ethics (Slate 2013). *The Huffington Post*, however, does have guidelines for respectful and engaging commentary by readers (*Huffington Post* 2013). On the other hand, a number of online news sites are very transparent about their operations, such as the Wisconsin Center for Investigative Journalism, which I discuss below.

Conceptual Insufficiency

Having sketched the concept of transparency in journalism, I return to the evaluation of transparency for journalism. Many points can be made quickly, because the argument was established above. I stress conceptual insufficiencies, because the empirical insufficiencies are obvious. Loopholes, blame avoidance, resistant institutional culture, and other factors are as possible in the relatively unregulated practice of journalism as anywhere.

Earlier arguments for the insufficiency of transparency provide reasons to doubt its sufficiency in journalism. However, in this section, we can explain in more detail why this insufficiency exists in journalism. A good place to start is the framework for journalism ethics (discussed at length in Ward 2010 and Ward 2013).

Journalists define their ethics not by starting with transparency but by starting with something more fundamental: (1) a commitment to use the power to publish responsibly, and (2) a commitment to further social aims such as serving a democratic public. To honor these dual commitments, journalists embrace principles such as truth-seeking, editorial independence, minimizing harm, and accountability. These principles are broken down into more specific values. For example, truth-seeking implies a commitment to accuracy and verification. Independence prohibits conflicts of interest. Minimizing harm may counsel not naming a young person in a story. Accountability asks journalists to explain decisions. Under accountability, transparency finds a place. (David Craig's chapter in this book also discusses the ethical responsibilities of journalists.)

Moral reasoning in journalism ethics adheres to the "web of norms" model. For any decision, responsible journalists weigh norms and facts to identify the best course of action.

Informing the public about the arrest of a public figure may harm that person's reputation but the story is justified because informing the public about the criminal justice system trumps the harm to reputation. Amid this balancing, transparency is one—and only one—of the core values to be weighed.

The journalist's commitment to responsibility and democracy is prior to transparency. We determine how transparent journalists should be by looking at their social responsibilities and aims. Nor is transparency an absolute value. Where transparency conflicts with other values, the other values may deserve our support. There are two areas where tensions occur: non-transparent measures to seek truth, and non-transparent measures to minimize harm.

Non-transparent methods in seeking truth have always been part of journalism. Journalists have used confidential sources, for example, whistleblowers, for centuries. In the United States, "shield" laws protect journalists from being forced to reveal their sources. Without promises of confidentiality, sources on wrongdoing would dry up. Therefore, the "doing" of journalism can conflict with the demand that journalists show everything.

Non-transparent methods to minimize harm are widely practiced. Journalists may not reveal a confidential source in an investigation of drug cartels because it would expose the source to retaliation. Journalists act in a morally sound manner when they reduce harm by not identifying the identities of children involved in a tragic story. They also act ethically when they do not publish private photos of public figures to sell the news.

Transparency, when used to justify opinionated journalism, comes into tension with journalistic impartiality. Many news organizations believe their journalists should act impartially to maintain public trust. The American public broadcaster National Public Radio (NPR) restricts how transparent NPR journalists are about their personal and political views. NPR is especially sensitive to what its journalists say when they appear on other media and when they comment on their websites. The NPR impartiality rule is clearly non-transparent: Never say in

public or on other media what you would not say as an impartial journalist on
NPR programs. For example, suppose an NPR journalist reports objectively on
a controversial new law by the governor. Later, she posts on her Twitter feed that
the governor is an "idiot" for bringing in such a law. Such partial and transparent
comments would violate the impartiality rule. Over the past few years, this policy
has been debated nationally due to controversial cases, such as NPR's firing of
Juan Williams for comments on a FOX talk show that he gets nervous at airports
when he sees Muslims in traditional dress. In response to the controversy, and to
additional media developments, NPR and other public media have updated their
editorial policies through a project called "Editorial Integrity for Public Media"
(Editorial Integrity for Public Media 2013). The commitment to impartiality
remains strong.

Over the past few years, skepticism about the ethical sufficiency of online values has grown in direct proportion to irresponsible uses of online media. Take, for
example, the role of online media during the bombing of the Boston Marathon on
April 15, 2013 (Kang 2013; for a detailed discussion see Alfred Hermida's chapter
in this book). Some bloggers and users of websites such as Reddit and social media
like Twitter set out to find a second suspect. In the end, they misidentified a Brown
University student, Sunil Tripathi, as the suspect. Tripathi had been missing for some
time, and his family was looking for him. They set up a Facebook site asking people
to help them find Sunil, and they put a photo of him on the site. Then, a number
of online users, acting as vigilantes and as breaking news reporters, thought they
saw a resemblance between grainy police photos and the picture of Tripathi on the
family's Facebook site. They identified him as the suspect. The family suffered cruel
online abuse. At one point, the family had to take down the Facebook site.

The moral is clear: Transparency and sharing information online should be
tempered by a commitment to responsible publishing and a concern for accuracy,
verification, and minimizing harm. The Tripathi case shows that good practice in
journalism requires much more than transparency. It requires the convergence
of two sets of things: knowledge and rigorous methods plus a web of norms that
determine how knowledge and method is put into practice.

To understand transparency's role in journalism's web of values, we need to
keep squarely before us the difference between doing and showing. The values of
truth-seeking, investigating, and verifying are standards for doing journalism. The
values of accountability, transparency, and explaining decisions are standards for
showing how we do journalism.

Perhaps this story might help. Some years ago, I attended a communications
conference in Dresden, Germany, with my wife, Glenda. Because of my wife's
love of Volkswagen cars, we took a tour of a Volkswagen plant. I was impressed
by the transparency. We could walk along the car production areas, separated from
the workers by panes of glass. Yet, there is more to making cars than showing
people the production areas. There is the skilled workmanship, the technology,

and the standards that guide production. The plant combined the values of doing and showing. But no one confused making cars with showing how to make cars.

The same distinctions apply to journalism. Doing journalism is gathering information, verifying it, and constructing and disseminating stories. Showing our journalism is being accountable and transparent. Although newsrooms don't provide tours for citizens behind panes of glass, citizens can "observe" how the journalism was done through the above-mentioned methods of transparency. But no one should confuse "making" stories with showing how the "making" happens.

Replacing Independence?

Not all arguments for transparency come from enthusiasts who overplay its efficacy. Better arguments come from respected ethicists and journalists, such as Tom Rosenstiel and Kelly McBride. As mentioned, they developed new ideas about transparency when updating the principles of the Poynter Institute. Their study resulted in *The New Ethics of Journalism* (McBride and Rosenstiel 2014). The book starts with the fact that journalism is done by many new agents, from citizen journalists to think tanks. This weakens the principle of editorial independence, which was meant for a well-defined class of professional journalists. Independence cautioned professionals against conflicts of interest and allowing allegiances to bias reports. Today, many journalists are non-professionals and they put their perspectives in stories.

In a separate article, Rosenstiel argues that seeking truth and reporting it remains primary for good journalists but the principle of acting independently is problematic (Rosenstiel 2013). Hence, act independently should be replaced by "be transparent." This transparency requires not only that journalists provide information on how they did their story but also how they approach journalism. Are they advocates, objective reporters, or otherwise? Of course, Rosenstiel wants these journalists to value accuracy and verification. His hope is that this idea of transparency, combined with traditional values, will separate journalism from propaganda.

This is an interesting proposal. However, for the reasons I have given, I cannot agree that the best response is to replace independence with transparency. First, transparency's conceptual insufficiency warns us about thinking that it can (or should) replace basic principles. A better strategy is to talk about *reforming* principles for new conditions, not abandoning them or replacing them. In addition, we should seek ways to incorporate new ideas about transparency under the principle of accountability.

Second, I think independence is conceptually different from, and more basic than, transparency. I do not think independence can or should fall under a broader notion of transparency. Independence is about doing journalism. It insists that journalists not let allegiances and sources weaken their commitment to independent journalism. Independence, not transparency, distinguishes journalism

Figure 4.1 WisconsinWatch.org

and propaganda, journalism and narrow advocacy. Appealing to an increase in the number of non-objective and advocational journalists does not undermine the ethical importance of independence. Rather, the reverse. We should challenge the new kids on the block to persuade the public that they are truly independent. At the same time, we should reform our conception of independence so it applies to new and popular forms of journalism. Without independence, much questionable journalism will fly under the flag of responsible journalism.

In summary, this chapter puts forward an interpretation of the role of transparency in today's journalism. However, it provides only a general understanding. In upcoming publications, we—ethicists and journalists—need to be more specific. We should develop concrete guidelines on how much weight to give transparency in different types of stories, and in different forms of journalism.

The hard work of developing a detailed ethics of transparency lies in the future.

Best Practices in Action: Wisconsin Center for Investigative Journalism

Skepticism that, in a new media world, transparency and independence cannot coexist is best met by producing examples to the contrary. There are forms of online journalism that support a "web of norms" model, are transparent, and maintain a commitment to independence. Take, for example, the Wisconsin Center for Investigative Journalism (WCIJ), located in the School of Journalism and Communication at the University of Wisconsin–Madison. It has won regional and national journalism awards.

The center is part of the growing domain of non-profit journalism where journalists are supported by non-traditional economic models, such as foundation funding, membership subscriptions, and individual donors. Journalists who direct such centers have conflicting roles—of fund raiser and news editor. These journalists do not enjoy a "wall" between editorial and business sections—a wall that once existed in large mainstream news organizations. That wall is either gone or crumbling. In non-profit journalism, there is little "distance" between journalists and funders (or fund raising), raising questions of independence and funder influence on editorial writings. The main ethical questions for non-profit journalism are about independence and transparency: Who will you take money from? Will you name all (or most) donors? Will you explain arrangements between funders and stories? Would you allow funders to attach "strings" to their gifts?

The center's approach is to use transparency to buttress editorial independence. Rather than "replace" independence, the center seeks to preserve it (and the public's trust) by *both* employing transparent measures and doing accurate and hard-hitting independent journalism. Showing and doing go together.

The center has extensive editorial guidelines that show how transparency and independence can be combined to create solid investigative journalism. Its website has a detailed policy on financial support which requires news coverage to be independent of donors and that all providers of revenue be identified (Wisconsin Watch 2012). The center has an elaborate conflict of interest policy to ensure that editorial decisions are made "solely in the interest of promoting the quality of journalism" (WisconsinWatch 2014). The policy includes a process for dealing with a claim of a conflict of interest made against anyone in the center.

I do not put the center forward as a perfect news operation. I mention it as an example of how journalism online and offline should treat transparency. It should be treated as an important value that supports, not replaces, the principles of verification and independence.

Discussion Questions

1. What is the value of transparency in general for organizations and agencies in a democracy? Is transparency in journalism different from or similar to transparency in other organizations? Can demands for transparency go too far?

2. Can you think of a non-transparent process (or practice) that is essential to some domain of society or to democracy?

3. What mechanisms exist to check on the transparency of social institutions and government? What mechanisms exist to test the transparency of news organizations? Should there be more (or fewer) mechanisms of transparency in journalism?

4. How transparent should websites be about how they do their journalism and how they are funded? Take, for example, the "About" pages of websites. What should they disclose? What types of information should be available on "About" pages?

References

Baume, Sandrine, and Yannis Papadopoulous. 2013. "Transparency as a Requirement of Good Governance: A Historical Perspective." Paper presented at the CAST Workshop on National Security, Risk Management, and the Transformation of Bureaucratic

Ethics, Boston, MA, May 23–24, 2013. Accessed February 27, 2014. http://cast.ku.dk/national-security-risk-management-and-the-transformation-of-bureaucratic-ethics/download/Baume___Papadopoulos_2013.pdf

BBC. 2013. "Editorial Values." Accessed December 20, 2013. www.bbc.co.uk/editorialguidelines/page/guidelines-editorial-values-editorial-values

Bentham, Jeremy. 1983. "Constitutional Code." In *The Collected Works of Jeremy Bentham*, Vol. I, edited by Frederick Rosen and James H. Burns, 45–71. Oxford: Clarendon Press.

CAJ. 2013. "Ethics Guidelines." Accessed December 20, 2013. hwww.caj.ca/?p=1776

Editorial Integrity for Public Media. 2013. "Public Media Code of Integrity." Accessed December 20, 2013. http://pmintegrity.org

Fung, Archon, Mary Graham, and David Weil. 2007. *Disclosure: The Promise and Peril of Transparency*. Cambridge, UK: Cambridge University Press.

Habermas, Jürgen. 1989. *The Structural Transformation of the Public Sphere*. Translated by Thomas Burger. Cambridge, UK: Polity Press.

Heald, David. 2006. "Transparency as an Instrumental Value." In *Transparency: The Key to Better Governance?*, edited by Christopher Hood and David Heald, 59–73. Oxford, UK: Oxford University Press.

Huffington Post. 2013. "Comments & Moderation." Accessed December 20, 2013. www.huffingtonpost.com/faq/#moderation

Kang, Jay C. 2013. "Should Reddit Be Blamed for the Spreading of a Smear?" *The New York Times*, July 25, 2013. Accessed December 20, 2013. www.nytimes.com/2013/07/28/magazine/should-reddit-be-blamed-for-the-spreading-of-a-smear.html?pagewanted=all&_r=0

McBride, Kelly, and Tom Rosenstiel, eds. 2013. *The New Ethics of Journalism*. Los Angeles, CA: Sage.

Naurin, Daniel. 2006. "Transparency, Publicity, Accountability—The Missing Links." *Swiss Political Science Review* 12:90–98.

Pollitt, Christopher, and Peter Hupe. 2011. "Talking about Government: The Role of Magic Concepts." *Public Management Review* 13:641–658.

Rosenstiel, Tom. 2013. "Why 'Be Transparent' Has Replaced 'Act Independently' as a Guiding Journalism Principle." *Poynter*, September 16, 2013. Accessed September 26, 2013. www.poynter.org/latest-news/the-next-journalism/223657/why-be-transparent-is-now-a-better-ethical-principle-than-act-independently/

RTDNA. 2013. "RTDNA Code of Ethics." Accessed December 20, 2013. www.rtdna.org/content/rtdna_code_of_ethics#.UkGeK1_n_wo

Slate. 2013. Accessed December 20, 2013. www.slate.com

SPJ. 2013. "SPJ Code of Ethics." Accessed November 17, 2013. www.spj.org/ethicscode.asp

Ward, Stephen J. A. 2010. *Global Journalism Ethics*. Montreal: McGill-Queen's University Press.

Ward, Stephen J. A. 2013. *Ethics and the Media: An Introduction*. Cambridge, UK: Cambridge University Press.

WisconsinWatch. 2012. "Fundraising Policy." Last modified August 31, 2012. www.wisconsinwatch.org/about/funding/fundraising-policy/

WisconsinWatch. 2014. "Ethics and Diversity at the Wisconsin Center for Investigative Journalism." Accessed March 8, 2014. www.wisconsinwatch.org/about/ethics/

5

FILTERING FACT FROM FICTION

A Verification Framework for Social Media

Alfred Hermida

UNIVERSITY OF BRITISH COLUMBIA, VANCOUVER, CANADA

The photo spoke volumes about the human cost of war. It showed neat rows of shrouded bodies, as a child jumped over one of the rows. The picture was published by the BBC News website on its report of the killing of at least 90 people, 32 of them children under the age of 10, in the Syrian region of Houla in May 2012 (BBC 2012). Supposedly, it was a visceral record of the barbarity of the Syrian conflict. But it wasn't. A Getty photographer had taken the photo in Iraq almost a decade earlier.

"I went home at 3am and I opened the BBC page which had a front page story about what happened in Syria and I almost fell off from my chair," photographer Marco di Lauro told the UK newspaper, *The Telegraph* (Furness 2013). The BBC took down the image within 90 minutes of publication and later admitted it had been a mistake. "Efforts were made to track down the original source and, having obtained some information pointing to its veracity, the picture was published, with a disclaimer saying it could not be independently verified," explained the BBC's social media editor, Chris Hamilton (2012). "However, on this occasion, the extent of the checks and the consideration of whether to publish should have been better."

Publishing a powerful image without certainty highlights the challenges for journalists faced with the widespread proliferation of raw information related to the news produced and disseminated by the public. Over the past decade some of the most dramatic images have come from people witnessing the news, from a shaky video of the London bombings in 2005 to the photo of a plane in the Hudson River in 2009 to the video of a bloodied suspect in the Woolwich killing of 2013. Journalists who once could claim a monopoly on the supply of everyday public information are contending with publics that are sharing eyewitness accounts, commenting on the news, or evaluating information on social media.

Navigating streams of public information requires journalists to draw on tried and tested methods, but also presents opportunities to develop new techniques and tools.

How Verification Comes to Matter

The ease by which a rumor can take hold and spread on social media has given greater urgency to the need for sources of accurate and reliable information. Journalists have traditionally filled such a role. Verification is at the core of the journalist's contention to objectively parse reality. It enables the profession to claim a special kind of authority and status, distinguishing what they do from other forms of public communication. In their seminal work, *The Elements of Journalism*, Kovach and Rosenstiel declared the discipline of verification as "the essence of journalism" (2007, 79).

A commitment to accuracy is deeply embedded in the journalism profession. The Pew Research Journalism Project lists an obligation to the truth as the first of its nine Principles of Journalism. Journalists strive for the truth through "the professional discipline of assembling and verifying facts," as "accuracy is the foundation upon which everything else is built" (Pew Research Journalism Project 2013). The pursuit of truth is inextricably tied to journalism's purpose "to provide citizens with the information they need to be free and self-governing" (Kovach and Rosenstiel 2007, 12). The democratic purpose ascribed to journalism goes back to Walter Lippmann, who argued in 1920 "there can be no liberty for a community which lacks the information by which to detect lies" (2008, 38). The practice of verification not only confers journalistic communication with a unique status, it also validates journalism as a profession.

A commitment to verification underlies core ethical values in journalism. The code of ethics from the Society of Professional Journalists emphasizes a professional duty to seek the truth and report it fairly. The code states journalists should "test the accuracy of information from all sources and exercise care to avoid inadvertent error" (Society of Professional Journalists 2014). The abundance and speed of real-time social media has strained these ethical considerations, giving rise to criticisms of erroneous reporting and the potential harm caused in the rush to be first (Coddington 2013).

Journalists have always had to balance the need to be accurate with the pressure of deadlines. Getting things wrong pre-dates the Internet. In a study of US newspapers in the 1980s, Philip Meyer found that three out of five stories contained at least one error (2009). As Meyer noted, "a newspaper with a zero level of factual errors is a newspaper that is missing deadlines, taking too few risks, or both" (2009, 89). The explosion in material from the public, coupled with the speed and reach of digital platforms such as Twitter, has placed additional strains on verification practices.

An early indication of the need for new skills and practices came during the London bombings of 2005. More than 1,000 photographs, 20 videos, 4,000 texts, and 20,000 emails were sent to the BBC within six hours of the attacks. National TV news bulletins led with grainy mobile phone video. "By day's end, the BBC's newsgathering had crossed a Rubicon. The quantity and quality of the public's contributions moved them beyond novelty, tokenism or the exceptional," wrote Richard Sambrook at the time, when he was director of the BBC's World Service and Global News division (2005). Since then, the BBC and other news organizations have either expanded or created units dedicated to sift through material from the public.

Slip-ups are more prevalent and more significant at times of breaking news, when reports are confused, contradictory, and changeable. Politicians or celebrities are prematurely declared dead or suspects in terrorist acts are misidentified. These are the times when reliable providers of information are most valuable, given the surfeit of speculation, rumor, and opinion on social media. Figuring out what is fact from fiction requires a mix of old-school journalistic skills, new technologies, and an understanding of how news flows in always-on media systems.

Best Practices for Verification

Bearing witness to events and documenting them for the public has been at the core of journalistic activity. News outlets will send a reporter to the scene of a breaking story, but at least one person back in the newsroom will be scouring the web for eyewitness accounts, photos, or videos. Social media can serve as an early warning system for events that merit further investigation. The information on social media is often closer to a news tip than a fact.

At the time of the shootings at Los Angeles International Airport on November 1, 2013, one of the first reports came from a host of the TV show "MythBusters." "Something just happened at #LAX. TSA and police running everywhere," wrote Grant Imahara in a tweet (2013). Simply because a piece of information is circulating online doesn't mean that it is true. It needs to be checked. It seems an obvious thing to say but it is worth stressing. During the LAX shootings, Canada's *Globe and Mail* published a story about the alleged death of the ex-NSA chief, Michael Hayden. The source was a hoax account called @HeadlineNews [sic], fashioned to look like the reputable @BreakingNews account. The online story then incorrectly ran with a combined Associated Press and Reuters byline. Even though a reporter, members of the editorial web team, a homepage editor, and a senior editor saw the hoax tweet, no one checked the information or its source (Kirkland 2013).

With any piece of information, journalists need to ask basic questions. How do people know what they purport to know? Did they witness it or hear it from a friend? How would they have access to such information? Who are they connected to? Keith Urbahn was viewed as a reliable source when he tweeted, "So I'm told by a reputable person they have killed Osama Bin Laden. Hot damn," as he had been the chief of staff for the former defense secretary Donald Rumsfeld (Hermida 2011, 671). Urbahn would have had the network to be in the know.

The quest for accuracy is central to modern journalism, and the essential fact-checking skills that have been used for the past 100 years are the starting point. Journalists have three basic methods at their disposal—observation, interviews, and documents. With digital data, there is one further layer. Every piece of information published on the Internet leaves a digital trail that can help assess its veracity. No single approach works for everything. Adopting several layers of analysis and triangulating the information can help to avoid unfortunate missteps.

Message-Based Analysis

The third baseman for the Toronto Blue Jays, Brett Lawrie, made headlines in 2012 but not for his performance on the field. He was caught up in a shooting at the Eaton Centre in downtown Toronto on June 2 in which two people were killed. His first tweet read, "Pretty sure someone just let off a round bullets in eaton center mall . . . Wow just sprinted out of the mall . . . Through traffic . . ." (Lawrie 2013a). A minute later, he sent out another tweet: "People sprinting up the stairs right from where we just were . . . Wow wow wow" (Lawrie 2013b).

Lawrie's quick-fire messages from the scene meant he was one of the first people to report the shooting on social media. His tweets were how many first heard of the tragedy. One of the reasons he was considered a credible source was the language used in the tweets. They were not the well-crafted news alerts that are sent out by professional news organizations. The poor grammar and punctuation lent an air of authenticity to the posts. The same errors in a story in the newspaper would undermine its credibility. The words and phrases used in a post are message-based clues to the veracity of the information. People in the middle of a dramatic breaking news situation tend to focus on specific details of what they are seeing and experiencing. Does a message read like it was written in the heat of the moment?

In such situations, the use of swear words is an additional indicator of credibility. Expressions of shock and surprise are usually accompanied by a swear word. When Mike Wilson (@2drinksbehind) survived a Boeing 737 crash in Denver in December 2008, the first words of his tweet were "Holy fucking shit" (quoted in Buttry 2013). Most people are unlikely to write in journalese, mimicking the media by using terms such as "breaking" or "confirmed." Similarly credible messages do not tend to use multiple exclamation marks to try to grab attention. It doesn't mean the information should be discounted, but rather treated with a degree of extra caution.

The same degree of attention needs to be paid to photos and videos. When Hurricane Sandy made its way across New York and the Eastern Seaboard in

October 2012, social media were inundated with photos of the natural disaster. There were images of sharks in waterlogged streets, a tidal wave striking the Statue of Liberty, and a scuba diver in a flooded Times Square station. They were all fake, as shown by journalist Alexis Madrigal on the website of *The Atlantic* (Madrigal 2012).

Fakes like these can be easy to spot. Harder are those that look real but may be from another time or place. A good starting point is to compare the location of the content against existing photos and maps. Distinctive buildings or geographic features can help to determine that a photo or video was taken at a specific place. Once the location is confirmed, the weather conditions can be checked against weather reports on the day for the area. Shadows in the content and the position of the sun can help to point to the time of day. The language and accents on a video can serve as another indicator of authenticity. During the Arab Spring of 2011, BBC journalists turned to their colleagues in BBC Arabic and BBC Monitoring to advise on local accents.

The social media news agency Storyful used these techniques as part of its effort to verify one of the most powerful videos during the Egyptian uprising in January 2011 (Little 2011). It showed a clash between riot police and protestors on the Qasr al Nile bridge in Cairo. Storyful producers used Google Earth to check the location of the bridge and confirm the vantage point of Mohamed Ibrahim el Masry, who shot the footage from a hotel overlooking the bridge. Checking out who was behind the video was a key part of the process of verification. For the Storyful producers, a vital stage in the process was speaking with Mohamed Ibrahim el Masry.

User-Based Analysis

Getting in touch with the source of digital material is a tried and tested method widely recommended by experts in user-generated content. Eyewitnesses are often willing to share their experience with the media, though in some situations, such as the Syrian conflict, it may be next to impossible to contact the original source or it may be necessary to protect their identity. At the BBC user-generated content hub, the golden rule is to try to get hold of the person behind a photo, video, or tweet, preferably on the phone.

There might be an email on a person's webpage, or a mention of the person's place of work. On Twitter, people can be sent a tweet, asking them to call in. Once in contact with a source, journalists can ask detailed questions about an individual's background, where the person is, what the person saw. They can apply proven interview skills to establish the credibility of the source and the material. Storyful sought out Mohamed Ibrahim el Masry to confirm that he had shot the footage of the battle on the bridge in Cairo. Contacting a source directly also means that you can request permission to use the material. The person might also have other material that hasn't been shared on social media or know of other people to contact.

Digital media also opens up a range of ways to check out a source beyond speaking to that person. Every social media account comes with a raft of data that can help to provide a sense of the validity of the source. A user's profile is the first step towards figuring out who is behind the account. The bio may mention an affiliation to an organization and help in reaching that person directly. Often, the bio includes a link to a website that may provide additional details. At times, though, the description may not be enough to identify or verify the source. But there are other pointers that can help, such as when the account was first set up.

Be wary of an account that has just been created. It might have just been set up to take advantage of something in the news or to fool the media. In the five days following the Boston Marathon bombings in April 2013, researchers found that almost 40,000 new Twitter accounts were opened that commented on the attacks (Gupta, Lamba, and Kumaraguru 2013). Two months later, 19 percent of these accounts were deleted or suspended by Twitter. "We observe that there are a lot of malicious profiles created just after the event occurs. Such profiles and accounts aim to exploit the high volume of content and interest of users in the event to spread spam, phishing and rumors," wrote the team.

The postings on a social media account tend to signal an individual's interests and biases. Poring over past messages can help to put together a sense of the person behind the account. You are what you share, and the research proves it. Scientists at the University of Pennsylvania who analyzed 75,000 Facebook accounts found they could predict gender with 92 percent accuracy and estimate age more than half of the time (Schwartz et al. 2013). By analyzing language, they could also work out if someone was more likely to be an extrovert or introvert. Such analysis provides one more piece in assessing the validity of a source.

The need to investigate an account's timeline was highlighted by a Twitter account purporting to belong to the Libyan prime minister, Ali Zeidan. The account, @AliZiDanPM, seemed real enough and looked like it had been verified by Twitter. The tweets were quoted in news reports and the account was followed by high-profile figures such as the British Foreign Secretary, William Hague. But it was a hoax account. Sky News journalist Tom Rayner looked at the previous tweets and sounded the alarm. "Hmm, @guardian live blog quoting @AliZiDanPM—not convinced it's legit. Aug 16th tweet says he will make all Libyans 'tree hugging hippies'" (Nolan 2013). Even with the informality of Twitter, it seems highly unlikely that any prime minister would make such a statement. The account was debunked, to the embarrassment of journalists and politicians following it.

The fake account might have been exposed sooner if journalists had been able to confirm the location of the user. Twitter allows users to geo-locate their messages. A hyperlink to the place where the message came from appears on the tweet if location services are enabled. Location information is off by default and few people tend to switch it on. However, a little digging into an account's history can help narrow down someone's location. On the night of the raid on Bin Laden's compound in Pakistan, software consultant Sohaib Athar sent out a string of messages on his @ReallyVirtual Twitter account of unusual night-time activity over the skies of Abbottabad. Messages from the past weeks mentioned power cuts and hailstorms in Abbottabad, suggesting that he was indeed in the city (Buttry 2013).

The fact that prominent figures followed @AliZiDanPM lent a veneer of authority to the account. It highlights how the network of connections can serve as an indicator of the authority of a user account. Whom does that person follow and who follows that person on Twitter? A person's social circle conveys a sense of that individual. Reliable sources tend to be individuals who are prolific sharers with a well-developed network of connections. Additional clues lie in the interactions with others. This can be tracked on Twitter through retweets and mentions. These interactions can offer pointers as to the reliability of a source. The exchanges form part of a wider conversation that can help reporters assess the authenticity of content from the public.

Topic-Based Analysis

Whenever there is a major event such as a natural disaster or tragedy such as a school shooting, there is a surge in chatter on social media. Individuals who are engaged with the topic come together to talk about the story. Some will have witnessed the news. Others will be filtering information, adding context and background. Some will be expressing support and sympathy. A loose and distributed community emerges through the messages shared on networks like Twitter. Analyzing these signals can help towards establishing the truth of the reports swirling online.

For journalists, this means not simply focusing on individual messages that may be outliers and instead considering the aggregate of posts. How many other people are talking about the same topic on social media? How many of the messages have the same links or the same word to tag the content? Are others questioning the information? During the London riots of August 2011, politicians, police, and the press blamed social media for helping to incite people to violence. While there were some such messages, they were the exception, rather than the rule. An analysis of 2.6 million tweets related to the riots found that the network was used to quickly knock down rumors circulating on social media (Bell and Lewis 2011).

Taking a bird's-eye view of overall activity of social media can provide a more reliable indicator of the truth than cherry-picking single messages. The public functions as a collaborative filter that can help journalists make sense of a fluid and fast-moving situation. Lies and deceptions on social media tend to be contested far more than credible reports. A study of tweets following the 2010 Chilean earthquake found that messages coming out of the area tended to confirm reports that were true and question those that later turned out to be false (Mendoza, Poblete, and Castillo 2010). In one case, for every false warning of a tsunami in Valparaiso, there were more than 10 updates denying it. A significant number of people questioning a particular report should raise the alarm in newsrooms.

The main difficulty for journalists seeking to detect the truthful signals in the noise is twofold. First is the sheer volume of material at times of major news events and the trend is upwards. There were 3,000 tweets per minute at the time of the Boston Marathon bombings in 2013, compared to 800 tweets per minute during the US tornadoes in 2010 (Starbird 2013). Second is the tendency of misinformation to spread much faster and wider than subsequent corrections. For example, there were thousands of tweets erroneously reporting the death of a young girl running in the marathon, compared to hundreds correcting the information. Similarly tweets misidentifying a bombing suspect far outnumbered corrections (Starbird 2013). Information scientists are working to develop tools to automatically assess the credibility of social media content, detect fake messages, and amplify corrections to reduce the spread of misinformation.

Propagation-Based Analysis

The way information spreads on social media provides additional signals to help assess the validity of information. Computer scientists more commonly employ these techniques of network analysis than journalists. One such group, at Indiana University, is working on a project called Truthy that examines how information propagates through social networks, blogs, and social media. Truthy churns through thousands of messages on Twitter looking for patterns that might help it discern fact from fiction. "There's a timescale at which things are propagating in social media that's so short," Filippo Menczer, one of the lead investigators on the project, told the *Columbia Journalism Review* (Silverman 2011). "We're talking seconds and minutes rather than hours and days."

But there are some giveaways that can be spotted by analyzing the data, as scientists found when they pored over close to 8 million tweets posted by 3.7 million users between April 15 and 19, 2013, about the Boston Marathon bombings (Gupta, Lamba, and Kumaraguru 2013). Accurate information tended to be spread at a steady pace from the start, as the messages usually came from users with significant numbers of followers. Fake messages were usually started by people with small numbers of followers. These messages spread far slower initially, until being retweeted by users with greater influence.

Similarly, suspicious social media accounts tend to be active within a short time of each other, sending and retweeting messages with very similar phrasing. At the time of the Senate race in Massachusetts in January 2010, the Democratic contender Martha Coakley was on the receiving end of a concerted dirty tricks campaign on Twitter. Computer scientists crunched the data and found that nine fake Twitter accounts, created within 13 minutes of each other, were behind the 929 tweets sent in 138 minutes promoting an anti-Coakley website (Mustafaraj and Metaxas 2010).

The use of such sophisticated techniques to manipulate information and fool the public exposes the limitations of a simply human approach to verification. A temporal spike in social media can create the impression of a groundswell of public opinion for or against a particular issue. The same information coming from multiple sources may increase its perceived veracity. Systems that can take apart the chatter on social media and watch out for patterns of propaganda would be invaluable in the pursuit of the truth.

Crowdsourcing Verification

The approaches to verification so far have focused on the use of social media for newsgathering, trawling it for photos, videos, or eyewitness accounts. Such material is often blended into an unfolding narrative through live update pages or live blogs (see Neil Thurman's chapter). An emerging practice is the notion of social media platforms as the newsroom, where journalists work with the audience to identify, evaluate, and highlight relevant information (Hermida 2012). Digital media systems as newsrooms means the process through which the truth is established takes place openly in collaboration with the public as facts, rumor, and speculation are authenticated or denied in a recurrent cycle.

At the time of writing, the most prominent illustration of a media professional operating in such a "social newsroom" was Andy Carvin, National Public Radio's social media strategist who left the organization at the end of 2013. He has been described as the "master at crowdsourcing verification" (Buttry 2013). How he worked with his network to debunk reports of the use of Israeli weapons during the Libyan conflict is a case study in collaborative verification.

In March 2011, reports were circulating on social media about a munitions shell used during the Libya conflict. A photo on the Facebook page of Al Manara, a Libyan expatriate news service based in the UK, triggered speculation that the mortar shell came from Israel. The shell had what looked like a Star of David on it, underneath a crescent-like shape, leading Al Manara to declare in the headline on its post, "Israeli industry against the Libyan people." News that Muammar Gaddafi was using weapons made in Israel against his own people would have enflamed the region. Carvin turned to his network on Twitter and outlined the process on the Storify website (Carvin 2011).

"The whole thing struck me as very odd, so I asked my Twitter followers to help me investigate it," recalled Carvin. He maintained a back and forth with his followers, steering the investigation, such as asking them to look for similar images on the web. They found Indian, British, and French shells that used comparable icons. Twitter user Amin El Shelhi solved the mystery by finding a NATO manual on the labeling of munitions. The star symbol identified it as an illumination round, used to light up a battlefield at night, while the crescent shape was the symbol for a parachute. Carvin tweeted out the link to the NATO manual, debunking the original claim by Al Manara. "A rumor perpetuated by several news sources was easily debunked by a group of people on Twitter who don't know each other and likely will never meet each other in person," wrote Carvin (2011).

What made this different from the work of the user-generated content hubs at the BBC or CNN is that Carvin viewed his network as his editors, researchers, and fact-checkers. "It's where I'm trying to separate fact from fiction, interacting with people. That's a newsroom," he said (quoted in Ingram, 2012). He has described his Twitter followers as "smart, curious, and skeptical" people who are "generous in sharing their time and skills to help me out when I need it" (2011). This is a very different type of newsroom from traditional enclosed spaces populated by professionals. On Twitter, the newsroom is open and distributed. The process of journalism—sourcing, filtering, contesting, and confirming information—takes place through exchanges in public on the network.

Developing an active, engaged, and diverse community online requires an investment of time and energy. Much as a journalist develops a range of sources in a physical community or around a topic, Carvin developed a variety of sources on Twitter. He started with people he knew and trusted, and then looked at their connections. On his network, Carvin would seek independent verification from a range of sources. Often, details about the veracity of a photo or video would come from people who didn't know each other. By cross-checking the information, he was able to piece together the fragments to reveal the whole picture.

There are risks with an approach that does not follow the standard mantra of verify then publish. Journalists have to be aware of how a retweet of an unconfirmed report may be interpreted by others. Even simply saying, "we are looking into" may be seen as lending credence to questionable reports, especially if it comes from an institutional media account, rather than a journalist's account. In Carvin's case, he gained a reputation for sharing images and video, mediating discussions, and reaching out to his followers to help him translate and verify information about events in the Middle East. Regular followers would know this is how he operates, but it leaves room for misinterpretation by those less familiar with his approach.

Treating Twitter as a newsroom requires journalists to be far more open and transparent about what they know and don't know in their interactions with the public. Journalists tend to be reticent about admitting ignorance. They also tend to fear tipping off the competition that they are looking into a story. The phrasing of an appeal for help is important to avoid being alarmist and to contextualize the reasons for reporting unconfirmed details. When Carvin retweeted a link to the photo on Al Manara's Facebook page, he prefaced it with: "They ID it as Israeli.

Maybe, maybe not. Need help to ID it. Anyone?" He was candid about not knowing whether the report was true but suggested it was worth investigating.

As part of the process of being transparent, journalists need to be ready to admit mistakes quickly and address erroneous information. The truth in journalism emerges over time, as more is known about an event. Social media have contributed to accelerating news cycles, putting additional pressure on the need to be both fast and accurate. In fluid situations where reliable information is scarce, such as during the Libyan uprising, news is messy and chaotic. It is important, then, for journalists to be prepared to acknowledge how things may have changed and be upfront with audiences about corrections.

Conclusion: The Limits of Verification

Journalists are continually checking what they know since accuracy is a universal ideal. Verification is built into the everyday routines of reporters to the extent that it has become a "strategic ritual" (Shapiro et al. 2013, 669). But there is not one consistent standard applied across the board and not all facts are equal. Instead there is a "spectrum of facts" (Shapiro et al. 2013, 663). Names, places, and potentially defamatory statements are subjected to far more rigor than characterizations and explanations. Journalists have to evaluate the consequences of getting something wrong.

At times of breaking news, they will rush to find out what happened, get updates from the police, and search social media for more. The process of assembling the facts often now takes place through constant updates with the latest

Figure 5.1 Aftermath of the Boston Marathon bombing, April 15, 2013; courtesy of Flickr user Rebecca_Hildreth.

morsel. But there are times when the consequences of getting it wrong far out-weigh any advantage gained from being first. The reputation of major news orga-nizations, including the BBC, CNN, and NPR, took a significant hit in January 2011 when they mistakenly reported the death of US Congresswoman Gabrielle Giffords after she was shot in the head.

Journalists should never forget their responsibility to the people they are report-ing on. Getting something wrong can be devastating for the audiences served by the media. When Giffords' husband heard on TV the reports of his wife's death, he "just walked into the bathroom and broke down" (quoted in Stelter 2011). Journalists make judgment calls all the time about what to publish and what to hold back. Part of the process of parsing information is assessing the human cost of getting a crucial fact wrong. At times, restraint is the best policy.

Best Practices in Action: Boston Marathon Bombings

Rumors, misinformation, and reporting errors flowed on news outlets and social media in the hours and days following the Boston Marathon bombings on April 15, 2013. The media struggled to make sense of the confusing information swirling about the attack and hunt for the perpetrators (Coddington 2013). CNN and other news organizations reported an arrest when there was none, while the *New York Post* mistakenly identified two men in a front page photo it said were wanted by law enforcement.

Twitter and Reddit came under fire for fanning the flames of speculation. There was false chatter on social media of a possible device at the JFK Library and speculation that it was the work of right-wing supremacists and of Muslim terrorists. One study found that rumors and fake reports accounted for 29 percent of tweets during this period, with only 20 percent relaying accurate information. The bulk of tweets, 51 percent, were people commenting on the attacks (Gupta, Lamba, and Kumaraguru 2013).

In breaking news situations, events are in constant motion, facts are in flux, and reporting is messy. In a digital media system, gathering, verifying, and reporting the news is done in public. Journalists are one of the many voices, sharing the media space with official sources such as law enforcement and emergency services, wit-nesses to the event, and those across the world responding and reacting to the news.

It amounts to a profound shift as verification moves out of the private space of the newsroom and into the public arena of the Internet. Among the best practices:

- Be precise in your reporting. Some of the worst errors come from reporters making assumptions and jumping to conclusions. Some of the early confu-sion in the hunt for the marathon bombers resulted from conflicting media reports about whether a suspect was in custody or whether the person was under arrest.

- Be clear about what you know but also about what you don't know. In the stream of constant updates, consider adding notes of caution given the rapidly changing situation.
- Be careful to place new information in context, acknowledging the source and its reliability. In the rush to be first, mistakes will happen. Acknowledge and correct the error quickly and openly.
- Be aware that people will want to talk about the news, share what they know, and want to help. Rather than dismissing the chatter on social media, engage with it and seek to channel the conversation unfolding online.
- Be mindful that exchanges on social media are not the equivalent of publication. It is information in flux. During the marathon bombings, conversations on community news site Reddit were ongoing discussions where the community collectively tried to figure out what happened and who was responsible. In the rush to find someone to blame, some posters on Reddit misidentified a missing student as a suspect. But at the same time, many others urged caution about speculating on the identity of the bombers.
- Be conscious of the emotional impact of an event. During tragic events such as the marathon bombings, there will be an outpouring of shock, sadness, and anger, much of it through social media. The information spread by the media shapes the public mood, reinforcing the duty of journalists to provide responsible and trustworthy reporting.

Discussion Questions

1. Describe the competing factors that journalists have to balance in an era of social media.
2. What best practices could journalists use to verify a piece of information on social media?
3. How could a social media platform such as Twitter be used for novel approaches to the gathering, production, and dissemination of news?
4. How does social media allow journalists and audiences to work together in the verification of information?
5. In what contexts would it be justified to publish unverified information on social media?

References

BBC. 2012. "Syria Massacre in Houla Condemned as Outrage Grows." BBC News, May 27, 2012. Accessed October 2, 2013. www.bbc.co.uk/news/world-middle-east-18224559

Bell, James, and Paul Lewis. 2011. "Twitter and the Riots: How the News Spread." *The Guardian*, December 7, 2011. Accessed October 13, 2013. www.guardian.co.uk/uk/2011/dec/07/twitter-riots-how-news-spread

Buttry, Steve. 2013. "How to Verify Information from Tweets: Check It Out." *The Buttry Diary*, January 21, 2013. Accessed October 13, 2013. http://stevebuttry.wordpress.com/2013/01/21/how-to-verify-information-from-tweets-check-it-out/

Carvin, Andy. 2011. "Israeli Weapons in Libya? How @acarvin and His Twitter Followers Debunked Sloppy Journalism." Accessed October 13, 2013. http://storify.com/acarvin/how-to-debunk-a-geopolitical-rumor-with-your-twitt2

Coddington, Mark. 2013. "This Week in Review: Verification Online and Off in Boston's Wake, and an Underdog Pulitzer Prize." *Nieman Journalism Lab*, April 19, 2013. Accessed September 24, 2013. www.niemanlab.org/2013/04/this-week-in-review-verification-online-and-off-in-bostons-wake-and-an-underdogs-pulitzer-win/

Furness, Hannah. 2013. "BBC News Uses 'Iraq Photo to Illustrate Syrian Massacre.'" *The Telegraph*, May 27, 2013. Accessed October 13, 2013. www.telegraph.co.uk/culture/tvandradio/bbc/9293620/BBC-News-uses-Iraq-photo-to-illustrate-Syrian-massacre.html

Gupta, Aditi, Hemank Lamba, and Ponnurangam Kumaraguru. 2013. "$1.00 per RT #BostonMarathon #PrayForBoston: Analyzing Fake Content on Twitter." Paper presented at IEEE APWG eCrime Research Summit (eCRS), San Francisco, CA, 17–18 September 2013. http://precog.iiitd.edu.in/Publications_files/ecrs2013_ag_hl_pk.pdf

Hamilton, Chris. 2012. "Houla Massacre Picture Mistake." The Editors, BBC News, May 29, 2012. Accessed May 29, 21012. www.bbc.co.uk/blogs/theeditors/2012/05/houla_massacre_picture_mistake.html

Hermida, Alfred. 2011. "Tweet the News: Social Media Streams and the Practice of Journalism." In *The Routledge Companion to News and Journalism*, 2nd ed., edited by Stuart Allan, 671–82. Abingdon, Oxon, UK: Routledge.

Hermida, Alfred. 2012. "Tweets and Truth: Journalism as a Discipline of Collaborative Verification." *Journalism Practice* 6(5–6):659–68. doi:10.1080/17512786.2012.667269

Imahara, Grant. 2013. (grantimahara). "Something just happened at #LAX. TSA and police running everywhere." November 1, 2013 [Tweet]. https://twitter.com/grantimahara/statuses/396312419879776256

Ingram, Mathew. 2012. "Andy Carvin on Twitter as a Newsroom and Being Human." *Gigaom*, May 25, 2012. Accessed October 13, 2013. http://gigaom.com/2012/05/25/andy-carvin-on-twitter-as-a-newsroom-and-being-human/

Kirkland, Sam. 2013. "Globe and Mail Falls for Hoax Tweet, Falsely Reports Ex-NSA Chief's Death." *Poynter*, November 1, 2013. Accessed November 1, 2013. www.poynter.org/latest-news/228255/globe-and-mail-incorrectly-reports-ex-nsa-chiefs-death-hoax-twitter-account-to-blame/

Kovach, Bill, and Tom Rosenstiel. 2007. *The Elements of Journalism: What Newspeople Should Know and the Public Should Expect.* 1st rev. ed. New York: Three Rivers Press.

Lawrie, Brett. 2013a. (blawrie13). "Pretty sure someone just let off a round bullets in eaton center mall . . . Wow just sprinted out of the mall . . . Through traffic . . .". June 2, 2012. [Tweet]. http://twitter.com/blawrie13/status/209047958304468992

Lawrie, Brett. 2013b. (blawrie13). "People sprinting up the stairs right from where we just were . . . Wow wow wow". June 2, 2012. [Tweet]. http://twitter.com/blawrie13/status/209048242187538432

Lippman, Walter. [1920] 2008. *Liberty and the News.* Princeton, NJ: Princeton University Press.

Little, Mark. 2011. "The Human Algorithm." Storyful blog, May 20, 2011. Accessed October 15, 2013. http://blog.storyful.com/2011/05/20/the-human-algorithm-2/

Madrigal, Alexis. 2012. "Sorting the Real Sandy Photos from the Fakes." *The Atlantic,* October 29, 2012. Accessed October 23, 2013. www.theatlantic.com/technology/archive/2012/10/sorting-the-real-sandy-photos-from-the-fakes/264243/

Mendoza, Marcelo, Barbara Poblete, and Carlos Castillo. 2010. "Twitter under Crisis: Can We Trust What We RT?" Paper presented at SOMA 2010: KDD Workshop on Social Media Analytics, Washington, DC, July 2010.

Meyer, Philip. 2009. *The Vanishing Newspaper: Saving Journalism in the Information Age.* 2nd ed. Columbia: University of Missouri Press.

Mustafaraj, Eni and Panagiotis Metaxas. 2010. "From Obscurity to Prominence in Minutes: Political Speech and Real-time Search." In *Proceedings of the WebSci10: Extending the Frontiers of Society Online,* Raleigh, NC, April 26–27, 2010.

Nolan, Markham. 2013. "Ticked off by Fake Libya Twitter Account." Storyful blog, October 10, 2013. Accessed October 23, 2013. http://blog.storyful.com/2013/10/10/ticked-off-by-a-fake-libyan-twitter-account/

Pew Research Journalism Project. 2013. "Principles of Journalism." Accessed October 2, 2013. www.journalism.org/resources/principles-of-journalism/

Sambrook, Richard. 2005. "Citizen Journalism and the BBC." *Nieman Reports,* Winter 2005. Accessed October 2, 2013. www.nieman.harvard.edu/reportsitem.aspx?id=100542

Schwartz, H. Andrew, Johannes C. Eichstaedt, Margaret L. Kern, Lukasz Dziurzynski, Stephanie M. Ramones, Megha Agrawal, Achal Shah, Michal Kosinski, David Stillwell, Martin E.P. Seligman, and Lyle H. Ungar. 2013. "Personality, Gender, and Age in the Language of Social Media: The Open-Vocabulary Approach." *PLoS ONE* 8(9):e73791. doi:10.1371/journal.pone.00

Shapiro, Ivor, Colette Brin, Isabelle Bédard-Brûlé, and Kasia Mychajlowycz. 2013. "Verification as a Strategic Ritual: How Journalists Retrospectively Describe Processes for Ensuring Accuracy." *Journalism Practice,* 7(6):657–673. doi:10.1080/17512786.2013.76 5638

Silverman, Craig. 2011. "Misinformation Propagation." *Columbia Journalism Review,* November 4, 2011. Accessed September 14, 2013. www.cjr.org/behind_the_news/misinformation_propagation.php?page=all

Society of Professional Journalists. 2014. "SPJ Code of Ethics." Accessed January 12, 2014. www.spj.org/ethicscode.asp

Starbird, Kate. 2013. "Crises, Crowds & Online Convergence: Crowdsourcing in the Context of Disasters." Paper presented at US Frontiers of Engineering Symposium, Wilmington, DE, September 18, 2013. Accessed November 7, 2013. www.naefrontiers.org/File.aspx?id=41201

Stelter, Brian. 2011. (brianstelter). "Giffords' husband says he heard it reported on TV that his wife had died. "I just walked into the bathroom and broke down." January 19, 2011. [Tweet]. https://twitter.com/brianstelter/statuses/27565217277812736

6

BEST PRACTICES FOR LINKING

Juliette De Maeyer

UNIVERSITÉ DE MONTRÉAL, CANADA

The ability to add links to a news story using hypertext is a feature generally considered to have the greatest potential impact on online journalism (Steensen 2011). But why exactly should linking matter in online news? And how should journalists think about the practice of linking?

Adding links to a news story can help journalism to better fulfill some promises rooted in ethical principles. A link in a news item is said to increase transparency by providing a direct gateway to source material. While "transparency" is more complicated than some commentators might allow (see Stephen Ward's chapter in this book), the transparency of newsgathering is among the "most prevalent and recurrent issues in journalism ethics" (Hanitschz, Plaisance, and Skewes 2013), and being able to directly show what you have sourced is therefore one of the most prominently professed advantages of linking.

Linking can also enhance the quality of news by allowing users to customize their experiences with the right level of depth and details. A link can provide useful background information for readers who need more context. Additionally, linking is said to enhance the diversity of the news by allowing us to point to a variety of voices, opinions, and information.

So much for the idealized vision of the link. How this is actually implemented by journalists is more complex. Since the late 1990s, journalists and online news experts have discussed the role of linking in the news, and such debates have repeatedly traversed the world of online journalism. Quite surprisingly, given that the old hyperlink does not qualify as a "new" technology anymore, the controversies never seem to end.

This chapter discusses some key best practice issues concerning linking in the news. It first focuses on what some have called the "ethic of the link," emphasizing that links can be used by journalists to increase transparency, to ensure correct attribution and sourcing, and to promote openness. It then briefly points out other functions of linking, and explains the economic dimension of linking, before addressing the question of how links can affect reading as well as concerns about accessibility and responsibility. Finally, a brief case study and some discussion points seek to illustrate that there is no such thing as one good way of linking. The practice embodies many journalistic issues that need to be weighed by every newsroom, journalist, or blogger in their individual way, according to their editorial goals or target audiences.

Sourcing and Attribution

Attribution is a prominent issue related to linking. The idea of using links in order to directly point to sources and raw material used by the journalists to produce news stories is vigorously defended by proponents of the "ethic of the link" such as Jeff Jarvis (2007, 2008) and Jay Rosen (2008), who see links as one of the many embodiments of transparency, as an attribution device and as an expression of the ideology of openness that characterizes the web. According to Jarvis, the "ethic of the link layer on news" allows journalists to "show readers how [journalists] arrived where [they] have in a story" (Jarvis 2008). As such, links are a way for writers to "show their work" because "readers and viewers should be able to examine the sources of [journalists'] information, both to provide depth and to strengthen credibility" (Buttry 2013). The proponents of the "ethic of the link" also make a moral argument about giving credit where credit is due, summarized in Jarvis's motto: "Cover what you do best and link to the rest" (Jarvis 2007). They also argue that linking is a fundamental expression of the web and its core values, such as openness and the free flow of knowledge (Rosen 2008).

But several controversies have shown that untangling the interrelated issues of linking and attribution actually forces journalists to reflect on fundamental concerns of how the news is made: the lines between aggregation, curation, and full-blown plagiarism might sometimes be thin. (The next chapter, by Fiona Martin, addresses some of these issues.) These issues are particularly salient when it comes to aggregation and reporting on what other media have published before— an inclination towards replication is sometimes called the "circular circulation of information" (Bourdieu 1998). In that context, a link to the original source appears as an obligation, as a good attribution practice: if one news outlet publishes a scoop on its website and if other outlets want to cover the same story, they should acknowledge the original reporting and provide a link to the news site that published it first.

Even if sourcing is one of the prominent functions of links, it should also be remembered that sourcing is not limited to adding a few links. There is an underlying assumption in the strict equivalence between links and sources: that all sources are available online, and that they are only one click away. But this is of course not always the case. Initiatives that have tried to transparently communicate all the sources of a news article to readers, such as ProPublica's "Explore Our Source" experimental feature (Shaw 2011) or *The New York Times'* "Source Notes" to the 2013 "Invisible Child" (Elliott 2013) story, show how comprehensively sourcing is a vast enterprise that goes beyond linking: the former implies that the author was able to digitize and upload many annotated documents that could be thoroughly linked to each time a statement referred to a source, while the latter lists an impressive number of diverse sources that simply do not exist digitally (such as scenes witnessed by the journalist, or statements made during interviews) and cannot be linked to.

Beyond Attribution: The Other Uses of Links

But showing sources is not the only function of links. Others include the following.

The Social Hyperlink

This practice is especially favored by bloggers (Coddington 2012), who argue that links are a way of displaying affiliations, friends, and references—a mesh of social ties that helps the readers to understand where the writer comes from. Or, as blogger Scott Rosenberg argues:

> The links you put into a piece of writing tell a story (or, if you will, a meta-story) about you and what you've written. They say things like: What sort of company does this writer keep? Who does she read? What kind of stuff do her links point to—*New Yorker* articles? Personal blogs? Scholarly papers? Are the choices diverse or narrow? Are they obvious or surprising? Are they illuminating or puzzling? Generous or self-promotional? Links, in other words, transmit meaning, but they also communicate mindset and style.
>
> (Rosenberg 2011)

The Contextual Hyperlink

Links can solve a "problems journalists routinely face" (Tremayne 2005, 31): how much is it necessary to recap previous or contextual elements before presenting new information? "On the web, the journalist could link to yesterday's news and dispense with a background paragraph," says Mark Tremayne (Tremayne 2005, 31). However useful links to contextual information might be, this practice raises two concerns. First, one of the missions of news media is to inform readers in an authoritative way (Anderson 2008). This leads to an expectation of self-sufficiency: readers should be able to be fully informed by a news item, without needing to follow links in order to put all the pieces of the puzzle together. Second, there is the issue of reliability of what is linked to, especially in the case of external links. If a news item relies on external sources to provide background and context, the linked content should comply with the journalistic standards and expectations of the host publication. When considering the addition of a contextual link, journalists or bloggers must also consider how much they think their audience already knows about the topic, in order to provide the right contextual clues without drowning the article in a torrent of superfluous links. There is, of course, no definite answer here as every reader might come with a different background. Still, a strong knowledge of audience might help journalists and bloggers to provide relevant links and to assess when they might be required.

The Wink

Finally, links sometimes solely exist as a knowing sign. They might be used as a wink to other writers: as most publishing platforms now allow tracking of referrers (i.e., the incoming links), producing a link can be seen as a way of discreetly waving to the authors of the linked content—a quality which might not be of prime interest for large, mainstream media, but which is often used by bloggers (Rosenberg 2011; Coddington 2012).

Caught in the *Link Economy*

Whatever its journalistic virtues, linking also has potential economic implications. For a link, first, is a potential reader transferred to the targeted website, hence a source of traffic that could be monetized in many ways. The worry that links, and especially external links pointing to other websites, might send traffic away and thus represent a direct loss for news sites keeps reappearing when news organizations discuss their linking policies. It is an old concern, often challenged and criticized as outdated in an era of free flows of information. Looking back at the dawn of online news, it is difficult to find discourses that explicitly defend the "walled garden" policy, but we find several examples of pieces criticizing that perspective. A 2003 *Online Journalism Review* article by Mark Glaser emphatically announced the end of the "proprietary vision" of the link: "There was a time in the not too distant past when news sites had a very proprietary view of their content. The focus was on collecting eyeballs, and any link that sent readers offsite was frowned upon. A link that went to a competitor's site was almost treasonous" (Glaser 2003). In the words of Jeff Jarvis, then president of Advance.net (a company running several regional news sites):

> If you serve your readers well, they will recognize that and come back to your site first (. . .) If you make your readers' lives difficult, they will start

elsewhere the next time they look for something. So "losing" one page view to someone else's story is only an investment in the relationship with the reader; it's far more important to gain readers' loyalty for frequent return visits than it is to underserve them once.

(Jarvis, quoted in Glaser 2003)

Does this mean that the issue of external linking was solved in the early 2000s? External linking certainly gained momentum in the years that followed, with media companies adopting and promoting concrete, link-friendly initiatives. For instance, *The New York Times* launched a feature called "Times Extra" in 2008. It was promoted as "an alternative view of the home page featuring news headlines with links from third-party sources" (*The New York Times* press release, quoted in Seward 2008). The feature could be activated on the homepage, and displayed external links alongside headlines. Around the same time, *The Washington Post* launched a section called "Political Browser" that primarily consisted of a list of links relevant to the political news, selected and commented on by journalists. Such initiatives, among others, created another wave of celebratory comments about the end of protectionist linking policies. In a 2008 *New York Times* article titled "Mainstream News Outlets Start Linking to Other Sites," Brian Stelter argued that the era of "link journalism" was beginning, and that news organizations were "embracing the hyperlink ethos of the Web to a degree not seen before" (Stelter 2008). Other countries soon followed, with news outlets in France, for example, introducing their own "link journalism" sections: French newspaper *Libération* talked about a "paradigm shift" (Roussel 2009).

But the enthusiasm was short-lived. "Times Extra" was terminated without much explanation in December 2009. Sections devoted to link journalism in mainstream news sites, such as *The Washington Post*'s "Political Browser," were shut down—even if portions of link journalism, in the form of curated lists of links, were then reshuffled in the whole site, the emphasis was certainly more discreet. In the meantime, empirical studies from different national contexts (e.g., Quandt 2008; Dimitrova et al. 2003; Engebretsen 2006; Tremayne 2005; Sjøvaag, Moe, and Stavelin 2012; Larsson 2013; Coddington 2012) have repeatedly shown that news sites produce few external links. It should be noted, though, that such results vary dramatically from site to site, and from one news item to another. There is no such thing as a standardized external linking policy.

The fear of losing direct readership is not the only economic interest at stake with links. There are also *indirect* economic interests, embodied by the role played by links in the way that search engines, and especially Google, rank resources on the web. To formulate it (too) simply: the more links point to a page, the higher it will be ranked by search engines such as Google. Receiving and distributing links therefore also affects how a news site might potentially be more visible in Google search results—a significant economic concern as visibility in search results also drives traffic. What is best for business might not correspond to what is best for the readers. In this context, there is no absolute right way to link, but only a series of editorial decisions. It's up to every newsroom, journalist, or blogger to balance those considerations.

Impact on the Readers

An important question is missing from the previous pages: Who clicks on links? And what effect do links have on readers?

American essayist Nicholas Carr provoked a heated debate when he argued that links could badly affect readers' concentration. The argument was set out in his book, *The Shallows: What the Internet Is Doing to Our Brains* (Carr 2010a), and further developed in a blog post entitled "Experiments in Delinkification": Links, he said, are

> tiny distractions, little textual gnats buzzing around your head. Even if you don't click on a link, your eyes notice it, and your frontal cortex has to fire up a bunch of neurons to decide whether to click or not. You may not notice the little extra cognitive load placed on your brain, but it's there and it matters. People who read hypertext comprehend and learn less, studies show, than those who read the same material in printed form. The more links in a piece of writing, the bigger the hit on comprehension.
>
> (Carr 2010b)

Is Carr correct? Research on this topic hardly provides a definitive conclusion. As Carr argues, there is empirical evidence that hypertext readers might encounter a feeling of disorientation—a phenomenon dubbed the "lost in hyperspace problem" (Theng and Thimbleby 1998). But the measurement of hypertext usability is in itself a controversial issue (Smith 1996): common usability measures are tailored to assess specific information-seeking tasks, they "assume that there is a particular task being undertaken, that there is a 'correct' way in which this task should be performed" (Smith 1996, 366) and that there is a clear answer to an informational need—a definition that does not fit with what is expected when reading the news. Besides, most experiments that conclude that hypertext has a negative impact on comprehension deal with the kinds of hypertexts that are radically deconstructed, literary experiments such as stories with no narrative thread whatsoever (Rosenberg 2010). Consequently, their findings cannot directly be applied to links in news content, where there remains a narrative structure and where hypertext is used as a way of complementing a story.

Journalists and bloggers should nevertheless try to avoid confusing readers when producing links, especially with respect to the various, co-existing functions of links that have been described above. Links are extremely simple: they consist of underlined words and a target URL. Their simplicity might explain why they have become such a fundamental part of the web, but they're not always good at conveying subtleties. To readers, all links look equal—whether intended for attribution, contextual, or social purposes. As a result, writers should try to maximize the use of each link to convey meaning, especially when choosing which words to underline. They should be as explicit and efficient as possible.

The placement of links can also be used to maximize clarity. Even if there are no standardized rules we can suggest a couple of basic best practice principles: links that serve attribution purposes should be presented as early as possible (and not hidden at the bottom of a story), whereas contextual links might be pulled out from the main text and placed in a list separate from the body of the text. Consequently, the body of the text would not be too link-heavy, and links with different purposes would be visually distinct, which would help the users to make sense of them. Where possible, links should point to specific pages (what is sometimes called "deep linking") where the information the writer wants to reference is to be found directly, rather than to generic home pages.

Barriers to Linking: Accessibility, Responsibility

Another issue is the obstacles that sometimes come in the way of free-flowing hyperlinks. For instance, how should journalists present links to content that is behind a paywall? How useful is a link when it leads to content that not everyone can access?

A 2010 *BBC Strategy Review* report argued that BBC websites should become "a window on the web" and propose links to external websites whenever it is "editorially relevant" (BBC 2010). Then, science blogger Ben Goldacre sparked a controversy on links to science journals: he denounced the way the BBC usually handled links in its science coverage, by primarily linking to a journal's homepage rather than linking directly to the article itself. One argument presented by BBC News staff, in reply to Goldacre's complaint, was that "many papers are available on the web via subscription only, while others give only an abstract summary. In these instances, the vast majority of our readers would not be able to read the full papers, without paying for access, even if we provided the relevant link" (Richard Warry, assistant editor, specialist journalism, quoted in Goldacre 2010).

In response, then editor of the BBC news site Steve Herrmann, launched a debate with users in a series of blog posts in order to come up with revised guidelines about linking at the BBC. These emphasized the importance of sources and context: "Linking to relevant source material and useful additional content is a key part of being a good online journalist" (BBC Guidelines 2010). The guidelines also specify that external links should, as a general rule, point to content that is "normally free" but add the following exception to the rule: "it may be appropriate, where there is a strong editorial justification, to link to a specific subscription site. If we do, where this is practical, we should normally indicate to our users that the link is to a subscription site" (BBC Guidelines 2010).

There are also legal issues with linking. When placing a link in a story, how responsible is the journalist for the content that is in the target of the link? This question obviously concerns links pointing to sensitive and illegal content, but also more broadly questions the role of the link as an (implicit) endorsement.

News organizations have therefore been cautious in the way they handle links. In 1996, *The New York Times* presented its readers with an explicit disclaimer that sites that the paper linked to were "not part of The New York Times on the Web, and The Times has no control over their content or availability" (quoted in Glaser 2004).

Most news sites today express similar caution more discreetly: the disclaimer is not right next to the link, but often somewhere in the website's terms and conditions. For example, the terms and conditions of lemonde.fr, the online edition of the French newspaper *Le Monde*, state that the website contains

> hyperlinks to other websites that were not developed by *Monde Interactif*. (. . .) The existence of a link from this site to another site does not imply a validation of this site or its content. It is the responsibility of the reader to use such information with discernment and a critical mind. The responsibility of *Monde Interactif* cannot be engaged because of information, opinions or recommendations made by third parties.
>
> (*Le Monde*, n.d.)

Sometimes news organizations deliberately choose not to include a link because of the nature of the linked content, even if that link could theoretically provide more contextual information or point to a source. This can arise when a news story is about online content that may be highly distasteful or plainly illegal (such as websites of hate groups or child pornography). Subtler ethical problems might also be at stake: for instance, in 2010, *The New York Times* explicitly refused to link to documents—the so-called Afghanistan war logs—released by Wikileaks. Bill Keller, then editor of *The New York Times,* explained why they decided, in that case, to "make a point of saying that [they] did not link to the material posted by WikiLeaks," even though they claim to usually link to source material when it is available online: it was "a gesture to show we were not endorsing or encouraging the release of information that could cause harm" (Sarlin 2010).

A case that suggests potential legal dangers of linking occurred in September 2013, when *Guardian* journalist Barrett Brown was charged with various counts by a Texan court for "transferring a hyperlink" (in this case, he published it in a chat room). The link was to files from an intelligence contractor that were hacked and subsequently posted on Wikileaks in order to denounce alleged ties between the intelligence contractor and governmental bodies. But the files also contained credit cards data and security codes, hence the indictment on identity theft and other charges. This was seen as a "criminalization of the link" by many commentators, including David Carr from *The New York Times* : "by trying to criminalize linking, the federal authorities in the Northern District of Texas (. . .) are suggesting that to share information online is the same as possessing it or even stealing it" (Carr 2013).

While there may be a lot of variation when it comes to some linking practices, journalists and bloggers should still keep these issues at the forefront when thinking about when to link and what to link to: Will the links you provide enrich the experience for your audience? Would the story make sense without the link? There is a balance to strike: you don't want the link to provide no new information at all (then the link becomes useless to the user), but you also don't want your story to entirely rely on the content that is linked to in order to provide meaning and information (as it is your article which becomes useless to the user who had better read the linked content directly).

Where should links be placed in an article, and what text should they cover? Clarity should be the main guiding principle, as links need to be as explicit as possible and leave no room for confusion about what readers are going to find once they click on the link. Writers may also ponder the different functions of the link they want to propose (is it a link to a source? Does it provide more contextual information?) and reflect these different functions in the way links are presented, by placing them separately or by offering textual cues—for example, contextual links are sometimes placed under a header that says "Read more about this topic . . ."

Best Practices in Action: Linking to Wikipedia

When journalists or bloggers aim to provide contextual links for background information, a website that often comes to mind is Wikipedia. The collaborative online encyclopedia indeed seems to offer a perfect solution to many of the challenges delineated above. It is freely accessible, provides extensive coverage on a wide range of topics, the encyclopedic genre perfectly fits the need for synthetic background information, and its collaborative nature as well as its overall policy aim toward a neutral, factual point of view.

Some news sites have experimented with links to Wikipedia. For instance, in 2008, the BBC implemented a feature that allowed writers to easily add contextual links to Wikipedia (among other sites). However, the experience was discontinued after negative feedback from the users (Herrmann 2008), who mostly complained about the design choices but also about the sources. Despite Wikipedia's claim to neutrality and its community's work to ensure quality, some readers expressed concern about the reliability of its content, arguing that the BBC should not link to it.

Reliability is an important concern for Wikipedia itself (Wikipedia 2014), which has developed a wide range of procedures to ensure it. Journalists and bloggers who want to use Wikipedia and link to it should therefore be familiar with the way it operates in order to be able to distinguish entries that are subject to controversy (which are often and fiercely edited) or biased or incomplete, from stable, well-documented, and more reliable articles.

Stability is also a concern that should be considered when linking to external content, but the issue is broader than Wikipedia: any website that is linked to can change over time or disappear.

Links to Wikipedia also raise the question of the "circular circulation" of the news. Wikipedia policy demands that articles are backed by sources, and especially encourages the use of secondary sources such as scholarly journals and news media. Traditional news media are among preferred sources—with the websites of *The New York Times*, the *BBC,* and *The Guardian* among the most cited domains (Ford et al. 2013). Using Wikipedia links to provide context in a news story can hence become a circular, self-referential phenomenon which presents a false impression of external authority—with journalists outsourcing parts of the contextual authority on Wikipedia, and contributors to Wikipedia encouraged to use journalists' work to produce their entries. At the worst, such a phenomenon—dubbed the "information loop" (Wikipedia 2014) problem by Wikipedia—could lead to factual errors, with inaccurate information from Wikipedia being replicated in news media, consequently becoming reliable according to Wikipedia's criteria (as they have been published by a trustworthy secondary source).

Discussion Questions

1. Read the Wikipedia entry entitled "Reliability of Wikipedia" (http:// en.wikipedia.org/wiki/Reliability_of_Wikipedia). Then look at a randomly chosen Wikipedia entry. How would you assess its reliability, if it were a topic you had to cover as a journalist or a blogger? Would you propose a link to this entry, and if so, why? What other sources can you think of, and how would you present these different sources or elements of context to your readers?

2. Watch Jay Rosen in the "Ethics of linking" clip at www.youtube.com/ watch?v=RIMB9Kx18hw (Rosen 2008). Which functions of links does he address? How does he balance the different concerns related to links?

3. Choose three different kinds of news outlets (e.g., a traditional masthead such as *The New York Times*, an online-only outlet such as Gawker Media or *The Huffington Post*, and a personal blog) and find, in each, a news story that contains links. Compare their linking strategies. Discuss how easy it was to find a story with links, as well as the different functions of linking that are involved in each case. Finally, think about which links you would have added and why.

4. A white supremacist group is involved in a current news event that you have to report. The group's website clearly states racist ideas. Would you include a link to this website in your news story? Discuss why, and how you would handle that issue. (What arguments are at play? Whom would you talk to in order to decide what to do?) How would you consider ethical duties of telling the truth and minimizing harm?

References

Anderson, Christopher. 2008. "Journalism: Expertise, Authority, and Power in Democratic Life." In *The Media and Social Theory*, edited by David Hesmondhalgh and Jason Toynbee, 248–64. New York: Routledge.

BBC. 2010. "Strategy Review—Putting Quality First." www.bbc.co.uk/bbctrust/our_work/strategy_review/index.shtml

BBC Guidelines. 2010. "BBC—Editorial Guidelines—Guidance—Links and Feeds—Part 1: Links." www.bbc.co.uk/guidelines/editorialguidelines/page/guidance-links-feeds-links

Bourdieu, Pierre. 1998. *On Television*. New York: New Press.

Buttry, Steve. 2013. "Plagiarism and Fabrication Summit: Journalists Need to Use Links to Show Our Work." *The Buttry Diary*, May 4, 2013. http://stevebuttry.wordpress.com/2013/04/05/plagiarism-and-fabrication-summit-journalists-need-to-use-links-to-show-our-work/

Carr, David. 2013. "A Journalist-Agitator Facing Prison over a Link." *The New York Times*, September 8, 2013. www.nytimes.com/2013/09/09/business/media/a-journalist-agitator-facing-prison-over-a-link.html

Carr, Nicholas. 2010a. *The Shallows: What the Internet Is Doing to Our Brains*. 1st ed. New York: W.W. Norton.

Carr, Nicholas. 2010b. "Experiments in Delinkification." *Rough Type (Nicholas Carr's Blog)*, May 31, 2010. www.roughtype.com/archives/2010/05/experiments_in.php

Coddington, Mark. 2012. "Building Frames Link by Link: The Linking Practices of Blogs and News Sites." *International Journal of Communication* 6:2007–26.

Dimitrova, Daniela V., Colleen Connolly-Ahern, Andrew Paul Williams, Lynda Lee Kaid, and Amanda Reid. 2003. "Hyperlinking as Gatekeeping: Online Newspaper Coverage of the Execution of an American Terrorist." *Journalism Studies* 4(3):401–14. doi:10.1080/14616700306488

Elliott, Andrea. 2013. "Invisible Child—Source Notes." *Nytimes.com*. www.nytimes.com/projects/2013/invisible-child/notes/

Engebretsen, Martin. 2006. "Shallow and Static or Deep and Dynamic? Studying the State of Online Journalism in Scandinavia." *Nordicom Review* 27:3–16.

Ford, Heather, David R. Musicant, Shilad Sen, and Nathaniel Miller. 2013. "Getting to the Source: Where Does Wikipedia Get Its Information From?" Paper presented at the WikiSym '13 Conference, Hong Kong, China, August 5–7, 2013. http://opensym.org/wsos2013/proceedings/p0203-ford.pdf

Glaser, Mark. 2003. "News Sites Loosen Linking Policies." *Online Journalism Review*, September 17, 2003. www.ojr.org/ojr/glaser/1063750500.php

Glaser, Mark. 2004. "Open Season: News Sites Add Outside Links, Free Content." *Online Journalism Review*, October 19, 2004. www.ojr.org/ojr/glaser/1098225187.php

Goldacre, Ben. 2010. "No Movement on the BBC's Bizarre Links Policy." *Bengoldacre—Secondary Blog*, August 4, 2010. http://web.archive.org/web/20101120010944/http://bengoldacre.posterous.com/no-movement-on-the-bbcs-bizarre-links-policy

Hanitzsch, Thomas, Patrick Lee Plaisance, and Elizabeth A. Skewes. 2013. "Universals and Differences in Global Journalism Ethics." In *Global Media Ethics: Problems and Perspectives*, edited by Stephen J. A. Ward, 30–49. Chichester, West Sussex, UK: Wiley-Blackwell.

Herrmann, Steve. 2008. "New Ways of Linking." *BBC—The Editors Blog*, August 15, 2008. www.bbc.co.uk/blogs/theeditors/2008/08/new_ways_of_linking.html

Jarvis, Jeff. 2007. "New Rule: Cover What You Do Best. Link to the Rest." *Buzzmachine*. Last updated February 27, 2007. www.buzzmachine.com/2007/02/22/new-rule-cover-what-you-do-best-link-to-the-rest/

Jarvis, Jeff. 2008. "The Ethic of the Link Layer on News." *Buzzmachine*. Last updated February 6, 2008. www.buzzmachine.com/2008/06/02/the-ethic-of-the-link-layer-on-news/

Larsson, Anders Olof. 2013. "Staying In or Going Out?" *Journalism Practice* 7(6):738–54. doi:10.1080/17512786.2012.748514

Le Monde. n.d. "Mentions Légales." www.lemonde.fr/service/mentions_legales.html

Quandt, Thorsten. 2008. "(No) News on the World Wide Web." *Journalism Studies* 9(5):717–38.

Rosen, Jay. 2008. "Ethics of Linking." *YouTube*, April 8, 2008. www.youtube.com/watch?v=RIMB9Kx18hw&feature=youtube_gdata_player

Rosenberg, Scott. 2010. "In Defense of Links, Part One: Nick Carr, Hypertext and Delinkification." *Wordyard*, August 30, 2010. www.wordyard.com/2010/08/30/in-defense-of-links-part-one-nick-carr-hypertext-and-delinkification/

Rosenberg, Scott. 2011. "In Defense of Links, Part Three: In Links We Trust." *Wordyard*, February 9, 2011. www.wordyard.com/2010/09/02/in-defense-of-links-part-three-in-links-we-trust/

Roussel, Frédérique. 2009. "Le Journaliste, Tisseur de Liens." *Ecrans.fr (Libération)*, October 2, 2009. www.ecrans.fr/Le-journaliste-tisseur-de-liens,6374.html

Sarlin, Benjy. 2010. "New York Times Strikes Back at WikiLeaks Founder." *The Daily Beast*, July 28, 2010. www.thedailybeast.com/beltway-beast/julian-assange-vs-the-new-york-times/

Seward, Zachary M. 2008. "Times Extra: The NYT Votes for Automated Aggregation." *Nieman Journalism Lab*, April 12, 2008. www.niemanlab.org/2008/12/times-extra-a-vote-for-automated-aggregation/

Shaw, Al. 2011. "Explore Sources: A New Feature to 'Show Our Work.'" *ProPublica*, December 15, 2011. www.propublica.org/nerds/item/explore-sources-a-new-feature-to-show-our-work

Sjøvaag, Helle, Hallvard Moe, and Eirik Stavelin. 2012. "Public Service News on the Web." *Journalism Studies* 13(1):90–106. doi:10.1080/1461670X.2011.578940

Smith, Pauline A. 1996. "Towards a Practical Measure of Hypertext Usability." *Interacting with Computers* 8(4) (December):365–81. doi:10.1016/S0953-5438(97)83779-4

Steensen, Steen. 2011. "Online Journalism and the Promises of New Technology." *Journalism Studies* 12(3):311–27. doi:10.1080/1461670X.2010.501151

Stelter, Brian. 2008. "Mainstream News Outlets Start Linking to Other Sites." *NYtimes.com*, December 10, 2008. www.nytimes.com/2008/10/13/business/media/13reach.html?_r=1&ref=media&oref=slogin

Theng, Yin Leng, and Harold Thimbleby. 1998. "Addressing Design and Usability Issues in Hypertext and on the World Wide Web by Re-Examining the 'Lost in Hyperspace' Problem." *Journal of Universal Computer Science* 4(11): 839–55.

Tremayne, Mark. 2005. "News Websites as Gated Cybercommunities." *Convergence: The International Journal of Research into New Media Technologies* 11(3):28–39. doi:10.1177/135485650501100303

Wikipedia. 2014. "Reliability of Wikipedia." Last modified January 24, 2014. http://en.wikipedia.org/wiki/Reliability_of_Wikipedia

7

THE CASE FOR CURATORIAL JOURNALISM . . . OR, CAN YOU REALLY BE AN ETHICAL AGGREGATOR?

Fiona Martin

UNIVERSITY OF SYDNEY, AUSTRALIA

As the world's stores of information expand, we are putting a high price on businesses that can collect, filter, contextualize, and link to relevant information online, or that help us to do it ourselves. *The Huffington Post*, a business built on aggregating blogs and snippets of political news, was valued at $315 million when it was bought by America Online in 2011. A year later Instagram, the photo-sharing application, sold to Facebook for $1 billion, while startup ventures Pinterest and Storify have already attracted equivalent angel investment in the democratization of social media curation (and in the hope of "monetizing" their users' labor).

Yet in some quarters encouraging aggregation and reuse is tantamount to supporting piracy and plagiarism. Legacy media companies have typically treated unlicensed news aggregators as thieves, or at least free riders. Not so long ago US media executives called Google and *The Huffington Post* "parasites" on journalistic enterprise (Downie 2010; Greenslade 2009). In 2008 Associated Press (AP) started to pursue bloggers, such as the *Drudge Report*, for copyright infringement after they excerpted AP headlines and stories (Pérez-Peña 2009), and later led legal actions against aggregators, including AllinOne Headlines and news monitoring service Meltwater (Isbell 2010; Jasiewicz 2012). In 2010 Rupert Murdoch's News Ltd websites blocked UK search engine Newsnow from indexing their content to prevent it being captured and reposted (Weaver 2013) and *The New York Times* briefly managed to get Apple to remove its Pulse newsreader from the App Store on copyright grounds (Singel 2010).

Despite the introduction of paywalls around newspaper content, there are signs of an old media retreat from flatly opposing aggregation. Murdoch's sites have reopened to search as a marketing strategy (Andrews 2012) and AP has dropped ongoing litigation against Meltwater, partnering with it in data services innovation (Beaujon 2013). But debates about how to do "remix" journalism in an appropriate manner are still mired in adversarial law and definitions of fair use.

This chapter sidesteps that impasse. Instead it explores how online journalists can best reuse and repurpose existing works in ways that avoid legal action, acknowledge authorial invention, and most important, enrich the networked relationships developing between them, their sources, subjects, and users. It looks at the significance of aggregation and reuse, and the ethical debates they present. It then examines the scope of filter publications and the nature of their reproductive work. Finally it suggests that some conflicts around reuse could be addressed by attention to reciprocity, a principle derived from an ethics of care, and presents suggestions for best practices in curation of digital media.

A New Ethics for the Remix Age?

Media aggregation and reuse ventures are big business because they are ideal modes of production for the Internet age. They exploit the fundamentals of digital information that underpin Internet communications, like the ability to make and circulate near-perfect copies of web pages and other files at zero marginal cost (see Lessig 2008). Aggregation produces cheap, shareable content that can fill new titles and channels with minimal labor costs (Martin and Dwyer 2010), while copy-paste journalism has driven the growth of content farms like Demand Media's eHow (Bakker 2012). Aggregation also provides an increasingly popular mode of consumption. Nearly as many US consumers very often get their news from a "news organizing website or app" (29 percent) as a specific news brand online (36 percent) (Mitchell, Rosenstiel, and Christian 2012).

Aggregation is often read as a bad practice because it relies on making data copies, and so is associated with exploiting others' creative rights. It has also destabilized the news media's economic status quo. In 2011, a year when hundreds of US newspapers closed, the UK's *Guardian* lost £44.2 million and *Times* Newspapers lost £11.6 million, the personalized social news magazine application Flipboard was valued at $200 million—despite having no revenue stream. No wonder then that old media companies are now carefully patrolling secondary uses of their content.

From a user perspective, however, aggregators provide practical benefit. They assemble a range of salient sources in an easily digestible, summary form, reducing users' search costs in terms of time and energy spent browsing multiple publications, allowing them to find specialist news (Chiou and Tucker 2011) as well as new information sources and historical context to ongoing debates.

There is hot debate about the impact of aggregation and curation on journalism standards. Some propose that lower barriers to public information access will force quality journalists to strive for higher standards of investigation and writing, so they can differentiate their offerings from aggregators and content farms. Others argue that widespread reuse creates a "spiral of sameness" (Boczkowski 2010, 173ff), where media diversity is lost, and a culture of self-referentiality, with echo chambers amplifying misinformation and fallacies.

Yet collating and excerpting have long been part of everyday journalism practice. The news agency business was built on supplying raw material to multiple news subscribers, who reused it in various ways (Paterson 2011). So it's the scale, scope, and speed of online aggregation that's now provoking legal and ethical anguish. In response, journalists need to establish agreed standards for negotiating the reuse of others' work and for acknowledging incremental and collaborative creativity, a new ethical framework for the evolution of a networked cultural form—*curatorial journalism*.

Curatorial Journalism

Curatorial journalism refers to the suite of digital content gathering, reuse, and repurposing practices that are used to build new stories and titles out of pre-existing materials. While cut-and-paste journalism has always been possible, more people now have ready access to software that automates, accelerates, and expands that capacity. Tools proliferate for capturing syndicated feeds, filtering, thematizing, excerpting, and linking to the source content, and publishing the resulting summaries in templated form. A genre roll call includes personalized news readers such as News360 and Netvibes; social media magazine compilers Zite, paper. li, Pulse, Flipboard, and RebelMouse; link aggregators like the *Daily Mail*, *Daily Beast*, and *The Drudge Report*; embedding service Repost; locative tweet visualizer Trendsmap; video news search engine Voxalead; and niche news services like *Gigaom* or *Science Daily*.

The meta-titles named here amount to a controversial business model—the *filter publication*. At issue is the way some of these titles republish so-called snippets of information under fair use conditions without a license or legal agreement with the originating publishers. In these instances users may read the filtered content without clicking through to the original story, diverting valuable page views and ad revenues from the content creators (Athey and Mobius 2012). That likelihood prompted Rupert Murdoch to argue that when journalism is "misappropriated without regard to the investment made, it destroys the economics of producing high quality content" (cited in Athey and Mobius 2012, 3). Yet as Google's chief economist Hal Varian has argued, it is not in aggregators' interest to undermine the health of the source news publications (Fallows 2010). For that reason alone it's imperative that filter publishers think about how to add, rather than subtract, value from their media ecosystem.

To understand that ecosystem it's important to consider how machine aggregation and human reuse intersect. Aggregators start with algorithmic collection, indexing, contextual grouping, and reposting of information contained in RSS (rich site summary) or Atom format web feeds. Scripts capture the Extensible Markup Language (XML) files prepared for these feeds and disaggregate the elements—usually headlines, summary or full body text, and sometimes image, sound, or video files. This data is then stored and reformatted for publication in a new web or mobile template, with an anchor link pointing to the original online file. It can then be used to fill multiple new titles, in the same way as licensed syndicated content. Personalized feed readers or burners, for example, automatically display headlines and leads from user-selected sources, and specialist filter titles like *Techmeme* focus on grouping topic-relevant information.

The most successful filter titles apply human editorial judgment to story selection and presentation, and add original features. *Drudge* and *Gawker* editors write catchy, search engine optimized headlines as links to source stories. These editors are renowned for repackaging aggregated excerpts with provocative commentary, or "snappy snarky snarking snark-snark shit" (Daulerio 2012), that ensures debate and cross-linking of their work. Social news services like Digg have editorially curated homepages and enable users to further filter by recommendation, and to suggest and comment on content. NewsVine, a news recommendation service, mixes AP syndicated content with "seeded" links to external stories and citizen journalism, allowing users to vote up the appearance of stories on the site.

As a cultural activity curation is associated with expertise, research and development, even conceptual innovation. Yet one of the chief complaints about self-proclaimed curators is that they simply repost others' work or produce copy/paste summaries, rather than adding value through analysis or original research. This is a valid criticism where story narratives are plagiarized, authors are poorly attributed, or original material is not contextualized.

At the same time we should not underplay the skill it takes to compile salient topic wraps, or the judgment needed to select important talking points for an ongoing debate or to identify and counterpose key quotes. Artful curatorial work is about creating interconnections between ideas, and bringing forth new ones: "linking objects, images, processes, people, locations, histories, and discourses in physical space like an active catalyst, generating twists, turns, and tensions" (Lind 2009, 63). Curatorial journalism ideally elaborates on source material through the inclusion of "context, relationships, background or impact" (Buttry 2012).

So in those senses aggregators and curators are not absolved from ethical responsibilities, or divorced from ethical interactions, just because it is easy to copy and republish digital content. Online their work is indexed and searchable, so it is subject to more intense public scrutiny and comment than offline reuse. They are bound in a network of creative relations based on appropriation and response, a "network of journalistic expertise" (Anderson 2013) that is still developing principles for social interaction.

An Ethics of Reciprocity

Studies of journalism ethics have historically tended to focus on conventional liberal and social responsibility models for acting at the expense of critical theories, which consider journalists as "social and political agents" (Ward 2009, 302). While conventional models are fine lenses for considering traditional paternalistic forms of mainstream journalism, based on top-down editorial processes, they do not always address the co-productive, contingent relations emerging online, particularly in blogs and social media services.

Online users communicate regularly with, and come to rely on, the opinions and recommendations of "intimate strangers." They collate, annotate, and critique journalism in tactical and ongoing knowledge communities. Given the diverse cultural relations and extended social ties we are developing across territorial borders—and the new informational interdependencies we are building—journalism standards could be better grounded in attention to the maintenance of those relational networks. One way to do this is through what feminist scholars have called an "ethics of care" (Noddings 2003; Watters and Johnson 2008).

Care ethics is "contextual, context-specific, based on maintaining and fostering relationships, and has empathy and responsibility as its central values" (Vanacker and Breslin 2006, 196). Like the more republican communitarian ethics (see Christians, Ferré, and Fackler, 1993), it shares an interest in the mutuality of journalistic creativity. Both frameworks challenge online journalists to respond to the articulated needs of their sources, subjects, and audiences—and audiences not as a general public, but as individual users within varying forms of social collective, with different degrees of cultural capital. Care ethics in particular prioritizes investment in interpersonal relations, on inclusion in social interaction, on affective responses to (and dialogue about) matters of conflict (Ess 2013, 363)—unlike the dominant ethical approaches, which Vanacker and Breslin argue produce an adversarial or "war model" for balancing competing claims (201). This is not to propose we should value care ethics above duty or virtue models but to consider, as Ess's work suggests, how notions of contextual responsibility to others might fruitfully operate in synthesis with industry codes and professional ideas of journalistic excellence. (See David Craig's chapter for additional discussion of ethical perspectives focused on duty, virtue, and care.)

Most studies of care examine face-to-face, interpersonal encounters, where social obligations and power relations are directly negotiated. Yet care ethics becomes an important rubric to consider in the journalistic building of online communities and user groups, the collaborative arrangements of crowdsourcing and the curatorial work of connecting and reworking others' stories. Here sharing, declaration, disclosure, and debate are the new foundations of participation and audience loyalty.

It may seem improbable to think care ethics could be implemented in algorithmic journalism or busy digital production environments where reporters have little contact with sources. Yet some basic principles of care for a networked community can be built into reuse publishing systems and production routines—for example, by standardizing and automating those aspects of source attribution that underpin communicative interaction. Linking excerpts to the original document, for example, benefits both source authors and, in turn, their hypermedia universe of sources, enabling the user to track the development of events and arguments. Chiou and Tucker (2011, 3) found that users of linked summary sites often consult source websites after visiting an aggregator, notwithstanding industry fears to the contrary, and are "more likely to be provoked to seek additional sources and to read further rather than merely being satisfied with a summary."

A care ethics framework suggests three procedural goals for curatorial journalists. First, they should attend to the impact of reuse on source authors and the online news ecosystem. Second, they should consider the implications of aggregation systems for users who want to access those source authors. This means linking not just to stories, but to author biographies and brands. Finally, they should pursue interaction to improve the accuracy, depth, and mutual benefits of their work—enlisting users to contribute to the diversity and evaluation of sources, or authors to correct errors of interpretation (say when a headline is rewritten for search engine optimization). Online journalists are becoming aware of the need to build better relations of trust between actors separated by time and distance. In these respects, care ethics is a framework that is keenly interested in *reciprocity*.

Reciprocity is a critical concept for networked media. On one hand it refers to the deontological expectation that we will treat others' creative work as we would want ours treated. As Stephen Ward has argued: ". . . in a fair society we believe that all will benefit from being reasonable, and hence we are motivated to act towards others in a reciprocal manner" (Ward 2010, 130). This idea of reciprocity, as Ward suggests, mediates between self-interest and altruistic actions, and helps us in setting benchmarks for social responsibility. We should attribute because we ourselves want to be credited for our creativity. Another way of thinking about reciprocity comes via Axel Honneth (1996), who posits the need for individuals to acknowledge and respond to others' communicative actions and desires, as the basis of self-realization and mutual political recognition. Reciprocity becomes an important ethical principle to consider when we share, comment on, or discuss others' work. Dialogic actions such as these anticipate a communicative response, whether or not we expect or get one. As Mikhail Bakhtin recognized, our thoughts about how our ideas will be interpreted and received shape the very act of speaking—or in the online case, writing (see Martin 2012) and thus our interest in participation. Thus reciprocity in aggregation or curation means anticipating when, how, and why people might want to respond to our re-presentation of their work.

How then could we put an ethics of care to work in developing more inclusive, productive, everyday reuse practices? Working with digital, internetworked media, as Charles Ess (2013, 315) observes, presents us with three ethical challenges. We need to recognize where:

> traditional ethical principles, such as attribution, might be applied to new
> forms of publication;

new practices and processes emerge, like linking or social media comment, that require we reinterpret those principles; and

novel relational problems demand a radical transformation of our professional thinking about journalism and society.

With these challenges in mind what follows is a checklist for best practice curation. It draws on ideas from the previous three chapters of this book and focuses on *attribution*, an existing journalism principle; *linking*, the expansion of attribution for hypertextual journalism; and a practice which is paramount in *curation*, the craft of connecting, recontextualizing, and elaborating in hypertext environments. Finally it explores the application of *reciprocity*, a new principle for doing collaborative, accountable journalism online.

Attribution

As Juliette De Maeyer notes in the previous chapter, source attribution has always been a fundamental acknowledgment of journalistic achievement. Attribution gains significance and value online through hyperlinking. Links are the quid pro quo of excerpting, directing traffic to the source material URL, and potentially increasing the creator's brand exposure. So a good curator always first identifies the source of her material and then links to the original document or file online—and not at the end of a long story, but early in the story text. Block quotes need to be clearly identified with indents or quotes, and again where possible linked back to the source story.

Ideally effective attribution would be built into story template design and the creation of attribution data fields: the headline text (linked to source URL), the masthead or publisher's name and/or logo (with homepage URL), and any Creative Commons licensing information (with URL to the license page)—especially for audio-visual material. A timestamp should be mandatory—how else can you trace the spread and evolution of stories through time and space? When you are tweaking a template or creating a custom layout, you could also add a byline to each headline entry, which can be linked to the author's online biography. The extent of linking on any one page is often a style or usability consideration, but ideally you should help the user to easily locate the source author. *The Huffington Post* includes a small font mini-bio with front-page story credits, but no link to the author's blog.

Attribution credits the creator and his or her brand but is also an act of *transparency* or openness (a concept Stephen Ward explores more fully in his chapter). Attribution reveals where ideas or source materials are drawn from, helping users make decisions about what they might trust and read. Users are known to seek out quality sources from aggregated material (Chiou and Tucker 2011, 24) and so author and/or brand attribution can be persuasive information, indicating reliability or geographic relevance. We can't assume that a user will click through on every headline, so that source data needs to be obvious, like a logo. *Techmeme* goes a step further than brand attributions, and publishes a leaderboard which gives ranked statistics on the relative percentage of content drawn from different publications, indicating their source "presence," and homepage links for those publications. This gives all users an indication of which publication is considered more influential in the aggregation stakes.

Linking

Linking is the critical second step in attribution, and again you can return to Juliette De Maeyer for a guide on suggested best practices for linking. Aggregators should hotlink story titles (to original works), bylines (to author biographies), and brand names or logos (to homepages). Curators should hotlink to the source story—which is where some bloggers trip up.

If you want to give credit where it's due, make sure that the source site you're linking to is actually the origin, and the copyright holder, of the material you want to republish. Before assuming this, you might check that the author of the material is clearly identified on the text itself, or in the metadata of the file. Tin-Eye reverse search engine is useful for cross-referencing the use of images and locating original files.

Determining authorship and copyright is time-consuming but essential for legal purposes—as Google News discovered when it aggregated news copy from Agence France Presse subscribers' websites, only to be sued by the news agency for republishing copyright material (Isbell 2010).

Linking also establishes the non-linear narrative and contextual paths that allow users to explore issues over time, via the perspectives of many, rather than one.

In that way, done effectively it can present a deeper and richer pathway into a debate.

Curation

A fundamental of effective curation is giving back to the community of authors and users who shaped the original material you cite. This may be simply by following journalism conventions such as verification and fact checking. Verifying or correcting information that has passed through many social media hands can address one of the great problems of reuse—the amplification of errors. Verification of source material is important, regardless of the publisher's credentials—unless you are prepared to produce a disclaimer stating you cannot vouch for the source (though the legal implications of this may vary in different countries). Similarly any modifications or paraphrasing must express the author's original intended meaning. Otherwise you may just as well quote the source.

In the art world curation involves different acts of invention, such as writing curatorial essays and providing interpretative materials. The intention is to elaborate on existing research, to cast it in a new light, and to produce original facts and reflections about the meaning of the work for new audiences. Veteran online editor Steve Buttry (2012) suggests journalists add value by doing original interviews, data analysis, commentary or critique, creating a wrap or roundup of a topic, and supplementing aggregated data with maps, tweets, or videos.

Curation is not just a matter of gathering, summarizing, paraphrasing, or riffing off what has already been said. You certainly cannot call yourself a curator if you are a "patchwork plagiarist" (McBride 2012)—that is, stitching together bits of original sentences and borrowed quotes with hastily rewritten clauses. As Poynter ethics specialist Kelly McBride notes, that level of basic appropriation may get you fired. Instead she asks digital journalists: "What can we provide to our audience that's different than what's already been published?"

At the very least, if you are only interested in the possibility you might face legal action for your reuse of online material, the U.S. Citizen Media Law Project (Isbell 2010) offers three points of advice that it says should reduce your risk:

1. Only reproduce those parts of a headline or article that are necessary to make your point or to identify the original story.
2. When possible, provide context for, or commentary on the material you use.
3. Don't republish all the material you can access from a single source.

An argument for aggregation based on the equivalent of fair use or fair dealing grounds will be much stronger if you follow these suggestions along with the attribution, linking, and curation practices just outlined. To take a step further, from good practice to best practice involves a little more work on the final care principle—reciprocity.

Reciprocity

Earlier I noted that one of the great debates in aggregation has been about the rewriting of headlines in order to exploit search engine ranking. When *Forbes* writer Kashmir Hill cleverly repackaged a whole *New York Times* article by veteran journalist Charles Duhigg and gave it a catchy Twitter- and SEO-friendly headline, she pulled in more Facebook likes and shares than the original article, and 600,800 page views in one day (Hill 2012). It's unclear how that last figure compares with direct accesses from the *Times*, but another *Times* reporter, Nick O'Neill, was so miffed by Hill's summary act he wrote a critical blog post called "How Forbes Stole a New York Times Article and Got All the Traffic" (O'Neill 2012). The post triggered a wave of social media discussion about the ethics of appropriation.

However, a subsequent feature by blogger Jim Romenesko, of Poynter Institute fame, showed graphically why journalists need to develop a better sense of reciprocity online. Romenesko contacted all parties for comment on the debacle and found that possibly the worst injustices Hill had committed were reworking someone's story idea without permission and failing to link to Duhigg's book, on which the article was based (Romenesko 2012). Duhigg himself was ambivalent about Hill's modification of his writing as long as his research got publicity, but thanked her for finally updating her story with an Amazon books link. Curiously, in rationalizing to Romenesko what they did, neither Hill nor O'Neill talks about the impact on Duhigg, the source of the story. They illustrate an everyday journalism focus on self and brand, at the expense of users and sources.

Journalism usually benefits from critique and consultation—through comments on stories or by offering readers the chance to report errors. In the last instance, Hill could have asked Duhigg about reaction to his article and considered linking to his website and book. In turn he might have revealed new insights he hadn't published in the *Times*. In setting up a filter publication, one of the first thoughts should be about the parameters for interaction and response. How can you know if you've posted something that contains an error? Can you solicit others' remixes or inspire theirs? How can you build the reciprocal relations that enable you to crowdsource information? And how might you encourage attribution of your work by others?

Creative Commons (CC) licenses have become one popular way of encouraging remix and republishing practices. For example, all *Gawker* gossip magazine articles are badged with an Attribution-NonCommercial license—which allows anyone to repost any original elements with proper attribution, on a non- or not-for-profit publication, and with the same CC licensing terms. However, a closer look at the terms of use reveals that you may only republish if "proper credit" is given to the source website and all content links remain in place. What proper credit means is not defined—so you would be wise to check. Gawker's terms of use also warn against republishing content that it may not own the copyright to—making it the republisher's responsibility to determine who owns copyright in their own jurisdiction (Gawker 2014). These limitations on reposting content from one of the world's iconic filter titles are a reminder that copyright has lost little of its underlying authority in a remix age.

Conclusion

It's tempting to sum up the value of aggregators with a quote from Steve Buttry (2012), who compares their promotional and educational benefits to public libraries:

> Society benefits from the existence of libraries, which boost reading and literacy. An author or publisher whining about the freeloaders who use

libraries would appear selfish and narrow-sighted, just as journalists whining about aggregators are selfish and myopic.

The people who are critical or dismissive of aggregation and curation fail (or refuse) to understand the value that [they] have in themselves. Pointing out things that people may be interested in has value. It's a great function of Twitter, Facebook, Pinterest, Google+ and other social media, which together drive huge traffic for news organizations.

Yet where public libraries were an institutional response to information scarcity, and state and philanthropist interest in educating ordinary people, aggregation is a response to information overload. It is a diversely constituted drive to make salient things visible and to share them for mutual benefit. Copyright is still the locus of concerns about reuse, but everyday conflict over misappropriation and misrepresentation often points to a failure to think about basic journalism principles such as attribution, accuracy, and accountability. Just as clearly it points to a lack of understanding about our connectedness to other online creatives and interest in those up and down the online chain of invention.

The world of aggregation—with its automated, no-pay, low-pay conditions— is ripe for an ethical overhaul, but unlikely to adopt the ideals set out here, except where they serve a legal purpose. Curatorial journalism, on the other hand, is in many accounts of media futures, part of a bigger, expanding set of networked journalism practices and so is rich territory for best practice development. Like citizen journalism, curation makes claim to collaboration, dialogue, and development. But greater social interaction via recommendation, friending, sharing, and cooperation requires an ethics of care—a concern for where the conversation's been and where it's going, who is involved and who needs to be. Without care, we will share plenty of information, but little history.

Best Practices in Action: Two Initiatives

In 2012 at the interactive media arm of the influential South by South West (SXSW) conference in Austin, Texas, two new proposals for digital ethics were given a run—one a bottom-up scenario and the other (relatively) top-down.

Freelance writer Maria Popova and designer Kelli Anderson launched their Curator's Code initiative: a symbolic system for standardizing attributions of reuse. Popova argued that while it was vital to attribute creators for their work, the "intellectual labor" of information discovery and amplification also needed better recognition. Only the year before Popova (2011) had likened Twitter curation to a form of authorship, involving moderation, filtering, and sense-making.

The heart of the Curator's Code is two new unicode symbols that bloggers can use to credit the "service" of information discovery:

ᔕ indicates a source you are re-posting with little or no modification

↬ stands for a hat-tip to the source that inspired you, or whose work you have significantly modified and expanded

Popova's rationale for the Curator's Code (2012) is a care ethics rationale—that the use of the symbols will better support a "link-love ecosystem" of information sharing. In a later update on reaction to the code she cites Albert Einstein's reflection as her inspiration:

> A hundred times every day I remind myself that my inner and outer life are based on the labors of other men, living and dead, and that I must exert myself in order to give in the same measure as I have received and am still receiving.
>
> (Einstein 1954, 1)

The Code site offers a bookmark widget, which enables users to copy and paste in the symbols—each wrapped in an anchor link to the Code to promote its wider use. The site also houses a badge for people to add to their blogs, to indicate their support for the move.

Despite the collegial intent, blogger reaction was swift and often unsupportive. Some people argued the proposal was unnecessary. Marco Arment (2012), the creator of Instapaper, noted that the word *via* (along with the tilde ~ symbol) and the acronym HT for hat-tip were already widely used to credit great shares or tip-offs. He also argued that Popova's symbols weren't legible—they did not convey a clear meaning and the different purposes weren't easily distinguished. Designer Ben Stott (2012) questioned the nature of the labor involved in reuse:

> . . . what we are doing is sharing—posting, linking and blogging somebody else's hard work. It is not our content, we didn't create it, we don't own it and we certainly don't have any rights over it just because we think we found it first.

The other ethical venture, led by media writer Simon Dumenco, was a standards think tank provisionally called the Council on Ethical Blogging and Aggregation. The group included senior executives from the Atlantic, Slate, Esquire, and Longreads, all of which have significant investments in forms of aggregation. Although Dumenco agreed in a Poynter chat that Council was a "dorky word," he said the name signaled a formal attempt to come up with "simple, common sense standards" for organizations that do aggregation and blogging "at great scale" (Myers 2012). He invited all interested parties to join and said the aim was to have an open development process.

In coverage for *The New York Times*, former editor in chief of *Salon* magazine Kerry Lauderman was supportive of the initiative:

> Increasingly, when people go online, it's like stepping through the looking glass. Whether you follow a link from Twitter, an e-mail, or Pinterest, you wind up on a site where you really don't know where you are. It would be nice if there was a way of signaling what the standards are and how trustworthy the information is.
>
> (Carr 2012)

Nevertheless subsequent reaction to the Council in legacy media and online publications was skeptical. *Gawker* rejected it as the blog police, while *Mediabistro* noted the absence of bloggers in the launch group. *The New York Times* media columnist David Carr envisaged the "digerati seizing with laughter at the idea a pew full of journalism church ladies is somehow going to do battle with the entire Internet" (Carr 2012). At the time of writing the Council did not have an online presence and no draft guidelines had been issued.

Discussion Questions

1. When digital journalism is such a permeable field, with so many forms of practice, how realistic is the idea of a normative code of ethics for aggregation and reuse?
    Is aggregation best regulated through law or ethical standards?
2. Where can you identify cases of best practice attribution, linking, and curation taking place?
3. You have been asked to compile a feature on the impact of the Occupy Wall Street movement by aggregating old stories, articles from rival publications, government documents, material from lobby groups, blogger critiques, and user comments. How might you apply the curatorial checklist to ensure key sources are included, accurately attributed, represented, and consulted?

References

Anderson, Christopher W. 2013. "What Aggregators Do: Towards a Networked Concept of Journalistic Expertise in the Digital Age." *Journalism* 14(8):1008–23.

Andrews, Robert. 2012. "Murdoch's Times Unblocks Search Engines to Seek New Subscribers." *paidContent*, September 26, 2012. Accessed February 25, 2014. http://paidcontent.org/2012/09/26/timesunblockssearch/

Arment, Marco. 2012. "I'm Not a Curator." *Marco.org*, March 12, 2012. Accessed November 6, 2013. www.marco.org/2012/03/12/not-a-curator

Athey, Susan, and Markus Mobius. 2012. "The Impact of News Aggregators on Internet News Consumption: The Case of Localization." Working paper. February 24, 2012.

Accessed November 26, 2013. http://faculty gsb.stanford.edu/athey/documents/local news.pdf

Bakker, Piet. 2012. "New Journalism 3.0: Aggregation, Content Farms and Huffinization: The Rise of Low-pay and No-pay Journalism." Hogeschool Utrecht. University of Amsterdam. Accessed September 28, 2013. www.mediafutureweek.nl/wp-content/uploads/2012/05/whitepaper-New-Journalism-30-HU.pdf

Beaujon, Andrew. 2013. "AP, Meltwater End Litigation, Will 'Collaborate on Innovating New Products.'" *Poynter.org*, July 29, 2013. Accessed February 25, 2014. www.poynter.org/latest-news/mediawire/219443/ap-meltwater-end-litigation-will-collaborate-on-innovating-new-products/

Boczkowski, Pablo J. 2010. *News at Work: Imitation in an Age of Information Abundance.* Chicago and London: University of Chicago Press.

Buttry, Steve. 2012. "Aggregation Guidelines: Link, Attribute, Add Value." *The Buttry Diary*, May 16, 2012. Accessed September 12, 2013. http://stevebuttry.wordpress.com/2012/05/16/aggregation-guidelines-link-attribute-add-value/

Carr, David. 2012. "A Code of Conduct for Content Aggregators." The Media Equation. *NYTimes.com*, March 11, 2012. Accessed September 22, 2013. www.nytimes.com/2012/03/12/business/media/guidelines-proposed-for-content-aggregation-online.html

Chiou, Lesley, and Catherine Tucker. 2011. "Copyright, Digitization, and Aggregation." Massachusetts Institute of Technology. NET Institute Working Paper No. 11–18. Accessed October 3, 2013. http://dx.doi.org/10.2139/ssrn.1864203

Christians, Clifford G., John P. Ferré, and Mark Fackler. 1993. *Good News: Social Ethics and the Press.* New York: Oxford University Press.

Daulerio, A.J. 2012. "Gawker Will Be Conducting an Experiment, Please Enjoy Your Free Cute Cats Singing and Sideboobs." *Gawker*, January 23, 2013. Accessed July 23, 2013. http://gawker.com/5878065/gawker-will-be-conducting-an-experiment-please-enjoy-your-free-cute-cats-singing-and-sideboobs

Downie, Leonard. 2010. *The New News.* James Cameron Memorial Lecture. City University London. *The Guardian*, September 22, 2010. Accessed September 28, 2013. http://image.guardian.co.uk/sys-files/Media/documents/2010/09/23/ DownieCameron.pdf

Einstein, Albert. 1954. *Letters and Opinions.* London: Alvin Redman.

Ess, Charles. 2013. *Digital Media Ethics.* 2nd ed. Cambridge, MA and Malden, UK: Polity Press.

Fallows, James. 2010. "How to Save the News." *The Atlantic*, May 11, 2010. Accessed May 5, 2011. www.theatlantic.com/magazine/archive/2010/06/how-to-save-the-news/308095/

Gawker. 2014. "Using Gawker Media Content." June 4, 2013. Accessed February 25, 2014. http://legal.kinja.com/using-gawker-media-content-511255350

Greenslade, Roy. 2009. "Thomson—Google Is a Parasite." *theguardian.com*, April 6, 2009. Accessed July 20, 2013. www.theguardian.com/media/greenslade/2009/apr/06/google-wallstreetjournal

Hill, Kashmir. 2012. "How Target Figured Out A Teen Girl Was Pregnant Before Her Father Did." *Forbes.com*, February 16, 2012. Accessed November 1, 2013. www.forbes.com/sites/kashmirhill/2012/02/16/how-target-figured-out-a-teen-girl-was-pregnant-before-her-father-did/

Honneth, Axel. 1996. *The Struggle for Recognition: The Moral Grammar of Social Conflict.* Cambridge, MA: MIT Press.

Isbell, Kimberley. 2010. *The Rise of the News Aggregator: Legal Implications and Best Practices.* Citizen Media Law Project. Berkman Center for Internet and Society Research Publication No. 2010–10. Cambridge, MA: Harvard Law School.

Jasiewicz, Monika I. 2012. "Copyright Protection in an Opt-Out World: Implied License Doctrine and News Aggregators." *Yale Law Journal* 122(3):837–50.

Lessig, Lawrence. 2008. *Remix: Making Arts and Commerce Thrive in the Hybrid Economy.* New York: Penguin Press.

Lind, Maria. 2009. "The Curatorial." In *Selected Maria Lind Writing*, edited by Brian Kuan Wood, 56–66. Berlin: Sternberg Press.

Martin, Fiona. 2012. "Vox Populi, Vox Dei: ABC Online and the Risks of Dialogic Interaction." In *Histories of Public Service Broadcasters on the Web*, edited by N. Brügger and M. Burns, 177–92. New York: Peter Lang.

Martin, Fiona, and Tim Dwyer. 2010. "Updating Diversity of Voice Arguments for Online News Media." *Global Media Journal*, Australian edition, 4(1). Accessed November 25, 2010. www.hca.uws.edu.au/gmjau/archive/v4_2010_1/dwyer_martin_RA.html

McBride, Kelly. 2012. " 'Patchwriting' Is More Common Than Plagiarism, Just as Dishonest." Everyday Ethics. *Poynter.org*, September 18, 2012. Accessed October 15, 2013. www.poynter.org/latest-news/everyday-ethics/188789/patchwriting-is-more-common-than-plagiarism-just-as-dishonest/

Mitchell, Amy, Tom Rosenstiel, and Leah Christian. 2012. "Mobile Devices and News Consumption: Some Good Signs for Journalism: What Facebook and Twitter Mean for News." In *State of the News Media 2012*. Project for Excellence in Journalism and Pew Internet Research Center. Accessed September 12, 2013. http://stateofthemedia.org/2012/mobile-devices-and-news-consumption-some-good-signs-for-journalism/

Myers, Steve. 2012. "Can We Agree about Aggregation Standards?" Media Wire. *Poynter.org*, March 13, 2012. Accessed April 23, 2013www.poynter.org/latest-news/mediawire/166315/live-chat-today-can-we-agree-about-aggregation-standards/

Noddings, Nel. 2003. *Caring: A Feminine Approach to Ethics and Moral Education.* 2nd ed. Berkeley: University of California Press.

O'Neill, Nick. 2012. "How Forbes Stole a New York Times Article and Got All the Traffic." *Nick O'Neill*, February 19, 2012. Accessed November 1, 2013. http://nickoneill.com/how-fortune-stole-a-new-york-times-article-and-got-all-the-traffic/

Paterson, Chris A. 2011. *The International Television News Agencies: The World from London.* New York: Peter Lang.

Pérez-Peña, Richard. 2009. "A.P. Seeks to Rein in Sites Using Its Content." *NYTimes.com*, April 6, 2009. Accessed February 25, 2014. www.nytimes.com/2009/04/07/business/media/07paper.html

Popova, Maria. 2011. "In a New World of Informational Abundance, Content Curation Is a New Kind of Authorship." *Nieman Journalism Lab*, June 10, 2011. Accessed October 27, 2012. www.niemanlab.org/2011/06/maria-popova-in-a-new-world-of-informational-abundance-content-curation-is-a-new-kind-of-authorship/

Popova, Maria. 2012. "Introducing the Curator's Code: A Standard for Honoring Attribution of Discovery across the Web." *Brainpickings*, March 3, 2012. Accessed October 27, 2012. www.brainpickings.org/index.php/2012/03/09/curators-code/

Romenesko, Jim. 2012. "NYT Reporter Defends Forbes Writer Accused of Stealing His Work." *Jimromenesko.com*, February 21, 2012. Accessed November 1, 2013. http://jimromenesko.com/2012/02/21/nyt-reporter-defends-forbes-writer-accused-of-stealing-his-work/

Singel, Ryan. 2010. "Did Apple Tell Times to Shove Its App-Takedown Letter? (Updated)." *Wired.com*, June 8, 2010. Accessed February 25, 2014. www.wired.com/business/2010/06/apple-times-pulse/

Stott, Ben. 2012. Trying To Understand The Curator's Code's Approach To Attributing Discovery. Comment on article by Daniel Howells. Howells. March 10, 2012. Comment posted March 14, 2012. Accessed October 27, 2013. http://howells.ws/posts/view/89/trying-to-understand-the-curators-codes-approach-to-attributing-discovery

Vanacker, Bastiaan, and Breslin, John. 2006. "Ethics of Care: More Than Just Another Tool to Bash the Media." *Journal of Mass Media Ethics* 21(2&3):196–214.

Ward, Stephen J. A. 2009. "Journalism Ethics." In *The Handbook of Journalism Studies*, edited by Karin Wahl-Jorgensen and Thomas Hanitzsch, 295–309. New York: Routledge.

Ward, Stephen J. A. 2010. *Global Journalism Ethics*. Montreal: McGill-Queen's University Press.

Watters, Kathleen, and Patricia Johnson. 2008. "Care Ethics and the Nurturing of Public Discourse: Language, Values, and the Voice of Ellen Goodman." *Teaching Ethics* 8.2: 29–42.

Weaver, Alexander B. 2013. "Aggravated with Aggregators: Can International Copyright Law Help Save the News Room?" *Emory International Law Review* 26(2):1161–1200.

8

REAL-TIME ONLINE REPORTING

Best Practices for Live Blogging

Neil Thurman

CITY UNIVERSITY LONDON, UK

Real-time online reporting has a history that can be measured in decades. Britain's *Guardian* newspaper was covering live soccer matches on its website as early as 1999 (Thurman and Walters 2013, 99). That story—a "minute-by-minute" report on Manchester United's game against Arsenal on February 17—was an early example of what, over recent years, has become a common and popular way for journalists to cover not only sport and other scheduled events, such as festivals and awards ceremonies, but also breaking news and ongoing political stories.

Contemporary live online reporting makes the most of converging technological platforms and includes not just text but a range of content including still and moving images and audio. Social media platforms are an important source of content, which is often embedded directly. The resulting news artefact is referred to using a variety of names, including "news streams," "live updating news pages," and "live blogs." This last term has been adopted for the purposes of this chapter. Live blogs are becoming increasingly common, with, for example, *The Guardian's* website publishing close to 150 per month (Thurman and Walters 2013, 82). They are also a relatively popular news format: a nine-country survey showed an average of about 15 percent of regular online news consumers use them on a weekly basis (Thurman and Newman 2014). Those levels of reach are complemented by a high degree of engagement, with readers spending, on average, between six and 24 minutes on any given live blog, more time than is typical for visits to online news in other formats (Thurman and Newman 2014; Thurman and Walters 2013, 87).

This chapter examines opportunities, risks, and best practices in live blogging. It ends with a suggested exercise involving a scheduled news event and a live blogging platform.

Opportunities and Risks

Live online reporting presents a number of opportunities, both to journalists individually, and to journalism as an institution. There are also, however, some attendant risks. Of the opportunities the most obvious is, perhaps, the way in which live blogs allow journalists—almost irrespective of the resources at their disposal—to report at speed, on an almost real-time basis. As well as empowering individual reporters and community or other small, specialist news outlets, live blogs enable news organizations with a background in print to compete against rivals with broadcast parentage in the coverage of breaking news and live events. They are also of value to broadcast news organizations by providing them with a format that works on devices, such as smartphones, and at locations of consumption, such as the office, where a purely audio-visual news presentation is less than optimal.

Less obvious, perhaps, is how live blogging seems to be offering news organizations an opportunity to rebuild trust with their audiences, and—should they so wish—to increase participation. Surveys of news consumers have shown that live blogs are perceived as being more balanced and/or factual than traditional articles because of the range of opinions they present, the links they provide to sources and supporting documents, and their "neutral" tone (Thurman and Newman 2014; Thurman and Walters 2013, 96). Thurman and Walters's study (97) also indicated that audiences are "more than twice as likely to participate in live blogs compared with other article types," although, at the time of writing, no other research had corroborated this finding. However, the volume of readers' contributions being submitted to some live blogs (Thurman and Rodgers 2014) indicates high levels of participation are possible.

The speed with which live blogging allows reporting to be conducted is an opportunity, but it also carries risks. Live blogs at *The Guardian*'s website are updated, on average, about every 10 minutes over the course of their six-hour duration (Thurman and Walters 2013, 90).[1] This places a considerable burden on the journalists involved—there are typically two or three (91)—and means that there is little time for factual verification. Editorial oversight may also be minimal because of technical factors (92). The most serious risk with live blogging then is that a serious error of fact or interpretation will be made in what *The Guardian*'s Paul Lewis[2] calls "the rush to do regular updates" (94). The potential for this to happen is, Lewis believes, compounded by how, in the practice of live blogging, a "new view" has emerged that tolerates the publication of unverified information (albeit labeled as such) accompanied by an invitation for readers to "determine how accurate it is" (Thurman and Walters 2013, 94).

One example of the publication of false information in a live blog occurred during *The Guardian*'s live coverage (Davis and Evans 2011) of the "March for the Alternative" protest against UK government cuts on March 26, 2011. A contributor, Chris Snell, a Google employee, took a photograph of the Lillywhites department store in London with smoke appearing to come from the back of the building, tweeting the picture with the text "Lillywhites on fire piccadilly circus" (Snell 2011). *The Guardian*, along with a number of other websites, included this tweet on their live blog, with the comment "There are reports on Twitter that the sports clothing store Lillywhites is now on fire." It turned out, however, that Lillywhites was not on fire: the source of the smoke was elsewhere (Davis and Evans 2011).

On other occasions, however, *The Guardian* has been one of the few news organizations *not* to be hoaxed. Following the death of Osama Bin Laden in May 2011, a picture purporting to show his dead body circulated in social and mainstream media (Newman 2011). *The Guardian*, suspicious of the photograph, decided not to use it (Paul Lewis, personal communication, June 8, 2011). The image turned out to be a fake.

Although, as has been shown, live blogs can engage some readers for considerable lengths of time, they are not universally popular. Research has shown their presentation of updates in reverse chronological order, as well as their fragmented structure, can confuse readers. Over 25 percent of regular online news consumers in the United Kingdom say live blogs are "difficult to understand" (Thurman and Newman 2014). Readers have also complained about decisions to use the format on stories that they believe did not warrant the intense scrutiny or informal tone that live blogs bring (Thurman and Walters 2013, 97).

A final risk relates to the costs of live online coverage which, as we have seen, can consume considerable amounts of journalists' time. As newsroom budgets are being reduced, what might have to be cut back to support any increase in live online reporting? As the editor of the BBC News website, Steve Herrmann, says, "there is still a need for self-contained, structured reporting and analysis and for narrative storytelling" (quoted in Thurman and Newman 2014). The BBC, in common with other news organizations, is still working out the editorial and financial implications of "trying to do both" (quoted in Thurman and Newman 2014).

Best Practices

Choosing What, and What Not, to Live Blog

With live blogs now often the default format for online coverage of breaking news, they may seem the obvious choice for many stories. However, journalists and editors should exercise discretion when deciding whether to deploy the format. Considerations include: the magnitude of the event; the resources available; and whether, for a particular story, a live blog—with its informal, conversational style—is appropriate. Some readers interviewed for Thurman and Walters's study (2013) expressed irritation when live blogs were used on what they saw as trivial stories, such as "Radiohead releasing an album" or "[the] Sarah Palin emails." Concern was also expressed about the live blogging of some sensitive events: one reader thought that the live blogging of the aftermath of a series of shootings in the English county of Cumbria in June 2010, when there were unidentified victims and an active police pursuit of the perpetrator (ultimately discovered to be Derrick Bird), was "ghoulish" (unpublished survey results, August 2011).

Choosing a Platform

Although, at its simplest, a live news stream need be no more than a series of time-stamped textual updates, it is now possible for—and audiences expect—such streams to contain:

- A headline
- A summary of the key story developments
- Pre-recorded and/or live video and audio
- Photographs and illustrations
- Maps and data graphics
- Embedded social media content such as tweets
- Hypertext links
- Readers' comments

The content management systems used in most online newsrooms can handle some or all of these elements, but most cannot bring them together in the manner expected of live blogs—that is, on a single page with updates presented in reverse chronological order. To do that, some news organizations, including Guardian.com and BBC News online, have adapted their existing content management systems, while others have bought in specialist live blogging software such as ScribbleLive or CoveritLive (Reuters, the *Wall Street Journal*, and CNN.com, for example).

The differing ways these various live blogging platforms handle key content elements—such as readers' comments—can have consequences on levels of reader participation, as well as on the feel and tone of the live blogs that result. For this reason the choice of platform is more than just a resource or technical decision. It should also be informed by, and will impact on, editorial considerations such as the prominence to be given to readers' contributions.

Preparation

Covering a live event successfully in any medium requires preparation. Although, with live blogging, "dead air" time can be longer than in live TV or radio, there will be periods during the coverage of a live event, particularly at the start, when previously researched and written posts will be vital. They help to set the context for the live coverage by providing background information on the people and place involved, and the purpose of the event. *The Guardian's* sports reporter Rob Smyth spends half an hour "constructing the preamble" before live blogging soccer matches (personal communication, July 6, 2011), and Heidi Stephens, who has live blogged *The Apprentice* TV show for Guardian.com, "always write[s] the intro section in advance" (Heidi Stephens, personal communication, June 14, 2011). Live online coverage of any scheduled event can be greatly enhanced if the verified social media feeds of any participants (individual or institutional) and attendees are identified and followed, along with any Twitter hashtags created for, or particularly relevant to, the event. Such feeds will provide leads and quotations or media content that can be incorporated directly into the live blog.

Aggregation and Links

Live blogs are characterized by the generous use of hyperlinks and a relatively high proportion of quoted material. Thurman and Walters (2013, 91) found an average of 16.25 hyperlinks per live blog at *The Guardian*. By comparison, Stray (2010) found the median number of links in regular news articles at 12 news sites he surveyed to be 2.6. Thurman and Walters's survey also showed that live blogs covering breaking news and ongoing public-affairs stories contained, on average, one third substantive quotes. Live blogs give journalists the freedom to aggregate comment and supplementary material on stories, and to exceed the 400–500 word limit of a typical news story.[3] Andrew Sparrow, *The Guardian's* Senior Political Correspondent, considers hyperlinks within live blogs to be "crucial," going as far as to say that "they are actually what [live blogging is] all about," because a "large chunk" of live blogs is aggregation (personal communication, June 13, 2011).

Best practice in this area is to attribute transparently, signposting quotations using, for example, block quotes and/or graphical devices such as large quotation marks. It is preferable if source material is linked to directly. Offering such links is, Andrew Sparrow suggests, "absolutely essential to the way web journalism ought to operate," because it adds value "in a way that newsprint can't." He warns, however, that this only "works if you are linking to stuff that is good and relevant and interesting" (personal communication, June 13, 2011). As we have seen, aggregating a range of opinions on a story, and providing links to sources and supporting documents, are characteristics of live blogs that contribute to readers' perceptions that the format is more balanced and/or factual than traditional articles. For much more on best practices in hyperlinking, see Juliette De Maeyer's chapter in this book.

Making Live Blogs Usable

A quarter of readers find live blogs difficult to follow (Thurman and Newman 2014). This is unsurprising because, first, unlike in a traditional news story written using an inverted pyramid structure, the most newsworthy information in a live blog may appear anywhere on the page. Second, live blogs are presented in reverse chronological order, with the most recent update first. This reversal of our expectation for stories to be told from beginning to end, can, understandably, be confusing.

To counter these problems of usability it is important that journalists follow best practice by providing contextual information in the form of a headline and summary of key developments. This contextual information should appear above the live story frame, in a prominent position at the top of the page, and should be rewritten as frequently as the story changes. The ScribbleLive platform makes the publishing of such contextual information relatively straightforward through its "LiveArticle" feature, which allows the headline and summary to be edited with the same tool used to control the live story, and to be embedded at the top of the live blog in a way that always shows the latest versions without the reader having to refresh their browser window. Both before and after live online coverage has finished, some readers like to read live blogs from beginning to end (Thurman and Walters 2013). To facilitate this, it may be useful, as *The Guardian* has done, to provide readers with the ability to view the live blog in chronological rather than reverse chronological order.

Sourcing and Verification

Live blogging journalists use a range of sources appropriate to the event being covered, including: social media networks, such as Twitter and YouTube; live television streams; news agency wires; subscription information services (such as Politicshome.com and Cricinfo); phone calls, face-to-face meetings, emails or text messages with contacts (who may or may not have official affiliation); and websites (sometimes via RSS feeds).

The speed at which live blogs are updated, the expectation that they will be on top of the latest developments, and their open, aggregating nature present a set of potentially conflicting demands on journalists. In journalists' attempts to keep abreast of developments, social media networks, particularly Twitter, are vital, but the volume of content on these networks, and the range of sources that the content emanates from, are such that particular tools and practices are required in order that material can be identified and some degree of verification can be carried out within the limited time available.

Editors and social media specialists in newsrooms use a range of tools, such as TweetDeck and HootSuite, which allow simple filtering and organization of social media streams (Schifferes et al. 2014). These filters do not, however, offer any means for journalists to assess the credibility of information. For that, some have experimented with tools such as Klout or PeerIndex in an attempt to gauge the reliability of contributors, but have mostly found these tools to be "insufficiently granular to help … make judgments on authenticity in a fast-moving news story" (Schifferes et al. 2014). Alfred Hermida's chapter on verification contains more information on some of the latest tools and techniques in this area.

In the absence of a set of tools able to adequately surface trends or assess the credibility of social media content, many live blogging journalists have relied on Twitter lists of known and trusted sources. Andrew Sparrow, who writes *The Guardian*'s "Politics Live" live blog, works "by and large … with a relatively narrow patch of usual suspects and I know who they are." A similar practice has been adopted by *Guardian* reporter Matthew Weaver, who is the primary author of its "Middle East Live" live blog: "I'll be doing Syria or Yemen, and I won't be looking at generic search terms, I'll be looking at lists of people who we know are there" (quoted in Thurman and Walters 2013).

With journalists often required to report at great speed via live blogs, such reliance on known sources is an understandable coping strategy. However, it is impossible to predict exactly where a new fact or observation will emanate from, so monitoring secondary networks and metadata (such as Twitter hashtags) is also important. How this is done depends, in part, on the resources available. Some live blogging journalists at *The Guardian* are supported by "community coordinators" who utilize social media tools more widely, feeding the results back to the journalists. As well as monitoring Twitter hashtags to build up a picture of a developing situation, the community coordinators also delve more deeply into social networks, as Laura Oliver, community coordinator, news, explained: "[Journalists] will have their own [Twitter] lists of correspondents which is a great place to start and then what we do … is look at the secondary network. Who are the correspondents talking to? Who are they linking to?" (personal communication, June 17, 2011).

The reliance on mediated communication is somewhat inevitable given that the practice of live blogging demands a fast, reliable Internet connection most often found in the office. However, as with any form of journalism, it is, as Paul Lewis cautions, always best to go and experience a story in person: "With live blogging … you have this view that there are lots of other people out there who are your eyes and ears. They can be really useful … but your vantage point is a computer screen in an office block in London, and as a journalist you always find out more when you're there. Always" (quoted in Thurman and Walters 2013).

The degree to which live blogs should publish unverified information (even with caveats) is, perhaps, the key ethical issue with the format. Some journalists are comfortable with how the conversational tone of live blogs, compared with the more authoritative "inverted pyramid" news story, allows the reader "in on the workflow of the journalist … saying 'Look this is out there, help us verify it' " (Matthew Weaver, quoted in Thurman and Walters 2013). Matt Wells, *The Guardian*'s US Blogs and Network Editor, is of a similar mind, saying that if something "might be quite important" but cannot be verified by the news organization it is okay to "flag it up" and ask the audience "to help verify it" (personal communication, June 17, 2011). Other journalists, however, are more cautious. Lewis says if "we're not sure whether or not this is true . . . don't put it out. Our job is to find out whether or not it's true, not to put it out and ask people to decide for us" (personal communication, June 8, 2011).

Audience Participation

Encouraging readers to help verify material that has been sourced on Twitter or YouTube and published on a live blog is one form of audience participation. Live blogs can, of course, be a direct source of material in their own right. This form of user-generated content is rather different from that found on social media channels because, as we'll see, it:

- Often comes via email
- May involve regular contributors
- Is prompted by the content and/or functionality of the live blog itself

Live blogging journalists covering certain fast-moving live events do not always have time to consult social media. For example, Heidi Stephens says that because *The Apprentice* "moves at a million miles an hour and there are no ad breaks, I haven't got time to check what people are saying on Twitter" (personal communication, June 14, 2011). Rob Smyth agrees: "[live blogging sports events] is quite a busy process and it would be difficult to keep an eye on Twitter" (personal communication, July 6, 2011).

As a result, email has become a way to keep in touch without being overwhelmed by information. For Rob Smyth, email is the source of 95 percent of incoming communication during a live blog (personal communication, July 6, 2011). Indeed, when *The Guardian* considered adding a comments section to cricket and football live blogs, there was resistance from some journalists because of the additional user-generated content that would result, and because of a feeling that "the quality of contributions you get via email is much higher" (Rob Smyth, personal communication, July 6, 2011). Some readers make regular contributions via email, becoming favored sources: "There is one chap . . . who really should be paid by *The Guardian* . . . he's quite witty and insightful . . . during a really busy game you look at your inbox and if you've got 50 emails you're immediately going to be drawn towards [him]" (Rob Smyth, personal communication, July 6, 2011).

Comments on live blogs, when enabled, can become a source in their own right. *The Guardian* blogs producer Paul Owen recounts that, during the 2011 protests in Bahrain, "readers posted really good first-hand accounts in the comments section" (personal communication, June 9, 2011). In live blogs of scheduled events, comments may also play a part (Heidi Stephens, personal communication, June 14,

2011), although volume is a problem. As Matt Wells explained, "if you get any more than a hundred comments it becomes impossible to write the live blog and read the comments" (personal communication, June 17, 2011). As a result, readers or community coordinators may be co-opted to help. "I haven't got time to check the comment box myself, so a lady called Hilary Wardle (another commenter who is a keen blogger on the side) keeps an eye on the comment box for me and emails over the best bits" (Heidi Stephens, personal communication, June 14, 2011). Part of Laura Oliver's role as a community coordinator at *The Guardian* is, she says, "to flag up useful things in the comment thread" (personal communication, June 17, 2011).

However, despite having such help, live blogging journalists at Theguardian.com use very few readers' comments in the live blog proper. In their analysis of 20 live blogs at Theguardian.com, Thurman and Walters (2013) found that, on average, the comments sections of live blogs contained 62 comments, but only 1.2 percent of those comments were taken "above the line." By contrast, Thurman and Newman (2014) have shown that a sample of live blogs ($n = 11$) published on the ScribbleLive platform contained between 21–50 percent reader contributions, partly because of the way that the ScribbleLive platform "puts reader testimony and comment on a par with that of journalists" (Thurman and Newman 2014).

Making Corrections

As we have already seen, the speed with which live blogs are updated, and their conversational tone, contribute to a "relatively loose culture of corroboration" (Thurman and Walters 2013). Indeed, some journalists appear to have accepted that unverified material will be posted. It is, therefore, important that correction practices are transparent and unambiguous. Tim Currie's contribution to this book covers handling mistakes via corrections and unpublishing in detail. The present chapter will highlight an example of best practice specific to live blogs, courtesy of *The Guardian*'s Andrew Sparrow:

> If I've got something substantially wrong I will acknowledge that—within the [live] blog—as quickly as possible in the most recent post. What I will also do is go back to the original post. I won't do an invisible mend [rather] I will insert a correction within the original post. If you just correct it in the most recent post—the nature of these [live] blogs is that they get very long and people skim read them rather than read them in detail—it's quite possible someone will see the original erroneous post but not pick up the subsequent correction.
>
> (quoted in Thurman and Walters 2013)

The use of the word "substantially" is important in Sparrow's statement. Where the error is minor (like a typo) Sparrow makes an "invisible mend." To put up a new post highlighting each minor error would adversely affect usability.

Conclusion

Some of the practices of live blogging outlined in this chapter hold out hope that the crisis of journalism's business models and the disruptions caused by the introduction of new technology will not inevitably lead to a crisis of ethics. As Lawrie Zion writes in the introduction to this book, "many practitioners are addressing questions about how journalism's mission to inform, enlighten, and entertain might be renewed in more open and collaborative ways." With live blogs, that openness has manifested itself in a number of ways. First, the finest examples of the format are not afraid to draw attention to error: best practice for making corrections in live blogs involves not only changing the erroneous post, but also flagging up the original error in the live stream, making the very fact of the correction a micro news story in its own right. A second manifestation of this openness can be seen in the adoption by the best live blogs of transparent attribution practices, and in their use of a relatively wide range of sources. The extent to which such sourcing practices are a genuine renewal of established professional norms is, however, still to be determined. Although, in some examples of the format, we see a significant move towards openness and collaboration; in other cases, despite technology having changed how journalists communicate with their sources, it has done less to change who those sources are.

Best Practices in Action: First Steps in Live Blogging

For anyone looking to learn some of the best practices in live blogging identified in this chapter, I would recommend selecting a scheduled news event. Seminars and conferences are ideal for a number of reasons:

- They have defined locations and start and end times, making attendance easy to plan.
- Because their programs are advertised in advance, it is easy to do background research on speakers and contributors. Such research is invaluable in order that pre-written background material can be prepared and used to provide context to the live coverage and to fill "dead air" time. It also means that contributors' social media streams (particularly on Twitter) can be identified ahead of time, for monitoring during the live coverage.
- They offer opportunities—depending on students' needs and abilities—for both passive coverage of the event as it plays out, and for more active coverage via, for example, interviews with participants and vox pops with attendees.
- They are usually at venues that are both safe and likely to have Wi-Fi and power, essential for journalists undertaking live coverage from an external location over a period of several hours.

ScribbleLive is a good platform for writing and publishing live stories online. Not only is it used by major news organizations, it is also relatively easy to learn, and available via a 30-day free trial. It is a hosted service that uses an online content management system (or CMS) that can be accessed through any web browser. The CMS supports a variety of levels of access, from "administrator" through "editor" to "moderated writer," and allows different editing privileges and levels of access to be assigned to different contributors. Social media content from YouTube, Twitter, and Facebook can be searched from within the CMS and, once identified, incorporated into the live story. Readers can also contribute directly by submitting comments via the live blog itself. These comments can be subjected to various levels of moderation, including automated filtering based on excluded keywords (e.g., racist or sexist terms), and full moderation by a human moderator. User contributions that pass the moderation process are published in the main section of the live story with the same level of prominence as posts from contributors with direct access to the CMS. The live story is hosted on ScribbleLive's servers and has its own dedicated URL, but can also be embedded (using simple HTML code) into any other website. The important contextual information that should surround any live blog—giving the story's current headline and summary of key developments—can be separately managed from within ScribbleLive's CMS via the "LiveArticle" function.

Discussion Questions

1. Should news organizations invest more resources in live blogging at the expense of traditional reporting?
2. In your view what sort of stories are unsuitable for covering via a live blog?
3. Do you agree that it is ok to publish unverified information on a live blog if it is labeled as such?
4. Do you believe that live blogs will turn out to be a more collaborative and pluralistic news format?
5. Overall, are live blogs ethically strengthening journalism in the digital era?

Acknowledgments

I would like to thank Anna Walters for conducting some of the interviews quoted in this study.

Notes

1 Some live blogging journalists, particularly on sport, try to post updates more regularly than this. Rob Smyth, for example, tries to leave "no more than two minute gaps" when live blogging soccer matches for Theguardian.com (personal communication, July 6, 2011).

2 At the time of the interview, Paul Lewis was Special Projects Editor at *The Guardian*; he has live blogged events including the inquest on the death of Ian Tomlinson, who died after being pushed to the ground by police in London during a protest march.

3 Thurman and Walters (2013, 91) found live blogs at *The Guardian* averaged 4,031 words.

References

Davis, Rowenna, and Alan Evans. 2011. "March for the Alternative—Saturday 26 March part 2." *Theguardian.com*, March 26, 2011. Accessed October 29, 2013. www.theguardian. com/society/blog/2011/mar/26/march-for-the-alternative-live-blog-updates

Newman, Nic. 2011. "Mainstream Media and the Distribution of News in the Age of Social Discovery." RISJ report. Oxford: Reuters Institute for the Study of Journalism. Accessed October 29, 2013. http://reutersinstitute.politics.ox.ac.uk/fileadmin/documents/Publications/Working_Papers/Mainstream_media_and_the_distribution_of_news_.pdf

Schifferes, Steve, Nic Newman, Neil Thurman, David Corney, Ayse Goker, and Carlos Martin. 2014. "Identifying and Verifying News through Social Media: Developing a User-centred Tool for Professional Journalists." *Digital Journalism*. doi:10.1080/216708 11.2014.892747

Snell, Chris. 2011. "Lillywhites on fire piccadilly circus." *Twitter.com*, March 26, 2011. https://twitter.com/chrissnelltweet/status/51719353791561728

Stray, Jonathan. 2010. "Linking by the Numbers: How News Organizations Are Using Links (or Not)." *Nieman Journalism Lab*, June 10, 2010. Accessed October 30, 2013. www.niemanlab.org/2010/06/linking-by-the-numbers-how-news-organizations-are-using-links-or-not/

Thurman, Neil, and Nic Newman. 2014. "The Future of Breaking News Online? A Study of Live Blogs through Surveys of Their Consumption, and of Readers' Attitudes and Participation." *Journalism Studies*. doi:10.1080/1461670X.2014.882080

Thurman, Neil, and James Rodgers. 2014. "Citizen Journalism in Real Time? Live Blogging and Crisis Events." In *Citizen Journalism: Global Perspectives*, Vol. 2, edited by Stuart Allan and Einar Thorsen, 81–95. New York: Peter Lang.

Thurman, Neil, and Anna Walters. 2013. "Live Blogging—Digital Journalism's Pivotal Platform? A Case Study of the Production, Consumption, and Form of Live Blogs at Guardian.co.uk." *Digital Journalism* 1(1):82–101.

9

LIVE TWEETING

The Rise of Real-Time Reporting

Jonathan Hewett

CITY UNIVERSITY LONDON

It might not have been intended as anything other than a simple social messaging platform, but Twitter developed rapidly as a tool used by journalists after its launch in 2006. Initially newsrooms concentrated on sourcing material for stories, particularly during major incidents. It then developed an expanding role in breaking news and other live coverage.

Breaking news often involves dealing quickly with incomplete, unconfirmed information emerging piecemeal and unpredictably. However inadvertently, Twitter offers the means to handle this by providing (almost) real-time communication, and a series of chronologically ordered, distinct but related containers for content. Add to this the scope for dealing with different forms of content (including photos), updates via mobile phones, linking and integration in web pages, and the appeal is clear.

Journalists' early experiments with Twitter often sought to address some of the huge changes in the media at that time (Pavlik 2013). Social media were competing for our time and attention, as well as for advertising revenue. A substantial online presence seemed essential for news organizations, which struggled to engage "users" in a more participative age. The rise of smartphones, and then of tablets, changed consumption patterns, too. But live tweeting was not a focus for most editors; promoting their organization's stories and brand, and exploiting Twitter as a pool of information, took priority (Broersma and Graham 2012, 404).

Only as the service became better-established as a resource for news—and increased its user base—did more journalists turn to Twitter for live reporting. It remains a specialist, if increasingly important, resource for many reporters. As a relatively new format, live tweeting is still evolving—and best practice remains a work in progress.

This chapter will briefly review the evolution of live tweeting and the forms it can take, and outline some pointers for formulating best practices, drawing on academic research, interviews with journalists, and examples of live tweeting. The discussion will point to areas of ethical challenge such as maintaining accuracy and continuity. It will concentrate on real-time coverage of news events, and conclude with a framework for students and teachers to use in learning to live tweet effectively.

Twitter Earns Its Wings

By 2007, just a year after Twitter was launched, Sky News, the BBC, and ESPN were experimenting with it. CNN was tweeting news updates, and *The New York Times'* Twitter page, which had "about 400 followers," was being updated "sometimes several times an hour, using RSS feeds from the paper's Web site" (Tenore 2007a).

When the *Orlando Sentinel* live tweeted a space shuttle launch in August 2007, senior editor John Cutter saw its scope for live reporting: "If we think, wow, this is something I'd want to know right now—the death of someone famous, a major road closure, charges in a significant ongoing case, something big from a major local company like Disney—then we would Twitter it, as well as send other alerts" (Tenore 2007b).

In October 2007, reporters used Twitter to provide updates on wildfires in southern California. Coverage of a series of major breaking stories—such as earthquakes in China (May 2008) and California (July 2008), the presidential election in the USA, terrorist attacks in Mumbai (both November 2008), and a plane crash in New York (January 2009)—all accelerated its take-up by journalists.

This was helped also by the continuing development of relevant technology (including the first iPhone, on sale from June 2007) and experiments in reporting. By May 2008, UK newspapers were live tweeting football matches (Oliver 2008) and local elections (Kiss 2008). Live tweeting arguably represented a greater shift—and opportunity—for newspapers than for radio and television news, where live coverage had long been a core feature.

Live tweeting was itself evolving. The typology I have developed in the table that follows identifies 10 different types of usage, although some of these overlap.

Table: Definitions: Towards a Typology of Live Tweeting

Live tweeting can be defined as using Twitter to report in (almost) real-time from the scene of a news event, scheduled or not (Broersma and Graham 2012). But this is a still-evolving format whose borders can be fluid. Below is a typology of live tweeting, which attempts to draw fairly wide boundaries while keeping a focus on journalistic uses.

Scheduled events	Speeches, conferences, and other meetings; launches (of reports, products, etc.), elections, court cases, sport.

Other breaking news	Natural disasters, crime incidents, politics.
Set-pieces	Investigations, features, own-initiative projects.
Ongoing news	Election campaigns, scandals, big news issues beyond one discrete story. Might be linked with live blog and/or other continuing coverage.
Explainers	Specialists adding context, insight, background.
Prepared exclusive	Partly publishing a story (or elements of it), partly promotional.
Chats	Based around a hashtag, often responding to questions tweeted in advance.
Behind the scenes	Showing part of the workings, process of a story, not routinely presented to public.
Retelling history	"Recreating" past events, typically at an anniversary, through pre-planned updates scheduled to retell stories in historic "real time."
Second screen	Accompanying TV or radio broadcasts, usually simultaneous with the broadcast (not necessarily live itself).

These categories can overlap, and may be covered by journalists in the field, in the newsroom, and/or working from home. They might draw on accounts from colleagues and other sources, and form part of other coverage. The priority accorded to engaging with other users can vary, as can the senses in which the activity is "live."

Taking Center Stage

The emergence of live tweeting as an integral part of journalism is clear from its role in award-winning reporting—including Pulitzer prizes, which were established to incentivize and honor excellence (Topping n.d.).

The 2013 award for Breaking News Reporting went to *The Denver Post* for coverage of a mass-shooting, "using journalistic tools, from Twitter and Facebook to video and written reports, both to capture a breaking story and provide context" ("The Pulitzer Prizes | Citation" 2013). It broke the news in a tweet at 1:47 a.m., nearly one hour before its first story on denverpost.com, followed by updates from reporters at the scene. Similarly, live tweeting formed an integral part of the 2012 winner, the *Tuscaloosa News*, for its tornado coverage ("The Pulitzer Prizes | Citation" 2012).

The criteria had been changed the previous year "by emphasizing real-time reporting of breaking news" ("The Pulitzer Prizes | Pulitzer Prizes for Journalism Move to All-Digital Entry System" 2011). Pointedly, perhaps, no Breaking News prize had been awarded that year, although the 2010 winner, *The Seattle Times*, had tweeted as part of its reporting of the shooting of four sheriff's deputies in

November 2009. The paper's journalists had previously used Twitter "relatively infrequently for breaking news" (Marchionni 2013, 257).

By 2010, most US news organizations were running Twitter accounts, primarily to drive traffic to their websites (Messner, Eford, and Linke 2011). But live coverage is usually done through named individuals' accounts; indeed, it made up almost one-third of the tweets sent by daily newspaper reporters, according to a 2011 study (Artwick 2013). This points to an unfamiliar situation that news organizations had to deal with—that although they might publish tweets on their website, the service is controlled by a third party, Twitter. Furthermore, live tweeting relies on individual journalists publishing directly, without the usual oversight from an editor, often from the field. While such characteristics may facilitate live tweeting in many respects, it also means that reporting in this format is perhaps more prone to error or misjudgment.

Twitter came of age as a tool for live reporting in the UK in 2011 as a result of its extensive use to cover riots in London and other cities in August. "Reporting" made up almost half of the tweets sent by two reporters—46.3 percent of the total from Paul Lewis of *The Guardian*, and 49 percent from Ravi Somaiya of *The New York Times*—according to an analysis of their tweets from four days and nights (Vis 2013). These consisted primarily of their own accounts as eyewitnesses on the scene (30 percent of total tweets for Lewis; 32.8 percent for Somaiya), but also included quotes from others present.

Pressures and Best Practice

Live tweeting has not always featured in social media guidelines provided to reporters, which probably reflects its relatively recent rise to prominence. In 2011, the American Society of News Editors (ASNE) appeared to position its "best practice guidelines for editors crafting social media policies" as geared principally to social media as "essential newsgathering tools" (Hohmann 2011).

One inadvertent effect of having such policies is that they may encourage journalists to regard social media as a separate realm where the usual rules do not apply. Some guidance addresses this explicitly, and the ASNE document usefully highlighted: "There's no reason that traditional ethics guidelines should go out the window." In similar vein, the importance of "adapting your instincts to digital/social" forms a section in AP's 2013 guidance ("Social Newsgathering in Sensitive Circumstances"). It encouraged its staff—familiar with best practice when operating in person or on the phone—to apply their "journalistic instincts." One part is worth reproducing here in full:

> Twitter, in particular, can present some challenges—with a tight character count and no way to modulate your body language or the volume and tone

of your voice, requests that are intended to be sensitive can come across as cold or even demanding. Think about how your tweet would come across if spoken with an angry voice, because that's just how the recipient may hear it in his head.

The competing demands of live tweeting and established journalism practice—speed versus accuracy, for example—can be seen in *The Denver Post*'s Pulitzer submission, which included hundreds of tweets. "We were determined to be aggressive but measured, fast but accurate," wrote editor Gregory L. Moore. "There were inaccurate rumors [...] that hit other outlets—but not one appeared on *Denver Post* platforms" (Moore 2013).

Checking and communicating factual information accurately has long been a core tenet of journalism—but not of social media, perhaps by its very nature. "The development of social networks for real-time news and information, and the integration of social media content in the news media, creates tensions for a profession based on a discipline of verification," notes Alfred Hermida (2012, 659; see also his chapter on verification in this book).

Unless reporters wish explicitly to prioritize speed over accuracy, best practice in live tweeting probably has to remain checking and double-checking—and where information is uncertain, to make this explicit. A survey of journalists in four European countries found most agreeing that accuracy was "the biggest problem with social media" (Gulyas 2013, 282).

The rise in commentary and opinion as part of reporting has been linked to social media in general and live tweeting in particular. Some researchers suggest that "the *form* of microblogging lends itself to freer personal expression" (Lawrence et al. 2013). The intimacy and immediacy of social networks can prompt confusion, too; "when tweeting, am I a reporter, an editor, a critic, or just chatting with friends," a journalist might wonder (Farhi 2009).

One large-scale US study found that nearly 43 percent of journalists' tweets included at least an element of opinion, and nearly 16 percent were primarily opinion (Lasorsa, Lewis, and Holton 2012). Consistent with Singer's 2005 findings for political journalism blogs (Singer 2005), the researchers concluded that journalists were adjusting "professional norms and practices to the evolving norms and practices of Twitter"—as well as normalizing Twitter to fit their own (Lasorsa, Lewis, and Holton 2012, 31).

The risks of compromised impartiality or integrity—and the perception of this—tend to permeate the social media policies of some news organizations. This is one reason why retweeting can be contentious, for example, although some guidelines do not regard it as a problem (see also Kelly Fincham's chapter in this book). AP's policy on retweeting was seen as overly cautious and restrictive by some social media editors (Sonderman 2012).

Using Key Features Effectively

Some best practices for live tweeting involve simply making good use of its features. A common mistake, for example, is starting a tweet with someone's @ handle (Twitter account name), typically as a form of attribution. This reduces—often drastically—the potential audience for the tweet, as it then functions as a "reply" usually visible only to users who follow both the sender and the account mentioned. Starting the tweet with a full point (before @) remedies this. Referring to others by their @ handle can be useful—but a name may be needed if this is unclear from their @ handle and/or Twitter profile.

Using hashtags (#) effectively can aid the visibility and reach of tweets as they will appear in search results for a particular hashtag—which may often emerge as a breaking news story takes shape. Journalists may initiate the use of hashtags, bearing in mind that they work best when short, unique, and easily recognizable. Checking hashtags can also help live tweeting reporters who need to monitor tweets—complicated by the possible use of a number of different hashtags. To find other relevant tweets (including those without a hashtag), journalists need to identify other key words to use in searches, save searches, and build Twitter lists of relevant accounts.

Monitoring tweets is much easier in Twitter management tools that allow users to create separate columns for tweets of different kinds, for example, for a specific list, search term, hashtag, and/or type of content, with optional filters for each column. Such features make TweetDeck, for example, popular among journalists who use Twitter intensively.

Advance planning can be crucial to make best use of live tweeting, says Kate Day, director of digital content at the *Telegraph* in London. For intensive coverage of a major scheduled event, the paper may allocate different reporters to focus on different strands of a story, as well as mapping out the expected timing of key stages and how live tweeting will form part of coverage on its website and other social media (Day 2013). Reviewing the analytics after the event, including the sharing of tweets and the traffic to the site from social media, has become a regular part of their practice, too.

Reporters' advance research will probably include that needed for any form of coverage—the names, titles, and correct spelling of the key people involved, for example, and likely angles for stories. But for live tweeting, they can usefully add the @ handles of participants; hashtags; relevant links (e.g., to previous articles and other background material); and setting up Twitter lists and searches. Creating a document containing these can save time during the later live coverage.

Presenting oneself explicitly as a journalist is considered fundamental in most reporting (undercover investigation is an obvious exception), so news organizations usually expect their staff to make their affiliation clear in their Twitter profiles. Sometimes this extends to @ handles as well; most BBC reporters with an official account include "BBC" in theirs, for example. Some employers may provide further guidance on the format for profiles, such as links, bio text, and style of photo. As the latter will appear next to every tweet sent, its significance should not be underestimated—it forms part of the branding of that journalist and his or her organization. If one envisages the face of a grinning reporter next to tweets containing the details of a disaster, it is not hard to see why a sober appearance prevails.

In some circumstances, it may be important to ensure that one feature is not used. This is where revealing the location of a reporter (and perhaps interviewees) could put safety at risk—as in conflict areas, for example. For this reason, remembering to turn off the GPS/location feature of phones used for tweeting is important in such cases.

Live Tweeting Court Cases

The reporting of court cases has developed as an important strand of live tweeting. Artwick found that court reporters live tweeted more than journalists on other beats (2013)—and in the UK, live tweeting has developed as the only way for journalists to report live from inside a courtroom. However, familiarity with the law is important not only for responsible live tweeting from court but for covering other events, too. In the UK, for example, a number of laws restrict not only commenting but also the disclosure of some facts (e.g., the identity of victims) in limited circumstances (Wheeler 2013).

Coverage of legal cases can also illustrate the challenges of handling complex outcomes when live tweeting. It can require specialist knowledge and experience, advance research, familiarity with the case, and care in producing tweets that are both accurate and timely. Even then, mistakes are made.

The decision of the US Supreme Court in June 2012 on President Barack Obama's Affordable Care Act was keenly awaited, a major news event—with live coverage on Twitter as well as broadcast. A number of news organizations reported wrongly that the court had struck down the "individual mandate" element of the law—including CNN on its Breaking News Twitter account, as well as on its website. After 13 minutes, it sent a tweet correcting the mistake.

The confusion was apparently caused by one point in the court's ruling—that the law was unconstitutional in terms of the "Commerce Clause"—emerging before another important one: that it allowed the law to stand as a tax. In its statement, CNN hinted at the pressures of breaking the news quickly: "CNN regrets that it didn't wait to report out the full and complete opinion regarding the mandate. We made a correction within a few minutes and apologize for the error." ("CNN Correction: Supreme Court Ruling" 2012. See also Tim Currie's chapter on corrections in this book.)

Some news accounts automatically tweet the headline of a story when it is published online. This simplifies the process but removes flexibility. Human error can occur at different stages, of course, indicating the importance of checking and, where feasible, involving more than one set of eyes. The Associated Press's main Twitter account tweeted inaccurately in December 2013: "MORE: Celebrity cook Nigella Lawson and her former husband are cleared of fraud charges," with a link to its story published online. The latter, also visible in the in-line Twitter card preview, had the correct headline: "Nigella Lawson's ex-assistants acquitted of fraud." Lawson and her former husband faced no such charges and a tweet correcting the error soon followed (Hewett 2014).

Continuity and Narrative

The short format of tweets can have particular implications for live coverage, which is necessarily spread across separate tweets—which, unlike most news stories, cannot include much context. Social media trainer Sue Llewellyn advises that, in general, reporters should assume that every tweet will be seen in isolation (Llewellyn 2013). It might also be read some time after the time at which it was first sent, particularly if passed on and/or republished.

One approach to signal a series is to include "1/3," "2/3," "3/3" (or similar) in successive tweets, but that requires the reporter to know—before sending the first tweet—the total number of tweets involved in this series. Another technique involves the use of an ellipsis (. . .) or "cont" (for continued) where more follows or continues.

These techniques still do not prevent any tweet from being read on its own. One work-around is provided by services such as TwitLonger that enable messages longer than the standard Twitter length to be posted—with a link from a tweet to the full text usually on that service's website. However, most journalists—perhaps recognizing the difficulties of relying on users following such links—seem to avoid this approach.

If the narrative of a story or breaking news event is sufficiently strong and engaging, this may help to "carry" a story even when relayed through a series of tweets. This was the experience of BBC correspondent Matthew Price when he tweeted the story of a survivor from a boat carrying more than 200 migrants capsized in the Mediterranean Sea in October 2013.

Having located and interviewed this survivor for BBC radio and television news, Price picked out key elements for a series of 16 tweets telling his story. He typed "Survivor:" to introduce each tweet, thus also attributing the short, vivid sentences that followed:

> "Survivor of boat sinking: boat was small but it was too late. We had no home. Couldn't live in Syria. Banned in Egypt. Libya too dangerous."
> "Survivor: they shot the engine room that's when water started to get into the boat. We tried to fill the holes. The water was so strong."

"Survivor: we carried on. Girls started screaming. We called Italians. They told us we were in Maltese water. We called Malta."

"Survivor: Malta told us they'd come in 30 minutes. The waves got high. The boat let in water. People for scared. More water."

"Survivor: another wave. The boat leaned right. All the people were on the right. The boat capsized. We got on life jackets."

"Survivor: I could see the people swimming to reach each other. We were in water for an hour or more. Then they came to save us."

Price says his tweets were prompted partly by the strong response he received to an earlier tweet that day breaking a key story element (Price 2013): "Survivor of Lampedusa boat sinking Friday tells BBC that Libyan gunmen fired on the boat causing it eventually to capsize." Another had also engaged users, encapsulating the tragedy of the incident in four short sentences: "Syrian couple floated for an hour in Med after boat sank. Clutching their 9mth old girl. Couldn't also hold their son. He drowned." More than 300 people drowned after their boat sank the previous week, and the wider issue of migrants to the European Union had received coverage in the media for a few years.

This example of live tweeting overlaps several of the types outlined earlier in the chapter. It was live not in the sense that Price was tweeting as he interviewed the survivor—but in the sense that it was breaking the news of that man's account of the event soon afterwards. Some parts were included in news packages already broadcast by the time of the tweets, but these preceded the fuller account that was published online the next day. It was a "prepared exclusive" in some ways, and partly promotional in that it probably generated interest in the online story, as well as having elements of "ongoing news," as part of the bigger story of migrants trying to reach the EU by boat.

In this case, Price used the translated English transcript of the man's words in Arabic as the basis for his series of tweets. "I knew it was a compelling story that I wanted as wide an audience as possible to see," he says. "Using Twitter meant I could get it out there myself before the online version could go up the next day" (Price 2013). The timing of the tweets also played a part, he believes, by finding interested users at accessible times; it was near the start of the working day in much of Europe, and mid-afternoon for the US East Coast.

"One of the challenges of reporting via Twitter is not just condensing the facts into 140 characters, it's also about how you construct a narrative over a series of tweets and add context," says BBC journalist Dominic Casciani (2013). He has been experimenting with what he calls "signposting" tweets—alerting users at the start of the day to what he'll be covering later, for example, or providing a reminder of key points to add context and/or to help those who have not been following the story. On the morning of November 29, 2013, for example, Casciani tweeted: "Good morning from the Old Bailey where we are expecting the start of the trial of the men accused of the murder of Fusilier Lee Rigby." (The Old Bailey is the Central Criminal Court of England and Wales, which handles many important cases; the term is well known in the UK.)

This kind of approach can be important in telling a story—but in large news organizations it also provides a valuable signal internally. In Casciani's case, it helps the BBC's social media team running the BBC's main Twitter accounts (such as @BBCBreaking, with 8.5 million followers [Jan. 2014]) to pick out updates to retweet, and/or flag up his account for live coverage of a particular story.

Context and Explanation

As a specialist correspondent in a high-profile area (home affairs), Casciani also uses tweets for what one might call "explainers"—providing the background and context to help readers to make more sense of a breaking story. As well as explaining the why or how of a situation, he also highlights key points that might not appear in, say, the headline of a story. Covering Ecuador's granting of asylum to Julian Assange, the founder of Wikileaks, and the surrounding legal and political issues, he tweeted pertinent details, links, and quotes, before explaining the position in six tweets (August 16, 2012), numbering the first five and then summarizing with the sixth:

> "So, here's the legal deal. 1) Assange has asylum—but that doesn't equal immunity from prosecution for non-political crimes."
> "2) He's wanted in UK for breaching bail—and UK Supreme Court backed extradition on allegations of rape. (That's non-political crime)."
> "3) He can't come out—because he will be arrested by the Met Police outside."
> "4) The coppers can't go in—unless the UK decides to revoke the embassy's status as a lawful diplomatic mission."
> "5) Even if he successfully got into a diplomatic car (which can't be searched) what next? Police could surround and stop it."
> "So this is one serious serious stand-off."

It is worth noting the use of informal language (e.g., "legal deal" and "coppers"—police officers), which helps to reinforce the idea of Twitter as a conversational medium.

Showing the Human Side

As well as the core content they tweet, journalists need to think about showing that they are human, says trainer Sue Llewellyn. "These are the little bits you could share, the photos from behind the scenes, the amazing scenery where you've just reported from, the other-side-of-the-camera shots, your hobbies. I think it makes you more real, and makes your feed more interesting. It might not be directly relevant to your audiences, but it's helping them think 'OK, now I know a little bit more about this person and feel more connected to them'" (Llewellyn 2013).

For the live tweeting journalist out and about, there may be scope to show people something of the process of reporting that is not normally visible. "We like the idea of the 'glimpse behind the curtain'; people like that," says Casciani. At the end of a complicated trial involving 13 separate charges, he tweeted a photograph of a whiteboard he used to help him keep track when reporting the outcome to camera. He has also tweeted images of evidence presented in court (provided to journalists by state prosecutors), including documents, stills from CCTV footage, and photos.

Choosing Equipment

Working from a desktop or laptop has some advantages, such as easily tracking others' tweets for relevant information, along with other online sources. The multiple columns and filtering/search features available in some Twitter clients help here. In the field, however, journalists may find themselves relying on smaller mobile devices. Phones are easy to carry, but some reporters prefer the larger screens (and on-screen "keyboard") of tablets—with the option of an add-on physical keyboard. An external battery pack can be a vital back-up.

Despite improved wireless, 3G, and 4G coverage, Internet access can still be patchy in some locations, and signals can be impeded by buildings, become unreliable—or have bandwidth overloaded by demand. Reporters therefore need to know how to tweet by text message (SMS). This involves linking the mobile phone to the relevant Twitter account (which can be done via SMS, as well as the web interface) and then posting updates by texting it to a dedicated number.

Settings enable selected notifications (e.g., direct messages, replies, and mentions) to be received by text, too—although there may be a risk of these overwhelming a reporter's phone in some situations. It may be preferable to turn on such notifications only for specified users, for example, an editor in the newsroom who can monitor replies to and mentions of the reporter's account (e.g., to pick up other leads, potential UGC, etc.) and respond to these if appropriate. Reporters likely to live tweet via SMS should familiarize themselves with the range of Twitter commands available, too—and note the risk of inadvertently making public an intended direct message (or part of it). This can happen if the sender omits the "D [username]" needed at the start of the message, or if the SMS exceeds

160 characters and so is split into multiple messages—when any material after the first will post as a normal tweet.

Best Practices in Action

1. Examine the social media policies of some news organizations (Hohmann 2011 and Kelly Fincham's chapter in this book offer some starting points, or you can find your own). Review these to identify the elements of the guidance that are most relevant to live tweeting—and supplement these from your perspective as a reader by drawing on your own experience of following live events and breaking stories on Twitter.
2. Identify some cases of live tweeting, ideally some scheduled examples you know are about to take place, and follow them. They might feature one individual reporter, a number covering the same story, the accounts of one or more news organizations, and/or based around a specific hashtag. A large class could have different people looking at different kinds of live tweeting (see the typology earlier in the chapter).

After the event, review the tweets for content, tone, and other relevant points. Consider them both as individual updates and as a stream. Take account also of the publicly available metrics, such as retweets, mentions, and replies. Comparing tweets from different journalists covering the same story (as well as with reports in print, online, and on broadcast media) can prove interesting. If you follow the live tweeting as it happens, taking notes at the time can helpfully complement a review of coverage at a later stage.

Identify what you think worked well and what you found less effective, focusing on the reasons underlying your evaluation. If you found differences between individual reporters live tweeting the same event or story, what were they and why do you think they occurred? How does the coverage fit with the best practice pointers in this chapter and elsewhere?

3. Identify some suitable (scheduled) events to cover, taking account of the level of journalistic experience that might be needed to live tweet it effectively. A local public talk is likely to prove more straightforward than a complex legal case, for example. As in point 2 above, it can be useful to have more than one person live tweeting the same event—and/or to have an editor who might help plan coverage. There is scope also to use live tweeting as part of a live blog (see Neil Thurman's chapter in this book) and/or to curate them using tools such as Storify.

Prepare in advance—think about how to cover it, check you have key details about the event, key individuals, links, Twitter handles, hashtags, and so on, as well as the practicalities of equipment. You may need to check with event organizers that they are happy for you to live tweet it, and what the venue is like.

With a large group, try live tweeting different events and different forms of live tweeting (see the typology earlier in this chapter). Have some reporters ready to cover breaking news, too—preferably those with previous experience of live tweeting a scheduled event.

It can be useful to save the tweets for review. For simple, short coverage, copying and pasting them from timelines and/or hashtag searches can suffice. Otherwise, save them using a tool such as Scraperwiki or the Twitter Archiving Google Spreadsheet (TAGS) (Hawksey 2013).

If you're teaching, why not join in? If you have previously live tweeted events and/or breaking stories by live tweeting, there is scope to model good practice. Otherwise it could be a valuable opportunity to catch up and join in the learning experience alongside your students.

4. After the live tweeting, review both the output (as in point 2 above) and the experience. Asking those not directly involved in covering that event can help to capture the perspective of an audience—and try asking followers for their feedback, too. Drawing up a list of learning points, and recommendations for the next time, can form a useful focus, consolidate the learning, and feed it forward into future practice.

Curating tweets after the event can be a valuable exercise; it requires the review and selection of tweets, and can integrate other online coverage of the same story, too. Using Storify, one can also add reflections and other comments on the experience of live tweeting as well as the output(s)—and publishing the results can encourage others to review, learn from, and comment on it. Publication in this form can also attract useful attention and input from practicing journalists, just as Twitter itself can act as an important professional networking and learning tool (Hewett 2013).

References

Artwick, Claudette G. 2013. "Reporters on Twitter." *Digital Journalism* 1(2):212–28. doi:10. 1080/21670811.2012.744555

Broersma, Marcel, and Todd Graham. 2012. "Social Media as Beat." *Journalism Practice* 6(3) (June):403–19. doi:10.1080/17512786.2012.663626

Casciani, Dominic. 2013, December 13. "Interview by Jonathan Hewett."

"CNN Correction: Supreme Court Ruling." 2012. CNN. http://cnnpressroom.blogs.cnn. com/2012/06/28/cnn-correction/

Day, Kate. 2013, December 13. "Interview by Jonathan Hewett."

Farhi, Paul. 2009. "The Twitter Explosion." *American Journalism Review* 31(3):26–31.

Gulyas, Agnes. 2013. "The Influence of Professional Variables on Journalists' Uses and Views of Social Media." *Digital Journalism* 2:270–85. doi:10.1080/21670811.2012.744559

Hawksey, Martin. 2013. "Twitter Archiving Google Spreadsheet TAGS v5." http://mashe.hawksey.info/2013/02/twitter-archive-tagsv5/

Hermida, Alfred. 2012. "Tweets and Truth: Journalism as a Discipline of Collaborative Verification." *Journalism Practice* 6:659–68. doi:10.1080/17512786.2012.667269

Hewett, Jonathan. 2013. "Using Twitter to Integrate Practice and Learning in Journalism Education: Could Social Media Help to Meet the Twin Challenge of Both Dimensions?" *Journal of Applied Journalism & Media Studies* 2(2):333–46. doi:10.1386/ajms.2.2.333_1

Hewett, Jonathan. 2014. "Tweeting Headlines for Breaking News." http://hackademic.net/2014/03/04/tweeting-headlines-for-breaking-news/

Hohmann, James. 2011. "10 Best Practices for Social Media: Helpful Guidelines for News Organizations." *American Society of News Editors.* http://asne.org/Files/pdf/10_Best_Practices_for_Social_Media.pdf

Kiss, Jemima. 2008. "Using Real-time News Tools." *theguardian.com.* www.theguardian.com/media/pda/2008/may/14/usingrealtimenewstools

Lasorsa, Dominic L., Seth C. Lewis, and Avery E. Holton. 2012. "Normalizing Twitter." *Journalism Studies* 13(1):19–36. doi:10.1080/1461670X.2011.571825

Lawrence, Regina G., Logan Molyneux, Mark Coddington, and Avery Holton. 2013. "Tweeting Conventions." *Journalism Studies.* Published online September 20, 2013. doi:10.1080/1461670X.2013.836378

Llewellyn, Sue. 2013, December 19. "Interview by Jonathan Hewett."

Marchionni, Doreen. 2013. "Conversational Journalism in Practice." *Digital Journalism* 1(2) (June):252–69. doi:10.1080/21670811.2012.748513

Messner, Marcus, Asriel Eford, and Maureen Linke. 2011. "Shoveling Tweets: An Analysis of the Microblogging Engagement of Traditional News Organizations." Paper presented at the International Symposium on Online Journalism, Austin, TX, April, 2011.

Moore, Gregory L. 2013. "Cover Letter for Denver Post Entry to Pulitzer Prize." Pulitzer Prizes. www.pulitzer.org/files/2013/breaking-news-reporting/denverpostentryletter.pdf

Oliver, Laura. 2008. "Local UK Newspaper to Use Twitter for Live Sport Reporting | Media News | Journalism.co.uk." www.journalism.co.uk/news/local-uk-newspaper-to-use-twitter-for-live-sport-reporting/s2/a531458/

Pavlik, John V. 2013. "Innovation and the Future of Journalism." *Digital Journalism* 1(2):181–93. doi:10.1080/21670811.2012.756666

Price, Matthew. 2013, January 15. "Interview by Jonathan Hewett."

Singer, J.B. 2005. "The Political j-Blogger: 'Normalizing' a New Media Form to Fit Old Norms and Practices." *Journalism* 6:173–98. doi:10.1177/1464884905051009

"Social Newsgathering in Sensitive Circumstances." 2013. Associated Press. www.ap.org/Images/Social-Newsgathering_tcm28–12860.pdf

Sonderman, Jeff. 2012. "AP Adds New Social Media Guidelines on Live-tweeting, Friending/following Sources | Poynter." *Poynter.* www.poynter.org/latest-news/mediawire/182517/ap-adds-new-social-media-guidelines-on-live-tweeting-friendingfollowing-sources/

Tenore, Mallory Jean. 2007a. "Newsies Twittering on Twitter | Poynter." *Poynter.* www.poynter.org/latest-news/top-stories/84048/newsies-twittering-on-twitter/

Tenore, Mallory Jean. 2007b. "Experimenting with Twitter: How Newsrooms Are Using It to Reach More Users | Poynter." *Poynter.* www.poynter.org/latest-news/top-stories/84153/experimenting-with-twitter-how-newsrooms-are-using-it-to-reach-more-users/

"The Pulitzer Prizes | Citation." 2012. Pulitzer Prizes. www.pulitzer.org/citation/2012-Breaking-News-Reporting

"The Pulitzer Prizes | Citation." 2013. Pulitzer Prizes. www.pulitzer.org/citation/2013-Breaking-News-Reporting

"The Pulitzer Prizes | Pulitzer Prizes for Journalism Move to All-Digital Entry System." 2011. Pulitzer Prizes. www.pulitzer.org/digital_entries

Topping, Seymour. n.d. "The Pulitzer Prizes | History of The Pulitzer Prizes." Pulitzer Prizes. www.pulitzer.org/historyofprizes

Vis, Farida. 2013. "Twitter As a Reporting Tool for Breaking News." *Digital Journalism* 1(1) (February):27–47. doi:10.1080/21670811.2012.741316

Wheeler, Brian. 2013. "Twitter Users: A Guide to the Law." BBC. www.bbc.co.uk/news/magazine-20782257

10

HANDLING MISTAKES

Corrections and Unpublishing

Tim Currie

UNIVERSITY OF KING'S COLLEGE, HALIFAX, CANADA

In the heady moments following the mass killing at the Washington Navy Yard in September 2013, journalists from both NBC and CBS rushed to identify the shooter on Twitter—but named the wrong person.

Their newsrooms realized their mistake within minutes. The two journalists who first posted the error announced or retweeted a retraction and returned to posting new updates. Meanwhile, a growing chorus of users in their tweet streams demanded an apology and derided their credibility.

An NBC reporter who had retweeted his colleague's misstep replied to a few of the haters insulting and lecturing him on his failure to get confirmation first. He attempted to explain the source of the error but stopped soon after, stating: "I know folks are relishing an opportunity to get out their hatred for media; I'm just trying to provide context for what we got wrong" (Todd 2013b).

Each of these journalists deleted their initial tweets, but only the NBC reporter mentioned that he did (Todd 2013a). Twitter users demanded that editors take ownership of the error and examine the practices that led to the error. But neither newsroom tweeted an apology or engaged their Twitter audience to explain in detail how the error happened—or how they would deal with it. Instead, the caustic Twitter comments linger like graffiti on the newsrooms' walls—angry words left in empty conversations that characterize the news outlets as distant and unaccountable.

How can journalists better use evolving platforms to limit the effect of errors? David Craig's chapter highlighted the concepts of duty, virtue, and care as core elements of ethical thought. This chapter looks at how those concepts can be applied to corrections and unpublishing. It discusses the obligation to duty contained in two sets of guidelines issued by the Canadian Association of Journalists. It considers the virtue of humility in acknowledging error. It examines the importance of care in using social media to minimize harm.

In applying these concepts, this chapter looks at how journalists can build a stronger, more trusting relationship with their audience before and after things go wrong.

Toward a Better System for Corrections

Mistakes happen. Hopefully not many more journalists will identify the wrong person as a mass killer. But even careful journalists will occasionally succumb to human error.

News organizations, however, have traditionally been laggards when it comes to accounting for their mistakes (Maier 2009; Porlezza and Russ-Mohl 2013; Silverman 2007). Research suggests that the items on a newspaper's corrections page account for less than 2 percent of the actual number of errors in the paper (Maier 2007b). Further, there is evidence sources are reluctant to report errors because, while they view many errors as inconsequential, they feel a sense of futility with the sheer number of mistakes and they lack confidence that a correction will actually remedy the error (Maier 2007a).

Broadcast outlets have been even less forthcoming. The on-air correction is still a rarity. Broadcasters have traditionally acknowledged errors infrequently, often only under threat of legal action (Friend and Singer 2007; Silverman 2012b). In short, news organizations have rarely corrected errors because it has been easy to hide them (Porlezza and Russ-Mohl 2013).

Over the last decade, bloggers have sought to lessen the stigma attached to corrections. Criticized by mainstream media for inaccuracies, bloggers themselves have collectively viewed corrections as a sign of transparency, not a mark of dishonor. Their values have evolved to see virtue in accepting fault, acknowledging it publicly, and updating content quickly (Singer 2007).

Many news organizations have taken these cues and made significant efforts to strengthen transparency over the past decade. But overall, news outlets haven't fully realized these ideas (Silverman 2007).

Even a basic commitment to encouraging submissions remains a challenge for many news organizations. In a pair of 2010 studies, only about half of news websites had a corrections policy and, of those, half required users to search for a link to it (Cornish 2010; Follman and Rosenberg 2010). As Maier (2009) states, "A clear standard for handling online errors is lacking."

Why are journalists so bad at issuing corrections? Craig Silverman, a blogger on the subject of journalistic accuracy and author of the book *Regret the Error* and the blog of the same name, has made an effort to tie our correction practices with the emotions and values that guide them. "Too often a correction is confusing or vague because the goal in drafting it was to mitigate damage and blame," writes Silverman (2013a, 159). The root of these errors, he argues, lies in feelings of embarrassment and pride that override journalists' obligations to their audience.

Silverman, who has written extensively on the subject of online corrections, argues a lack of sincerity and genuine remorse for errors is a key factor in disdain directed at news organizations. Journalists too often resort to robotic statements of regret that lack humanity and fail to account for the impact of their missteps. Just as often, journalists fall back on the norms of their craft, explaining error instead of feeling it.

During the Washington Navy Yard shootings, the Twitter conversations were littered with comments from users who felt the news organizations refused to accept responsibility. When the NBC journalist tried to explain how the error originated with newsroom sources, one user in the conversation thread demanded he "admit it was a screw up" and "stop defending" poor procedures (Army Vet Chic 2013). Regarding those unnamed newsroom colleagues, another user noted sarcastically, "Yes blame them!" (S.M. 2013).

The frustration audience members feel with journalists in these situations is a symptom of a greater disconnect with the audience that a journalism training institute has tried to address. The Poynter Institute for Media Studies has sought to elevate the importance of audience interaction by recasting its guiding principles for journalists.

In its 2013 update, the pursuit of truth is still its first objective. However, the institute has broadened the other two. It now recommends the aim of transparency instead of independence, calling for "an openness that encourages constant conversation between journalist and citizen, newsroom and community" (McBride and Rosenstiel 2013, 4). Its third objective expands the aim of minimizing harm into a broader goal of engaging community, with the "promise to act in the interest of informing a community and upholding democracy" (McBride and Rosenstiel 2013, 5).

This goal of greater engagement and conversation is a key theme in a pair of recent documents that provide ethical guidelines to journalists issuing corrections online. The reports, released by the Canadian Association of Journalists, start from the premise that full accountability begins with not just accepting user reports of error but actively welcoming them. A robust approach to corrections requires an aggressive effort to seek out the audience and build an open environment to support a continuous drive for accuracy. Silverman (2013a, 152) states:

> Rather than viewing corrections as a necessary evil, news organizations should treat them as a means to help create a strong connection to the people they seek to inform. With that correction comes trust and a more honest relationship.

Further, journalists must forget the syntax for corrections rooted in print and broadcast traditions—the often-buried, robotically phrased addendum to packaged news—and refashion their practice for evolving delivery platforms.

General Guidelines for Digital Corrections

The Canadian Association of Journalists' first document offers general guidelines for making digital corrections (English et al. 2011). Its core elements advocate for an approach that is open, clear, responsive, social, and comprehensive.

1. Transparency

A primary element of transparency is that journalists correct all errors that come to their attention. This may seem self-evident in an industry that places a high value on accuracy. However, there is evidence that print editors publish corrections for only a small number of the errors reported by sources (Maier 2007a). Still, journalists themselves believe they are good at correcting errors. A 2005 study by the Annenberg Public Policy Center found that 74 percent of journalists surveyed believe their colleagues quickly report mistakes, as opposed to ignoring them or covering them up (Annenberg Public Policy Center 2005).

Journalists' commitment to transparency, however, is better demonstrated by how they make those corrections. Simply making a correction and pretending the error didn't exist in the first place is a common and particularly deceptive journalistic practice, according to Silverman. "Scrubbing is, in effect, a cover-up. It's unprincipled and disingenuous," states Silverman (2007, 234).

Scrubbing is a practice rooted in the dark emotions of shame and fear. Further, it's a repudiation of fundamental journalistic values. Journalists frequently expose the failures of people with power and hold them to account. However, when journalists conceal their errors they reveal themselves to be hypocrites and cowards. The result is a "corrosive effect on our relationship with the public" (Silverman 2013a, 157). In practice, it's nearly impossible to hide errors (Porlezza and Russ-Mohl 2013). Readers grab screenshots and share errors in social media. Search engines cache copies. Many news organizations' own publishing systems write the initial headline of an article into its URL.

It's crucial to acknowledge error. But it's just as important to explain it well enough so the user understands how the correction differs from the original error. In a content analysis of three major newspapers in different countries, editors at only one—*The New York Times*—made a significant effort to explain the changes they made to online stories (Karlsson 2010).

However, explaining the error can be difficult without repeating it, an act some journalists are reluctant to do. Critics argue repeating the error, especially in social networks, amplifies the misinformation. Steve Buttry, a former editor for Digital First Media, has disagreed, arguing journalists should repeat the error with the aim of clarity: "If you don't say what was wrong, you aren't really correcting, just vaguely admitting error" (Buttry 2010).

For example, *The Guardian* mentioned in September 2013 that its editors had published a headline that stated almost the opposite of what the main source was quoted as saying. *The Guardian*'s correction notice mentioned both the original wrong headline and the corrected headline (Fotheringham 2013).

Crucially, the wording of a correction needs to be explicit. Journalists should avoid writing to "clarify" the original story if a fact was plainly wrong. A short, straightforward correction might read: "An earlier version of this story misidentified the CEO of White Point Investments as Claire Bowen. Her name is in fact Claire Bowden."

Does every error need to be corrected? There is a growing consensus among digital journalists that they don't need to declare corrections to ordinary typos and grammatical errors (McAthy 2013). Corrections are generally reserved for a mistake that introduces a factual error or changes the meaning of a story. However, personal names and the names of organizations are particularly important to readers and, consequently, to journalists themselves (English 2013; Shapiro et al. 2013). As a result, many journalists argue corrections to these errors should also be declared.

Finally, in breaking news situations, journalists should be open about what they know and don't know—and when they know it. Contradictory information can arise, and when it does, journalists should aim to explain how new information differs from that issued previously.

2. Visibility

Many news organizations place corrections at the bottom of the story. It's a practice that frames documents as linear media with a change representing an addendum or a postscript. *The New York Times* used to put corrections at the bottom of the page with a short alert warning of the correction at the top. However, it was a structure the paper's public editor has said was "a very bad system for the Web" (Sullivan 2013). The correction was too distant from the error and far below social media sharing buttons, where users could exit the story.

A commitment to accountability would aim to have as many people see the correction as see the error itself. This would involve, as a general principle, placing the correction as close to the error as possible. This idea is acknowledged in new guidelines at the *Times* and at *The Washington Post*, which issued a revision in January 2013 stating: "Placement for corrections reflects gravity of error" (Romenesko 2013).

When the error substantially affects the focus of an entire story, editors might place a correction at the top. When it pertains to a specific fact, it might go in the body of a sentence. Similarly, an apology of egregious error might also appear on a site's homepage. This practice scales effectively with the increasing trend among mobile- and social-focused news outlets to present content in chunks, rather than narrative blobs. Buzzfeed presents many of its articles in "listicle" format with social sharing tools attached to individual pieces of content such as images. The mobile-focused news outlet Circa presents narrative stories as a series of image and text screens that smartphone users swipe through. Each screen's "object-oriented" content is also shareable, as parts of the entire story. Keeping the corrections close to the error increases the chance of the correction being seen by social media users. (Note: Buzzfeed at the time of publication issues corrections at the bottom of the page.)

In the opening chapter of this book, Lawrie Zion notes that most of the people publishing content today have no journalistic training. Indeed, many bloggers have developed their own practices independent of the mainstream journalism industry (Porlezza and Russ-Mohl 2013; Whitehouse 2010). For example, bloggers use strikethrough text so users "will instantly notice that a change has been made but still be able to see what was corrected" (Friend and Singer 2007). However, mainstream media appear to regard this practice warily. According to Cornish (2010) no major online news sites use the strikethrough function in news stories.

A key aim with any correction should be visibility. NPR, for example, puts corrections in a large box below the byline that rivals the headline in importance (Beesley 2013).

An error in audio or video files can be particularly difficult to correct. It's often impossible to re-shoot a piece of video or re-edit audio to fix an error. Consequently, many news organizations simply place the correction on the web page where the video appears. But this can be an ineffective practice on video platforms that have tight integration with social media. For example, when a Facebook user shares a link to a YouTube video, that video is embedded in users' stream with little context. Other Facebook users playing the video within their own news feed are likely to see only the video title and the first few words of its description. They might never know a correction exists.

In social media, journalists must think of other ways to get the correction close to the error. Twitter and Facebook, for example, group posts into conversation threads. A correction mentioned in the same thread as the initial error makes a visual connection. As well, replies to the thread, on services such as Facebook, generate a notification to other users who replied previously (user preferences permitting). A correction issued in this way can be communicated effectively to people already engaged with the content.

3. Timeliness

Journalists should issue corrections as soon as they determine there is an error. If possible, they should put a timestamp on the correction to tell readers when the change was made. In social media, they should repeat a major correction at a later time so more people see it.

4. Engagement

If you want readers to report errors, you should ask them to. That was the logic behind a campaign launched in 2010 to encourage news organizations to include a "Report an Error" button on their website (Rosenberg 2010). However, the idea hasn't had widespread appeal (Karlsson 2010). Aside from the *Toronto Star* and a handful of other news organizations, few major news outlets appear to have taken up the challenge. Many news organizations are promoting personal channels to resolve errors over institutional ones, offering instead the ability to email the reporter, contact her on Twitter, or leave a comment in the discussion area.

Social media offer powerful ways for journalists to invite reports of error and spread notice of corrections. Journalists can mention sources by username on services such as Twitter to notify them when they publish a story. Journalists can engage with the audience in social media and in website comments to debate their stories. Further, when they know they have committed an error, they can reach out to make sure a correction is noticed (Porlezza and Russ-Mohl 2013; Silverman 2012a).

Accountability "means checking to see who retweeted an erroneous tweet or a tweet linking to a post or story with a major error and tweeting at those people to ask them to also retweet the correction," argues former Digital First editor Steve Buttry. "Accountability means posting the correction in comments on reposts where people have shared your post on their Facebook pages" (Buttry 2013).

Former NPR strategist Andy Carvin made that effort after he tweeted his newsroom's mistaken alert that Rep. Gabrielle Giffords had died in an Arizona shooting incident. Carvin learned the site Lost Remote had mentioned his tweet in its story about wrong reporting of the event. In a long post in the site's comments, he explained how and why he issued the tweet. He ended, stating: "I apologize to all of the people on Twitter who received the tweet, and I am terribly sorry for sending them incorrect information" (Carvin 2011b). A discussion of the merits of deleting tweets eventually climbed to more than 60 other posts.

Journalists can also engage the reader by issuing minor corrections in an entertaining way that encourages others to share them in social media. In 2013, a *Tampa Bay Times* reporter attended a dating event at a comic book convention. However, the reporter failed to accurately record the moderator's subtle Star Wars humor when she asked participants: "Are you ready to find love in Alderaan places?" In its correction, the paper playfully described the reporter as "not strong in the ways of the Force" for missing the pun about Princess Leia's home planet (Silverman 2013b).

5. Thoroughness

A correction made to a website story is only partially effective if the error still appears uncorrected on other platforms. A basic effort to contain the spread of error would include ensuring it is corrected in every channel in which it initially appeared (Silverman 2013a, 160).

For example, a video uploaded to YouTube might note the correction within the YouTube description field, in addition to the website story page where it is embedded.

In September 2013, NPR ran a Q&A on health-care funding and its source misstated the name of a medical plan. NPR noted the correction in the website story, the website transcript of the audio, and in its app (NPR 2013).

Guidelines for Unpublishing

Unpublishing is the act of permanently removing online content after having tugged at a journalist's cold heart. It can involve scrubbing errors—but more specifically it concerns removing factually accurate content because sources request it.

The inboxes of managing editors and public editors are increasingly filled with emotional—some heart-wrenching—stories from people who can't escape the shadow of being mentioned in a news story (Watson 2012). Here are some actual requests made to news organizations:

- A woman voluntarily relates her efforts to overcome her gambling addiction in a feature story. She recounts in detail how she gambled away money from family members and struggles to overcome depression and anxiety. A year later she says continued publication of the story online "is a disaster for me" and is harming her ability to get a job and overcome her health issues.
- A law student is charged in connection with a prank relating to a bomb threat but those charges are ultimately dropped. His lawyer says he was simply "in the wrong place at the wrong time." A year later, the student is job hunting and says the story, returned prominently by search engines for his name, is damaging his reputation.
- A young woman who discussed her divorce in a lifestyle feature is embarrassed by her comments a year later and wants them removed.

The cases are drawn from requests to the *Toronto Star* and also from newspapers across North America as part of a 2009 study conducted by Kathy English, the public editor at the *Star* (English 2009). English found that about half of the 110 editors surveyed had created policies and procedures for handling unpublishing requests. Most declared a strong reluctance to delete content but three-quarters said news organizations should be able to do so under some circumstances.

Managing editors and producers have coined the phrase "source remorse" to describe the motivation of people who grant an interview to a journalist and later feel they made a serious mistake. Their comments linger on for years in Google search engine results for their name—often elevated to the top because Google considers the news site a popular and credible information source.

One of the hardest jobs a journalist can do is refuse to help people in distress over their reporting. Simply removing the story would make the tears go away. However, unpublishing for ill-considered reasons can cause serious harm to a news organization's reputation and should never be undertaken lightly.

The Canadian Association of Journalists' guidelines on unpublishing provide recommendations based around the following points (English, Currie, and Link 2010).

1. In General, Do Not Unpublish

News organizations are in the publishing business, not the unpublishing business. They add information to the historical record and have an obligation to their community to retain it. As a general rule, they should not remove their content.

Andy Carvin's tweet "Rep. Giffords (D-AZ), 6 others killed by gunman in Tucson" is still online years later (Carvin 2011a). The stories plagiarized and fabricated by Jayson Blair are still available on *The New York Times* site, with corrections notices attached (New York Times 2003).

Leaving an erroneous tweet or a story online requires courage. But when coupled with a rigorous corrections strategy, it's a much more transparent way to handle errors (Porlezza and Russ-Mohl 2013).

Source remorse is not a reason to unpublish. Information gathered fairly and reported accurately is an important part of the public record. *The Washington Post* and *The New York Times* are among the growing numbers of news organizations that have blunt policies on the issue. "We have a strict policy on unpublishing: We don't," states the *Times'* public editor (Sullivan 2013).

In his book *Delete: The Virtue of Forgetting in the Digital Age*, Mayer-Schönberger wonders "Will our children be outspoken in online equivalents of school newspapers if they fear their blunt words might hurt their future career?" (Mayer-Schönberger 2009, 111) This is a worthy question, but one news organizations are ill suited to resolve.

2. Update Stories to Maintain Accuracy

Unpublishing requests increasingly concern criminal charges from the daily police blotter (English 2009). However, news organizations have not typically reported on the outcomes of those charges—whether they were dropped or the person was acquitted—in minor cases.

The lack of a reported resolution to those charges can cause ongoing damage to a source's reputation. Consequently a news organization may consider further reporting. This can take the form of a short note in the story, especially to report the resolution of criminal charges. Another option is to write a separate follow-up story. This may be appropriate when a source was interviewed at a low point in her life, perhaps in the midst of drug dependency or debt, and has dramatically improved her situation since. Both practices have been used by news outlets (Tenore 2010).

3. Communicate Policies and Engage with the Public

A decision to reject an unpublishing request can seem arbitrary to a source who feels wronged. It's important for news outlets to have a policy in place to show readers their rationale. It's even better if the readers can find that statement themselves online. Cornish (2010) found that few news organizations had an easily findable corrections policy. A statement on unpublishing would explain the news organization's commitment to integrity and credibility, and how retaining information online serves the community.

As well, many sources simply may not understand that the news outlet will publish their story online. A journalist arriving with a TV camera is more likely to be asked what time the piece will air than where the story will appear online. It's not the journalist's job to educate people about the Internet. But journalists need to tell sources if their story will go online.

4. Act Humanely—and Legally—in Extreme Situations

Rare circumstances may arise when publication of a story has breached ethics or broken laws. The story may break a publication ban, be defamatory, or have been obtained through deception. Legal counsel should be sought when necessary and every effort should be made first to correct or update the story transparently. If the violation is severe, the news organization may remove the story. However, it should leave the URL untouched and place a notice of removal in place of the story. As with scrubbing, it's near impossible to remove a story without a trace, so transparency should be a guiding concern.

There may be other rare situations where continued publication profoundly affects a source's well-being. It may be fair—and humane—to remove a story especially where publication appears to threaten a source's life. Where possible, the news organization should seek to obtain evidence of harm, for example, in the form of a doctor's diagnosis. At all times, the news organization should keep in mind that these situations are frequently complex, with no single cause or easy resolution.

5. Unpublish by Consensus

A study of journalists' attitudes toward corrections found that news workers believed they were capable of being accountable for their errors and able to fix them (Joseph 2011). However, a decision to unpublish should always be undertaken by a group of senior journalists. No single journalist should have the power to act unilaterally as an organization's censor.

As Silverman (2013a) points out, these guidelines work only when news organizations follow a corrections workflow that involves clear rules and responsibilities, coupled with an honest effort to share and promote the correction in the same manner as other content.

Best Practices in Action: NowThis News

NowThis News is a media outlet that aims to tailor multimedia content to the needs of mobile audiences. Launched in September 2012 the news outlet distributes bite-sized chunks of news for the smartphone-tailored platforms of Vine and Instagram. It distributes its video-heavy content on its app and its website, and also on Twitter, Facebook, Google+, and Tumblr.

NowThis creates a welcoming environment for corrections, explaining to website users how to report an error and telling them in direct language: "we want to know" about them (NowThis News, 2013).

Shortly after its launch, users took the site up on its offer. In November 2012 NowThis tweeted incorrect information about the political scandal involving US General David Petraeus (NowThis News, 2012a). As users began to question the information, NowThis replied to them, describing, in real time, how it was attempting to re-verify its report. More important, it made some of its replies visible to all of its followers, to let them know the situation.

When NowThis realized its mistake, it quickly tweeted a correction and explained how it made the error (NowThis News, 2012b). In subsequent tweets, it credited the first Twitter user to question its report (NowThis News, 2012d). Then, as users began mentioning NowThis's mistake, it began retweeting them and replying individually to at least nine of them. It took the further step of tweeting an apology to the news source it misquoted. Finally, it left its original erroneous tweet untouched (NowThis News, 2012c).

On Instagram, NowThis committed a less-serious mistake when it misrepresented its video mashup of statements by Barack Obama and Ronald Reagan in August 2013. Instagram offers minimal means of annotating its content, so NowThis regularly used the comment section to describe its video. A commenter quickly called out NowThis for misleading its audience and NowThis replied to the user with a correction. This action had the effect of prominently displaying the correction to other Instagram users and also of showing that NowThis was

Figure 10.1 NowThis News sets the record straight.

listening to its audience. It effectively stopped the spread of misinformation and encouraged others to report additional mistakes they might find.

In his discussion of this particular error, Silverman (2013c) describes how NowThis tries to create content, and issue corrections, that are authentic to each platform. This means using "the contextual area around the piece"—the comment area in Vine, the description section in a YouTube video, or the text field issued to a content partner such as Buzzfeed—to deliver the correction in the most visible and effective way.

As a result, NowThis doesn't have a special corrections section on its platforms. It doesn't try to attach complex descriptions of errors to individual pieces of content. Instead, it acknowledges the technological space in which it operates—a mobile environment characterized by small screens, atomized content, easy sharing, and real-time notifications.

It integrates corrections into the ordinary conversations it has with its users—and tailors them to the user's environment. It builds trust with its audience by being gracious to its critics and humble about its mistakes. It builds accountability by being transparent about its work and by publicizing its missteps as thoroughly as new content.

Discussion Questions

1. Under what circumstances would you consider unpublishing a website story?
2. In a post on your organization's Facebook page, you placed a link to a story. But now you realize the headline of that story is wrong. Your followers have started to comment on the error. What do you do? Consider your answer in terms of transparency, visibility, and engagement.
3. A correction to an online story you have written is a mark of shame. It's an indication to readers and future employers that you are a sloppy reporter. Discuss. Consider the ethos of bloggers and the role of emotion highlighted by Silverman.

References

Annenberg Public Policy Center. 2005. *Annenberg Media: Journalist Component.* Accessed September 24, 2013. http://web.archive.org/web/20070404081456/http://www.annen bergpublicpolicycenter.org/naes/2005_3_questions_for_press_release_v2_5.24.05.pdf

Army Vet Chic. 2013. Twitter post, September 16, 2013, 3:00pm. https://twitter.com/ habitual_grump/status/379666008442564608

Beesley, Kevin. 2013. "For Saudi Women, New Subway Will Mean More Than a Cool Ride." *Poynter,* July 31, 2013. Accessed September 22, 2013. www.npr.org/blogs/ parallels/2013/07/30/207077269/for-saudi-women-new-subway-will-mean-more-than-a-cool-ride

Buttry, Steve. 2010. Twitter post, November 17, 2010, 9:49pm. https://twitter.com/ stevebuttry/status/5074979922120704

Buttry, Steve. 2013. "Advice for Editors: Stand for Accuracy and Accountability." *The Buttry Diary*, May 8, 2013. Accessed September 21, 2013. http://stevebuttry.wordpress.com/2013/05/08/advice-for-editors-stand-for-accuracy-and-accountability/

Carvin, Andy. 2011a. Twitter post, January 8, 2011, 3:12pm. https://twitter.com/nprnews/status/23819307624435712

Carvin, Andy. 2011b. Website comment, January 9, 2011. Accessed September 21, 2013. http://lostremote.com/how-an-incorrect-report-of-giffords-death-spread-on-twitter_b14351#comment-126540166

Cornish, Sabryna. 2010. "Online Newspaper Sites Need to Establish Uniform Process for Making Corrections." *Newspaper Research Journal* 31(4):93–100. Accessed August 17, 2013.

English, Kathy. 2009. "The Long Tail of News: To Unpublish or not to Unpublish." Accessed August 17, 2013. www.journalismproject.ca/sites/www.j-source.ca/files/attachments/Long%20Tail%20report_Kathy_English.pdf

English, Kathy. 2013. "If Star Misspells Your Name, We Will Correct: Public Editor." *Toronto Star*, September 6, 2013. Accessed September 24, 2013. www.thestar.com/opinion/public_editor/2013/09/06/if_star_misspells_your_name_we_will_correct_public_editor.html

English, Kathy, Bert Bruser, Tim Currie, Rod Link, Craig Silverman, Shauna Snow-Capparelli, and Scott White. 2011. "Best Practices in Digital Accuracy and Correction." *Canadian Association of Journalists*, November 16, 2011. Accessed September 12, 2013. www.caj.ca/?p=1866

English, Kathy, Tim Currie, and Rod Link. 2010. "The Ethics of Unpublishing." *Canadian Association of Journalists*, October 27, 2010. Accessed September 12, 2013. www.caj.ca/?p=1135

Follman, Mark, and Scott Rosenberg. 2010. "The Wrong Stuff." *Media Bugs*, November 8, 2010. http://mediabugs.org/pages/the-wrong-stuff

Fotheringham, William. 2013. "Sir Bradley Wiggins Satisfied with World Time Trial Silver Medal." *The Guardian*, September 25, 2013. Accessed September 27, 2013. www.theguardian.com/sport/2013/sep/25/sir-bradley-wiggins-world-time-trial

Friend, Cecilia, and Jane B. Singer. 2007. *Online Journalism Ethics*. New York: Sharpe.

Joseph, Nicole L. 2011. "Correcting the Record." *Journalism Practice* 5(6):704–18. Accessed August 16, 2013. doi:10.1080/17512786.2011.587670

Karlsson, Michael. 2010. "Rituals of Transparency." *Journalism Studies* 11(4):535–45. Accessed September 13, 2013. doi:10.1080/14616701003638400

Maier, Scott R. 2007a. "Setting the Record Straight." *Journalism Practice* 1(1):33–43. Accessed August 16, 2013. doi:10.1080/17512780601078845

Maier, Scott R. 2007b. "Tip of the Iceberg: Published Corrections Represent Less Than Two Percent of Factual Errors in Newspapers." Paper presented at the Association for Education in Journalism and Mass Communication, Washington, DC, August 2007.

Maier, Scott R. 2009. "Our Process for Online Corrections Needs Serious Correcting." *Nieman Reports*, Fall. Accessed August 16, 2013. www.nieman.harvard.edu/reportsitem.aspx?id=101903

Mayer-Schönberger, Viktor. 2009. *Delete: The Virtue of Forgetting in the Digital Age*. Princeton, NJ: Princeton University Press.

McAthy, Rachel. 2013. "Made a Mistake? Advice for Journalists on Online Corrections." *Journalism.co.uk*, January 21, 2013. Accessed September 7, 2013. www.journalism.co.uk/news/how-to-handle-online-news-corrections/s2/a551784/

McBride, Kelly, and Tom Rosenstiel. 2013. "New Guiding Principles for a New Era of Journalism." In *The New Ethics of Journalism*, edited by Kelly McBride and Tom Rosenstiel, 1–6. Washington, DC: Sage.

New York Times. 2003. "Correcting the Record: Times Reporter Who Resigned Leaves Long Trail of Deception." *The New York Times*, May 11, 2003. Accessed September 21, 2013. www.nytimes.com/2003/05/11/us/correcting-the-record-times-reporter-who-resigned-leaves-long-trail-of-deception.html?pagewanted=all&src=pm

NowThis News. 2012a. Twitter post, November 9, 2012, 3:59pm. https://twitter.com/nowthisnews/status/266993500095135745

NowThis News. 2012b. Twitter post, November 9, 2012, 4:48pm. https://twitter.com/nowthisnews/status/267005755947880448

NowThis News. 2012c. Twitter post, November 9, 2012, 4:51pm. https://twitter.com/nowthisnews/status/267006487870722050

NowThis News. 2012d. Twitter post, November 9, 2012, 6:04pm. https://twitter.com/nowthisnews/status/267024810192818176

NowThis News. 2013. "About Us." Accessed September 24, 2013. www.nowthisnews.com/info/about_us/

NPR. 2013. "Questions Rise As Health Care Exchange Draws Near." NPR. Accessed September 27, 2013. www.npr.org/2013/09/24/225747068/health-care-q-a-do-you-have-to-do-something-now

Porlezza, Colin, and Stephan Russ-Mohl. 2013. "Getting the Facts Straight in a Digital Era." In *Rethinking Journalism: Trust and Participation in a Transformed News Landscape*, edited by Chris Peters and Marcel Broersma, 45–59. New York: Routledge.

Romenesko, Jim. 2013. "Washington Post Updates Its Online Correction Policies." *JimRomenesko.com*, January 16, 2013. Accessed September 24, 2013. http://jimromenesko.com/2013/01/16/washington-post-updates-online-corrections-policies/

Rosenberg, Scott. 2010. "'Report an Error' Button Should Be Standard on News Sites." *PBS IdeaLab*, December 1, 2010. Accessed September 27, 2013. www.pbs.org/idealab/2010/12/report-an-error-button-should-be-standard-on-news-sites334/

Shapiro, Ivor, Colette Brin, Isabelle Bédard-Brûlé, and Kasia Mychajlowycz. 2013. "Verification as a Strategic Ritual: How Journalists Retrospectively Describe Processes for Ensuring Accuracy." *Journalism Practice*. Accessed September 12, 2013. doi:10.1080/17512786.2013.765638

Silverman, Craig. 2007. *Regret the Error: How Media Mistakes Pollute the Press and Imperil Free Speech*. New York: Viking.

Silverman, Craig. 2012a. "How Journalists Can Do a Better Job of Correcting Errors on Social Media." *Poynter*, July 26, 2012. Accessed September 12, 2013. www.poynter.org/latest-news/regret-the-error/181508/how-journalists-can-do-a-better-job-of-correcting-errors-on-social-media/

Silverman, Craig. 2012b. "NBC's Failure to Correct Zimmerman Audio On-Air Highlights Lack of TV News Corrections." *Poynter*, April 23, 2012. Accessed September 7, 2013. www.poynter.org/latest-news/regret-the-error/171310/nbcs-failure-to-correct-zimmerman-audio-on-air-highlights-lack-of-tv-news-corrections/

Silverman, Craig. 2013a. "Corrections and Ethics." In *The New Ethics of Journalism*, edited by Kelly McBride and Tom Rosenstiel, 151–61. Washington, DC: Sage.

Silverman, Craig. 2013b. "Tampa Bay Times Correction Admits Reporter 'Not Strong in the Ways of the Force.' " *Poynter*, April 10, 2013. Accessed September 7, 2013. www.

poynter.org/latest-news/regret-the-error/209772/tampa-bay-times-correction-admits-reporter-not-strong-in-the-ways-of-the-force/

Silverman, Craig. 2013c. "How NowThis News Handles Multi-platform Corrections." *Poynter*, September 12, 2013. Accessed September 27, 2013. www.poynter.org/latest-news/regret-the-error/223147/ed-okeefe/

Singer, Jane B. 2007. "Contested Autonomy." *Journalism Studies* 8(1):79–95. Accessed September 17, 2013. doi:10.1080/14616700601056866

S.M. 2013. Twitter post, September 16, 2013, 2:10pm. https://twitter.com/redsteeze/status/379653510104879104

Sullivan, Margaret. 2013. "Make No Mistake, but If You Do, Here's How to Correct It." *The New York Times*, January 16, 2013. Accessed September 21, 2013. http://publiceditor.blogs.nytimes.com/2013/01/16/make-no-mistake-but-if-you-do-heres-how-to-correct-it/?_r=1

Tenore, Mallary. 2010. "5 Ways News Organizations Respond to 'Unpublishing' Requests." *Poynter*, July 19, 2010. Accessed September 17, 2013. www.poynter.org/latest-news/top-stories/104414/5-ways-news-organizations-respond-to-unpublishing-requests/

Todd, Chuck. 2013a. Twitter post, September 16, 2013, 2:05pm. https://twitter.com/chucktodd/status/379652181323808768

Todd, Chuck. 2013b. Twitter post, September 16, 2013, 3:00pm. https://twitter.com/chucktodd/status/379666133508702208

Watson, Dan. 2012. "Unpublishing Requests Are on the Rise." *Columbia Journalism Review*, April 9, 2012. Accessed September 21, 2013. http://cjr.org/the_news_frontier/unpublishing_requests_are_on_t.php

Whitehouse, Ginny. 2010. "Newsgathering and Privacy: Expanding Ethics Codes to Reflect Change in the Digital Media Age." *Journal of Mass Media Ethics* 25(4):310–27. Accessed September 25, 2013. doi:10.1080/08900523.2010.512827

11

COLLABORATION

Lily Canter

SHEFFIELD HALLAM UNIVERSITY, UK

The concept of "us and them" is one that is rapidly losing its legitimacy as publishers and the public join forces online. Instead, collaborative projects between traditional journalists and their amateur counterparts are increasingly populating the virtual space of news organizations as they experiment with new ways of engaging audiences via innovative forms of digital storytelling. This process of welcoming the public and other—sometimes competing—organizations into the exclusive journalism fold is fraught with complex challenges both ideological and practical.

This chapter seeks to provide an overview of the processes involved in collaboration and how interested parties can form successful partnerships. It attempts to define what collaboration really means in the digital media context and what might be achieved when seemingly disparate content producers come together. Yet these collaborative relationships are not without their pitfalls, and a level of management is required to meet the various needs of all those involved. Guidance is therefore provided here to suggest ethical rules of engagement that might be adopted by news organizations entering into collaborative projects. The discussion is placed within the context of real-life examples and addresses the untidy ethical issues that such initiatives can raise.

Defining the Relationship

The world of digital journalism is emerging at such a rapid rate that it is often difficult for the terminology to keep up with evolving and new practices. Journalism has often relied on a set of conventions including a familiar vernacular—specific to each organization—to describe different types of "copy" (hard, soft, feature, down-page, NIB, anchor), yet the online world brings with it a new vocabulary that is less clearly defined. News can be delivered via pages, tickers, blogs, tweets, posts, hyperlinks, feeds, and so forth, while audience engagement is no longer restricted to letters and phone-ins and instead encompasses a broader range of participation including comments, user-generated content, blogging, and citizen journalism. A recurring problem in this field is the lack of consensus between journalists and scholars alike in categorizing terms such as *collaboration* (Deuze 2008), *participation* (Singer et al. 2011; Blood 2006), *user-generated content* (Hermida and Thurman 2008), and *citizen journalism*. They are often described in contradictory manners (see the varying definitions of citizen journalism in Allan 2007; Charman 2007; Nip 2006) or new terms are created such as *alternative journalism* (Atton 2009), *meta-journalism* (Goode 2009), *mass self-communication* (Castells 2007), *open and closed journalism* (Deuze 2008), *networked journalism* (Jarvis 2008), and *participatory journalism* (Hermida 2011; Bowman and Willis 2003)—among others.

This lack of clarity reflects the fluid nature of digital journalism and the impotence of definitions in this virtual sphere. In order to set out a satisfactory understanding of collaboration within digital journalism, it is useful to strip back the word to its basic definition which assumes a working between two or more different parties. Collaboration—or working together—has been incorporated into the ethos of certain types of websites in the form of the wiki, often for journalistic purposes. Wikis allow users to add, remove, and edit content in a process of "collaborative authoring" (Bradshaw and Rohumaa 2011). The two best-known examples are Wikipedia and Wikileaks—the former a contemporaneous encyclopedia which includes news section Wikinews, and the latter a not-for-profit media organization that allows sources to leak information to the site's journalists. Meanwhile mainstream news organizations have taken more arms-length approaches to collaboration, which enables them to maintain a level of control. These consist primarily of:

1. Harnessing the public to investigate online data or submit information which is then incorporated into the work of journalists (e.g., *The Guardian* newspaper website in the UK)
2. Placing multimedia reports or blogs from the public in a distinct section of the news website (e.g., *The Cincinnati Enquirer* "CincyMoms" online section, or the community pages on Newsquest websites)
3. Creating a separate community website within the news organization brand (e.g., *Local People* portals in the UK run by publisher Local World).

News organizations are also increasingly looking to join forces with other institutions to work on collaborative projects, rather than simply working with hundreds of disparate members of the public. For example, the Georgia Project in the United States is a $5.6 million experiment which joins a university journalism center with the Macon local newspaper and Georgia Public Radio station. The aim is for students to work under the guidance of professional journalists to produce local news at a low cost to the news organizations while giving the aspiring journalists invaluable work experience.

As the aforementioned examples illustrate collaborative journalism implies a relationship between professional, paid for journalists, and others—at an organizational or individual level. The author's previous research (Canter 2012) defined collaborative journalism as the combination of professional and amateur content within the field of journalism. This incorporated user-generated content, citizen journalism, and participatory journalism where it was distributed either within a professional organization or involved the work of professional journalists. However, this definition overlooks the increasing collaboration between news organizations—between professional journalists and professional journalists—sometimes with the input of the "amateur" public as well. Three American news outlets, *Frontline*, ProPublica, and National Public Radio, collaborated on large-scale investigation Post Mortem, while Wikileaks has worked in partnership with various news organizations including *The Guardian*, *The New York Times*, *Al Jazeera*, and *Le Monde*. Furthermore in Australia, the national broadcaster, the Australian Broadcasting Corporation, has also partnered with *The Guardian*, Fairfax Media, and News Corp. for investigative stories.

Collaborative journalism can therefore operate both horizontally and vertically, with peers and the public. However, the biggest challenge arguably lies in navigating the uncharted waters of journalist-to-public collaboration where journalistic norms and conventions have little or no standing.

Benefits and Motivations

The stoic notions of objectivity, neutrality, and balance are often cited as the demarcation lines between traditional journalism and all other forms of communication, with journalists painstakingly striving to represent a fair account of events. But in reality traditional journalism is filled with much opinion and subjectivity, often originating from the powerful elite while simultaneously millions of voices are left unheard. As Jones and Salter (2012) suggest, collaboration can move away from the model of "objective" journalism to Bruns's (2008a) model of multi-perspectival journalism, leading to a more transparent and accountable form of reporting. Rather than audiences receiving one objective viewpoint collated by a journalist or editor, collaborative projects can enable audiences to receive multiple perspectives giving them a better overall picture. Through collaboration with the public, collective intelligence can be gathered via crowdsourcing enabling journalists to tap into the knowledge and skills of a large and diverse talent pool rather than a small and similar one.

Pierre Levy—who coined the term *collective intelligence*—described it this way: "None of us can know everything; each of us knows something; and we can put the pieces together if we pool our resources and combine our skills" (Jenkins 2008, 4). This is what Gillmor refers to as journalists accepting that readers collectively know more than media professionals do (2006, 111). The collaborative effect of the press and the public working together in the digital world is far more powerful than a single journalist working alone. According to Alan Rusbridger (2010), editor of one of the world's most popular English-language news websites, guardian.co.uk (Halliday 2011), and its associated newspaper *The Guardian*, news organizations are turning to the public to share the news-making process, particularly in the handling of large amounts of data or overcoming legal restrictions. This mass collaboration (Mansell 2009) sees a large and diverse labor pool constantly come up with better solutions than the most specialized workforce (Howe 2009). The *Guardian* used the power of the crowd on Twitter to overturn a secret injunction enabling it to legally report a story about oil trader Trafigura dumping toxic waste off the Ivory Coast in 2009.

> *The Guardian* story announcing that it had been restricted by an existing high court order from reporting certain parliamentary proceedings had been published online for just a matter of minutes before *internet* users began tearing apart the gag . . . blogs and the *social networking* site *Twitter* buzzed as users rushed to solve the mystery of who was behind the gagging attempt . . . 42 minutes after the Guardian story was published, the internet had revealed what the paper could not . . . All the while, efforts were continuing to persuade Trafigura to alter the terms of the order to allow the Guardian to report the parliamentary business, and at 12.19pm Carter Ruck emailed the Guardian agreeing to do so.
>
> (Booth 2009)

The same year *The Guardian* launched a crowdsourcing application asking the public to trawl through thousands of pages of documents relating to expenses of members of Parliament. The tools enabled readers to dig through the documents of MPs' expenses to identify individual claims, or documents that merited further investigation ("Investigate Your MP's Expenses" 2009). This illustrates how in many situations collective intelligence is a far greater tool than the selective information held by an individual reporter or newspaper.

This merge of audience and journalist has created what many refer to as prosumers or produsers—users or consumers involved in the production of news (Bowman and Willis 2003; Bruns 2008b). And within the local British newspaper industry many editors view collaboration as a potentially effective way to connect to audiences while also gaining free content (Maguire 2011). Dickinson (2011) proposes that local journalists are more likely to embrace this form of innovation because they "find themselves on the front line of an industry in crisis and therefore more aware of the need to cement relationships with audiences" (8). In their report to the Media Trust, Fenton et al. (2011) concluded that collaboration between local newspapers and communities was also vital for democracy.

> Establishing a more collaborative relationship between news organizations, individuals, and civil society should be encouraged in order to enable participation, increase effective engagement, expand the public sphere, and enhance democracy.
>
> (Fenton et al. 2011, 9)

Yet there is skepticism about such collaboration with claims that publishers are attracted to the shimmer of free labor and the public is motivated by narcissistic and private interests. However, recent research suggests that audiences are motivated to collaborate for a variety of reasons, many of them more altruistic or democratic than journalists would first assume (Canter 2013). The individuals who take an active role in collaborative journalism are often motivated by a desire to inform (Bowman and Willis 2003) and to harness the potential of the web for democratic debate (Rusbridger 2010; Gillmor 2006; Bowman and Willis 2003). On the opposite side of the collaborative coin, motivation for journalists and publishers is more complex. A constant friction exists between the social goals of journalists and the commercial pressures to make and maintain profits (Garnham 1986). This has been heightened in the Web 2.0 era as newspaper profits decline and companies seek ways to cut costs by gaining content from readers for free (Örnebring 2008). With limited resources journalists can use audience collaboration as a means of gaining exclusive, quick, and free information which helps them to remain competitive. But can a balance of exploitation and opportunity be struck? Despite an underlying economic motivation, a collaborative approach to journalism has the potential to harness the aforementioned collective intelligence and give a platform to previously unheard voices, serving an important democratic and civic function.

Managing the Masses

Working in partnership with the public creates a series of dilemmas and uncomfortable changes for journalists who have long resided in ivory towers picking and choosing letters to print and keeping the public out of a central role in story development. The very notion of letting the audience into the news production process is counterintuitive to many journalists and editors and appears to go against the nature of the profession. Professional ideology implies that journalists are distinct from the public due to their exclusive role and status, which is played out via a particular set of conventions and standards. Across the globe journalists in democratic states work to a set of unwritten obligations, underpinned by a public service tradition and a social role to ascertain truths (Donsbach 2010). Journalists also define themselves by their pursuit of autonomous principles and adherence to a professional code of ethics that often includes "a commitment to truth, accuracy and freedom of speech, the public's right to know, unbiased reporting and independence" (Webb, Schirato, and Danaher 2006, 183). These professional values are outlined in more detail by Deuze (2005), who identifies professional journalism ideology as being made up of the five ideal traits of public service, objectivity, autonomy, immediacy, and ethics. Journalists fulfill these traits by observing and informing, commentating, and providing a platform for outsider voices (Heinonen 2011).

But in order for collaborative projects to succeed, journalists need to be able to cast aside some of these traditional notions of "professional" journalism. Furthermore, professional norms and practices are not enshrined in law and unlike other more rigid professions (e.g., teaching, medicine, law), it is relatively straightforward in theory, to change the conventions—if journalists are willing to do it.

Members of the public do not operate by a set of professional norms and practices—they may not write tight copy or take perfectly lit photographs, but what they do provide are free resources, new perspectives, and an abundance of enthusiasm. Yet it is understandable that journalists, and editors in particular, are nervous about opening the gates to the public and potentially giving "amateurs" free reign over news production. There are issues of brand identity and trust with an expectation from audiences that a news organization's content will maintain high standards and be a trusted source of accurate information. There is also a wealth of legal restrictions which the public often appears to turn a blind eye to or is not aware of, but can cause considerable damage to a news organization's reputation and pocket if breached—and in the most extreme cases can land a journalist in custody. Therefore when initiating collaborative projects, it is useful for news organizations to set the boundaries from the beginning following a few simple rules: be open, be realistic, be fair, and be safe.

Rule 1: Be Open

Taking an open approach is central to any working partnership and can be interpreted in a number of ways. News organizations should seek to be transparent about the rules of engagement in collaborative projects and where the responsibility lies. But more than that, they need to be open to new approaches and amenable to bending the (unwritten) rules. As discussed in David Craig's chapter on ethics and best practices, professional discussions of the duties of journalists have underlined the importance of transparency and accountability, particularly in the digital media era. Therefore it is vital that the boundaries between collaborators, whatever form they may take, are clear from the outset.

The first step is to think about the issue of control and how much you are willing to open up the news production process. How much input do you want your collaborators to have and at which stage of the production cycle do you want them to be involved? Do you want collaborators to collect information, produce and edit news, disseminate news, respond to the news, or a combination of all these processes? Furthermore how much moderation does your news organization intend to do? Do you want to edit and approve all contributions or should the responsibility lie with the contributor, or the online community? There are a number of different approaches that can be taken and it is up to each organization to decide what is most appropriate for them by factoring in time, resources, and the ultimate aim of the collaborative project. For some news organizations the quantity of contributions and the emphasis on community engagement is more important than the quality of news stories that they produce. But for other news organizations maintaining high standards is of the utmost importance and they are prepared to put resources into facilitating collaborative projects that produce quality content which matches the work of journalists.

One approach is to enable the online community to act as editors and in effect hand control and duty of responsibility over to the public. For example, the website Wikinews is open to contributions from anybody and the public is also able to edit and correct stories after publication. However, there are some restrictions in place because after two weeks the news stories are only open to non-content changes which can only be carried out by the Wikinews administrators. And although Wikinews takes an open approach to editing and moderation, it still maintains a set of rules which are outlined in its editorial policy. This policy re-iterates the website's open approach by stating that all stories must be transparent and cite their sources. In doing so this enables the site to minimize harm caused to the public via false or inaccurate reporting as it enables traceability. This reinforces the journalistic ethical duty of truth telling and minimizing harm. Therefore setting up a readily available editorial policy from the beginning is an important ethical consideration because it lays the groundwork for all future collaboration and makes the rules transparent for all.

Rule 2: Be Realistic

Being open to collaborative projects also brings with it the need to be realistic about how these initiatives will work in practice. The quality of contributions may or may not match expectations and amateurs may or may not work well alongside professional journalists. Low-cost pilot schemes are often a good starting point to test the water and experiment with different ways of working. It may be that a news organization wants to collaborate with the public to cover local school events with written news reports but in reality the public is only interested in taking photographs of major annual events. The public will collaborate on issues and stories that are of interest to them and this may not always meet the interests of a news organization so compromises will always need to be made. News organizations therefore need to decide upon the scope of their hospitality, a form of virtue ethics, and the extent to which they are willing to open up ethical discourse to a wider range of voices, including dissenting ones.

Another pragmatic issue is the amount of help and support contributors require and whether this can be provided. It may not be realistic to expect an amateur to know how to find a story at a bureaucratic council meeting or how to take an engaging photograph, but providing some basic training may resolve this issue. Indeed as Craig illustrates in his earlier chapter, developing best practice via training is one of the ways in which media organizations can fulfill their ethical duties, and improve the quality of their output. This was the approach taken by the *Leicester Mercury*, a UK regional newspaper (see case study below) in its collaboration with volunteer media group Citizens' Eye, which offered training to community reporters but also took an open approach in setting the news agenda and initially allowed volunteers to cover stories of interest to them, but gradually provided them with more direction and specific events to cover.

A profusion of realism is also required when predicting the number of contributors or contributions a project is likely to attract. If you open the floodgates it does not necessarily follow that you will be flooded with news material, but instead a trickle or steady flow may be a more realistic expectation. It is therefore important for news organizations to understand the "long tail law" (Bradshaw and Rohumaa 2011), which states that a small number of users are responsible for the majority of material produced. Another useful equation is the 1:10:89 rule laid out by Howe (2009), which says that "for every 100 people on a site, 1 will actually create something, another 10 will vote on what he created, and the remaining 89 will merely consume the creation" (227). This rule together with Sturgeon's Law that 90 percent of everything is rubbish suggests that a realistic approach to collaboration is to expect only a tiny fraction of your audience to contribute and only a tiny fraction of that content to be good. The trick is to encourage enough contributions which can then be sorted and curated into valuable content.

Rule 3: Be Fair

In order to attract contributors and maintain successful collaborative projects it is crucial that your content producers be treated fairly. If someone has taken the time and effort to contribute to a news organization, whether it be working alongside a journalist on an investigative news story or trawling through documents online to spot anomalies, that person deserves recognition and news organizations have a moral duty to acknowledge this. The level of recognition will vary depending on the involvement of the individual. Some will want a sense of ownership over their creation while others will be happy to give anonymous support. It is important to give credit where credit is due as contributors will be keenly aware if they are being exploited. It is therefore important where appropriate to publish bylines, credits, or contributory acknowledgments. For example, the BBC endeavors to credit any submitted user-generated content it publishes or broadcasts and if the content is shared through a third-party website such as

Flickr or YouTube it tries to link back to the original location of that content. By acknowledging external content the BBC is able to reinforce the ethical duty of transparency, as explored above.

Rule 4: Be Safe

For many news organizations this is the most worrisome rule of all and indeed often a barrier to initiating collaborative schemes. There is anxiety around letting the untrained public produce or publish material which could be legally contentious. Furthermore people have vandalized others' online entries due to wiki-based websites allowing anyone to edit another piece of work. Therefore some form of moderation and editorial presence is necessary to ensure that contributors play by the rules—though a light-touch approach as described in the case study, or encouraging the community to police and moderate itself, can be more effective than a heavy-handed institutional response.

Another area of risk is the authenticity and accuracy of news stories coming from the unvetted and untrained public. Issues of verification, as discussed in Alfred Hermida's chapter, are a huge ethical concern for news organizations and safeguards and second checks need to be put in place even for the most innocuous of stories to prevent the public from being harmed or misled. If this is an unrealistic drain on resources, legal advice should be sought on the best way of ensuring that responsibility lies with the contributor rather than the publisher. However, a safe approach does not need to inhibit contributors, and a sensible, rather than overcautious, approach should be taken. For example, the UK *Telegraph* newspaper website actively encourages user moderation and feedback on its user-generated content policies, thereby involving users in this process rather than dictating what they can and cannot do. This hospitable approach allows ethical best practice to be scrutinized by the public and takes the caring approach alluded to in Craig's chapter. By opening up policy to user input the *Telegraph* is demonstrating that it cares about the concerns of the online community and how it is managed.

A further important factor to bear in mind is that items published online are subject not only to your own country's laws but laws of countries across the globe. But a good grasp of media law—in particular libel, contempt of court, and European Human Rights Act—should help news organizations steer clear of legal pitfalls. It is also increasingly important to be aware of copyright laws, data protection, and confidentiality (Hanna and Dodd 2012; Bradshaw and Rohumaa 2011).

These four simple rules act as ethical and practical guidance to news organizations embarking on collaborative partnerships and can be approached in a strict or lenient fashion depending on the project and the partners involved. But success is only likely to follow if a project is kept simple and all involved are willing to embrace a trial-and-error approach.

Figure 11.1 Citizens' Eye logo (citizenseye.org)

Best Practices in Action: Citizens' Eye

UK regional news organization the *Leicester Mercury* ran a pilot collaborative project with the independent Leicester news outlet Citizens' Eye (citizenseye.org) from 2010 to 2012 with the aim of allowing readers to provide copy for the newspaper and its website thisisleicestershire.co.uk. At the start of the project the *Leicester Mercury* had around 60 editorial staff while Citizens' Eye had a network of 450 volunteers with a core of 40 regular contributors. Citizens' Eye editor John Coster was recruited by the *Leicester Mercury* and paid a small undisclosed "retainer" for coordinating the volunteers on behalf of the news organization. The project involved members of Citizens' Eye providing text, photos, audio, and video for the newspaper, the newspaper youth supplement, and the newspaper website. The community reporters provided content in three ways, which each instilled the volunteer with a different role.

1. *Source*: Contacted by a journalist for information, content, or comment on a story. For example, a quote or a photo of a fire.
2. *Resource (independent and directed)*: Source story independently and create own content. Allocated a specific story by the newspaper news desk and asked to report on it. For example, attending a ward meeting.
3. *Collaborator*: Working alongside a journalist to provide complementary coverage of a story, arranged in advance. For example, providing video footage while journalists gather copy and photos.

The strategy of involving Citizens' Eye volunteers was implemented by *Leicester Mercury* editorial managers—in particular, the editor at the time, Keith Perch—and as such served a number of defined purposes for the news organization. A two-pronged approach was taken through which the project created more resources to cover a wider range of stories, in the hope that this would ultimately attract more readers. Citizens' Eye was seen as being particularly useful as a resource to report on stories that journalists did not have time to cover, such as community events, which then freed up reporters to concentrate on investigations. The editor of Citizens' Eye was acutely aware of the short-term economic fix his volunteers were providing the *Leicester Mercury*, but viewed it as mutually beneficial as it allowed Citizens' Eye to meet its goal of getting unheard voices into the mainstream media and he saw the collaboration as "a force for opportunity not destruction."

The project relied on an understanding that different types of stories were to be covered by Citizens' Eye reporters and *Leicester Mercury* reporters. The non-professional reporters were to cover low-level stories (or soft news) such as community or charity events, bottom-tier council meetings, self-interest news (such as promoting an event organized by the contributor), and expert opinions such as a classical music column previewing and reviewing local events. Stories which fitted into the high-level reporting category (or hard news) which should only be carried out by professional journalists were identified as court cases, top-tier council meetings, investigative journalism, major events, and breaking news. Tiers of reporting enabled a structure where the skills of a journalist could be maximized to add value to the news organization, and community/citizen/amateur journalists could add value by reporting on the community and giving expert opinion.

Further rules of engagement were verbally determined between the editors at both organizations. Citizens' Eye staff set their own agenda by sourcing stories that were important to them and they were also responsible for fact checking their stories, a role usually given to professionals. There was also flexibility in the writing style of Citizens' Eye reporters. They were not required to conform to the traditional formal style of news reporting. For example, stories often had no quotes, were subjective, and shifted between the third and first person. The light-touch moderation from journalists came into play when the content was placed in the newspaper or on the website. The journalists would decide where to place the content and on which day. The content would also be checked by editorial staff for accuracy, legal issues, and decency.

The project was not without its problems. There was a conflict between the two editors about the types of stories Citizens' Eye should cover, revealing that in practice the *Leicester Mercury* preferred community reporters to be assigned stories rather than write about whatever was important to them. By the end of 2012 the project had come to a gradual close due to staff leaving the *Leicester Mercury* including the editor and community projects co-ordinator.

Although the Citizens' Eye collaboration project was not entirely successful, it did help to open up the newspaper to more citizen journalism from a variety of outlets. By testing the field with an established community reporter organization, the *Leicester Mercury* was able to experiment, test, and define the boundaries between citizen and professional journalism. The *Leicester Mercury* continues to have a portion of its newspaper and website content provided by the local community for free, which enables a wider range of individuals and groups to engage with the brand.

Discussion Questions

1. The four rules recommend collaborative projects be open, realistic, fair, and safe. How could the *Leicester Mercury* improve its collaborative project by using these?
2. What other ethical considerations should be made?
3. To what extent does the *Leicester Mercury* collaborative project demonstrate journalistic ethics of duty, virtue, and care?
4. Is a mutually beneficial collaboration ethical if only one party is obtaining commercial gain?

References

Allan, Stuart. 2007. "Citizen Journalism and the Rise of Mass Self-Communication: Reporting the London Bombings." *Global Media Journal*, 1(1). Accessed November 11, 2009. http://stc.uws.edu.au/gmjau/iss1_2007/stuart_allan.html

Atton, Chris. 2009. "Alternative and Citizen Journalism." In *The Handbook of Journalism Studies*, edited by K. Wahl-Jorgensen and Thomas Hanitzsch, 265–77. London: Routledge.

Blood, Rebecca. 2006. "How Flickr Single-Handedly Invented Collaborative Photo-journalism." Rebecca Blood. Accessed October 26, 2011. www.rebeccablood.net/archive/2006/04/how_flickr_singlehandedly_inve_1.html#content

Booth, Robert. 2009. "Trafigura: A Few Tweets and Freedom of Speech Is Restored." *The Guardian*, October 13, 2009. Accessed January 10, 2014. www.theguardian.com/media/2009/oct/13/trafigura-tweets-freedowm-of-speech

Bowman, Shayne, and Chris Willis. 2003. *We Media: How Audiences Are Shaping the Future of News and Information. Hypergene.* Accessed October 27, 2009. www.hypergene.net/wemedia/weblog.php

Bradshaw, Paul, and Liisa Rohumaa. 2011. *The Online Journalism Handbook.* London: Pearson.

Bruns, Axel. 2008a. "Gatewatching, Not Gatekeeping: Collaborative Online News." Accessed May 2009. Accessed May 14, 2009. http://shrub.info/files/Gatewatching,%20Not%20Gatekeeping.pdf

Bruns, Axel. 2008b. *Blogs, Wikipedia, Second Life, and Beyond: From Production to Produsage.* New York: Peter Lang.

Canter, Lily. 2012. "Web 2.0 and the Changing Relationship between Newspaper Journalists and Their Audiences." PhD diss., University of Sheffield. http://etheses.whiterose.ac.uk/

Canter, Lily. 2013. "The Source, the Resource and the Collaborator: The Role of Citizen Journalism in Local UK Newspapers." *Journalism: Theory, Practice and Criticism* iFirst Article. 1–19. Accessed February 5, 2013. http://jou.sagepub.com/content/early/201/02/19/1464884912474203

Castells, Manuel. 2007. "Communication, Power and Counter-power in the Network Society." *International Journal of Communication* 1:238–66.

Charman, Suw. 2007. "The Changing Role of Journalists in a World Where Everyone Can Publish." The Freedom of Expression Project [online]. Accessed November 12, 2009. www.freedomofexpression.org.uk/resources/the+changing+role+of+journalists+in+a+world+where+everyone+can+publish

Citizens' Eye. "About." Citizens' Eye. 2011. Accessed June 9, 2011. www.citizens eye.org/about/

Deuze, Mark. 2005. "What Is Journalism? Professional Identity and Ideology of Journalists Reconsidered." *Journalism* 6:442–64.

Deuze, Mark. 2008. "The Professional Identity of Journalists in the Context of Convergence Culture." *Observatorio* 7:103–17.

Dickinson, Roger. 2011. "The Use of Social Media in the Work of Local Newspaper Journalists." Paper presented at the Future of Journalism conference, Cardiff, Cardiff University, September 2011.

Donsbach, Wolfgang. 2010. "Journalists and Their Professional Identities." In *The Routledge Companion to News and Journalism*, edited by Stuart Allen, 38–48. Abingdon: Routledge.

Fenton, Natalie, James Curran, Des Freedman, Angela Phillips, Nick Couldry, and Peter Lee-Wright. 2011. "Meeting the News Needs of Local Communities." *Media Trust*. Accessed October 14, 2011. www.mediatrust.org/get-support/community-newswire-1/research-report-3/

Garnham, Nicholas. 1986. "The Media and the Public Sphere." In *Communicating Politics*, edited by Peter Golding, Graham Murdock, and Philip Schlesinger, 37–54. New York: Holmes & Meier.

Gillmor, Dan. 2006. *We the Media: Grassroots Journalism by the People for the People*. Farnham, UK: O'Reilly.

Goode, Luke. 2009. "Social News, Citizen Journalism and Democracy." *New Media & Society* 11:1287–1305.

Halliday, Josh. 2011. "Mail Online Becomes World's Second Most Popular Newspaper Site." *The Guardian*, April 19, 2011. Accessed April 23, 2012. www.guardian.co.uk/media/2011/apr/19/mail-online-website-popular

Hanna, Mark, and Mike Dodd. 2012. *McNae's Essential Law for Journalists*. 21st ed. Oxford, UK: Oxford University Press.

Heinonen, Ari. 2011. "The Journalist's Relationship with Users: New Dimensions to Conventional Roles." In *Participatory Journalism: Guarding Gates at Online Newspapers*, edited by Jane B. Singer, 34–55. Chichester, UK: Wiley-Blackwell.

Hermida, Alfred. 2011. "Mechanisms of Participation: How Audience Options Shape the Conversation." In *Participatory Journalism: Guarding Gates at Online Newspapers*, edited by Jane Singer, 13–33. Chichester, UK: Wiley-Blackwell.

Hermida, Alfred, and Neil Thurman. 2008. "A Clash of Cultures: An Integration of User-Generated Content within Professional Journalistic Frameworks at British Newspaper Websites." *Journalism Practice* 2:343–56.

Howe, Jeff. 2009. *Crowdsourcing: How the Power of the Crowd Is Driving the Future of Business*. London: Random House Business Books.

"Investigate Your MP's Expenses." 2009. *The Guardian*. Accessed October 25, 2011. http://mps-expenses.guardian.co.uk/

Jarvis, Jeff. 2008. "Supermedia." *BuzzMachine*, June 6, 2008. Accessed June 10, 2010. www.buzzmachine.com/2008/06/06/supermedia/

Jenkins, Henry. 2008. *Convergence Culture: Where Old and New Media Collide*. New York: New York University Press.

Jones, Janet, and Lee Salter. 2012. *Digital Journalism*. London: Sage.

Maguire, Chris. 2011. "Social Media and the Regional Press." Lecture presented at the National Council for the Training of Journalists Digital Journalism Seminar, Press Association, October 2011, London.

Mansell, Robin. 2009. "Power, Media Culture and New Media." Paper presented at the German Communication Association (DGPuK) Media Culture in Change conference, University of Bremen, Bremen.

Nip, Joyce. Y. M. 2006. Exploring the Second Phase of Public Journalism. *Journalism Studies*, 7(2): 212–36.

Örnebring, Henrik. 2008. "The Consumer as Producer—of What?" *Journalism Studies* 9:771–85.

Rusbridger, Alan. 2010. "The Hugh Cudlipp Lecture: Does Journalism Exist?" *The Guardian*, January 25, 2010. Accessed June 10, 2010. www.guardian.co.uk/media/2010/jan/25/cudlipp-lecture-alan-rusbridger

Singer, Jane, Alfred Hermida, David Domingo, Ari Heinonen, Steve Paulussen, Thorsten Quandt, Zvi Reich, and Marina Vujnovic. 2011. *Participatory Journalism: Guarding Open Gates at Online Newspapers*. Chichester, UK: Wiley-Blackwell.

Webb, Jen, Tony Schirato, and Geoff Danaher. 2006. *Understanding Bourdieu*. London: Sage.

12

FOSTERING AND MODERATING CITIZEN CONVERSATIONS

David Domingo

UNIVERSITÉ LIBRE DE BRUXELLES, BELGIUM

Best practices in the moderation of audience participation in news websites have evolved over time from placing emphasis on filtering citizen input to avoid legal and quality issues, to fostering a virtuous spiral by selecting and highlighting positive contributions to the newsflow. Audience participation has long been part of journalism, from letters to the editor to talkback calls in radio programs. Online media have increased the amount, diversity, and ubiquity of input that citizens can contribute to news products, and social networks and blogs have expanded public conversations about current events beyond the boundaries of news websites.

The potential benefits are appealing: fostering a closer relationship with the audience, increasing their loyalty, getting new story ideas. But the challenges can easily overwhelm newsrooms: moderating comments in news has been a nightmare for many, and some journalists prefer to stay away from Twitter due to the lack of control over the conversations. Applying David Craig's proposal in Chapter 2 to moderation, best practices that foster virtuous journalism should create spaces where citizens feel that their participation is valued. Moderation strategies should encourage the quality of the contributions, rather than spending energy on deterring uncivil rant.

This chapter charts the challenges of managing audience participation and the strategies devised by different newsrooms to address and enhance them. The focus is on comments on news websites and the social media presence of journalists and news outlets, and how these foster conversations among citizens. These conversations complement (and sometimes trigger) news reporting by the newsroom.

Motivations and Attitudes toward Audience Participation

The reasons why newsrooms promote audience participation on news websites generally have more to do with marketing (fostering a feeling of belonging to the brand, increasing user traffic) than with journalism (Vujnovic et al. 2010; Goodman 2013), but the benefits for news work also rank highly when professionals are surveyed (Heinonen 2011): journalists mention the opportunities to know their audience better, to get new sources (experts, witnesses) that they would not have found through official channels, or to be more accountable (citizens may warn of factual errors in an article, challenge the point of view of the journalist). Audience participation can lead to better journalism. At the same time, it also poses many challenges: maintaining the quality and reputation of the news product, once it is open to contributions from thousands of users (Canter 2012; Loke 2012); preventing legal problems, as in many countries the editor of a publication is ultimately responsible for the content regardless of the authorship (Ruiz et al. 2011); or integrating moderation and user input in a news production workflow already under the pressure of immediacy and multiplatform publishing (Domingo 2008). For more than a decade, online newsrooms have been exploring strategies to find the balance between fostering the benefits and preventing the risks of involving the citizens in the news process. (For more discussion of collaboration with citizens, see the previous chapter by Lily Canter.)

As with other aspects of online journalism, there is not one solution that fits all. Different newsrooms in different countries and with diverse traditions adopt significantly diverse strategies. In a study of online newspapers in 10 countries, the editorial stand of *quality broadsheets* versus the *popular press* regarding their audiences determined more relevant variations than did national differences: there was, respectively, a tendency to isolate audience participation from the content produced by journalists (citizen journalism sections, stand-alone citizen blogging communities) versus an eagerness to incorporate citizen input into the news production process, rendering the collaboration visible by, for example, acknowledging user tips in journalist-authored articles (Domingo 2011; see also Jönsson and Örnebring 2010; Richardson and Stanyer 2011). On the contrary, analyzing specifically comments in news, Ruiz et al. (2011) found that the cultural context, the tradition of the media system (Anglo-Saxon or liberal vs. Mediterranean or polarized-pluralist), was what shaped the tone of the conversations in *quality newspapers* with very different moderation strategies.

Another axis of variation is to be found between online native media and the web presence of print and broadcast media. Many online-only news sites have developed from the professionalization of blogging, where the conversation with the community is an inherent part of the author's activity (Erard 2013a). That spirit carried on to the professional digital native websites: they tend to have a more open attitude towards fostering comments and participation within their websites than legacy media. Finally, a key ingredient that shapes audience participation across newsrooms is the individual attitude of the journalists, which can greatly vary within the same newsroom, depending on factors such as the age, experience with social media, and adherence to the principles of journalistic professionalism. The attitudes of journalists towards audience participation range between the "dialogical," who understand the news as a social conversation and welcome the input of their audience, and the "conventional," who defend the notion that journalism should stay detached from citizens to preserve its independence (Heinonen 2011).

Research also shows that newsrooms maintain a high degree of control over the publication of most of user-generated content (UGC), applying strict gatekeeping criteria for the material that is closest to the journalistic product: pictures of an event by witnesses, information tips (Hermida and Thurman 2008; Pantti and Bakker 2009; Williams, Wardle, and Wahl-Jorgensen 2011). Even comments in news are monitored to keep them within the limits of civility and legality determined by the newsroom in the guidelines for participation (Reich 2011; Ruiz et al. 2011). Newsrooms have embraced participation with caution, trying to avoid being overwhelmed by it, and maintaining the role of the journalist at the center of the news production routines (Williams et al. 2011). They do so by limiting the opportunities for participation to the entry point and the end of the production process: citizens are mostly welcomed to become sources and commentators, but seldom producers of news stories or selectors of what is news (Domingo et al. 2008). Beyond commenting on the news, citizens are invited to contribute content (pictures, testimonials) more often in lifestyle sections than in *hard news* sections: "users are mostly empowered to create popular culture-oriented content and personal/everyday life-oriented content rather than news/ informational content" (Jönsson and Örnebring 2010, 140).

Key Challenges of Audience Participation

The experience of online newsrooms indicates that their main worries when dealing with audience participation have to do with the quality of user contributions, the legal problems that inappropriate content may entail for the media company, and the integration of the material within the news production workflows. And only a minority of users contribute content to news websites: "Only 15 per cent [Internet users] said that they 'often' or 'always' comment on stories and this from an audience of people who are willing to take online surveys who likely would over-index for such behaviors" (Carmichael 2011). Most newsrooms admit that less than 10 percent of their audience comments on their news, and only around 1 percent do so on a regular basis or contributes other kinds of UGC (Reich 2011). However, in websites with millions of users the numbers are considerable and can overwhelm the moderation team: *The Huffington Post* received over an average of 25,000 comments per hour before its latest changes in registration policies (Sonderman 2012, see below). The moderators (a team equivalent to 30 full-time employees to cover the 24/7 cycle) only considered a quarter of the comments received to be publishable; the rest were deemed to be uncivil. Their job was devoted more to policing bad content than to promoting and making visible good discussions, and they have been exploring strategies related to registration policies to improve the situation (see below).

Research on online newspapers shows that most journalists do not usually think of comments in news as an agora of the public sphere, but rather as a challenge to the quality and the brand image of their news media (Loke 2012). Despite the signs of a more generally positive attitude towards fostering citizen conversations, community managers and editors in online-only news sites also devote much of their energy to eliminating uncivil contributions (Sonderman 2012). Moderation systems are quite effective at keeping most insults off the comment sections in news (Ruiz et al. 2011), but that does not guarantee by itself that they will become an effective platform for constructive public debate, as scholars had hoped (see Canter 2012). Researchers have singled out *theguardian.com* as one news website that gets closer to fulfilling this ideal (Graham 2013), with diversity of points of view in 23 percent of the threads analyzed and 40 percent of the comments engaged in a conversation with others (see the case study below). By contrast, other online newspapers, such as *ElPaís.com* or *LeMonde.fr*, barely had 1 percent of contributions with perspectives that differed from the political standpoint of the newsroom, and under 10 percent discussing other comments (Ruiz et al. 2011). When it comes to user-generated news stories, journalists tend to express disappointment because the nature of the material they get from citizens seldom falls under the category of *hard news*. For instance, Harrison (2009, 255) found that the UGC Hub in charge of selecting audience input at the BBC newsroom led to more "human interest" stories in the media of the public broadcaster, namely, "crime, calamities and accidents."

In social media, the challenges vary depending on the platform. On Facebook, news organizations have control over the posts on their official page, but they should be aware that this is an extension of the news website into a territory that users feel belongs to them. The etiquette of using their real names and being surrounded by their friends tends to render the conversations more civil, and that has inspired solutions for comments in news websites (see below). On Twitter, however, news organizations cannot delete mentions made by users, only report them to the social network, which may ban abusive users only in very extreme cases. In both cases, newsrooms do not have full control over the rules of what is expected and acceptable in these social media spaces. Journalists feel the need to be there because that is where their audience spends a lot of its online time, and conversations can spark much more naturally.

Another prime space for the discussion of current events outside news websites is platforms like Reddit, where users share articles and discuss them. Many journalists use social media and these platforms as sources for story ideas, even if they do not feel completely comfortable with the scrutiny that these news-avid communities do of their work (Johnson 2012).

Returning to conversations within news websites, the legal challenges vary greatly from country to country, and that shapes the attitudes and strategies of the newsrooms towards audience participation. The US offers quite solid protection to media companies as "providers of interactive computer services," making them immune from liability derived from "information provided by another information content provider," which in this case would be the user posting a comment or submitting other material (Section 230 of the Communications Decency Act of 1996). The situation is exactly the opposite in the European Union after the decision of the European Court of Human Rights, which held a media organization responsible of the defamatory (anonymous) comments published by a user on its website (Ridderhof 2013). The argument is that freedom of expression has its limit in the reputation of citizens referred to in any kind of content published on news websites, and newsrooms should have mechanisms to prevent libelous and defamatory comments. While there is a trend globally towards requiring registration of users with their full names (see below) to neutralize these legal risks, this requirement is problematic in the US where "[t]he First Amendment protects the right to speak anonymously" (Hermes 2013). Conversely, users in the US may find themselves in complicated situations if they are not conscious that the news media company may release information about them if required by a judge. Overall, what is most worrying of this diverse legal scenario is the "lack of awareness" both among journalists and citizens regarding the regulation of audience participation (Goodman 2013).

Besides these potential problems of audience participation, the biggest challenge for newsrooms is how to effectively integrate user-generated content into the news products, both to enhance the journalistic content and to reward citizen contributors, which can in turn motivate them to provide more relevant material in the future.

Basic Strategies for Comment Management

If we focus on comments in news websites, the struggle of online newsrooms to turn these spaces into a civil, useful dialogue has traditionally focused on two complementary practices: registration policies and moderation strategies. We will explore the diversity of these practices before moving on to consider advanced strategies for fostering the virtuous spiral of quality in citizen conversations.

Registration Policies

The media industry does not like anonymous comments: experience shows that if users think that their contributions cannot be traced back to them, they will feel less bound to the rules of participation (Reich 2011, 109). However, there is no consensus in the industry when it comes to requiring the use of real names or allowing for the use of pseudonyms. The discussion revolves around the compromise between quality of contributions and freedom of speech, and the trend since 2010 has been that more news websites are requiring some sort of registration in order to post comments. In a survey of 104 news websites in 63 countries, 53 percent required registration with an email address but allowed nicknames, 20 percent required real names, and 18 percent did not ask for registration before posting comments (Goodman 2013). The rise of social media has persuaded many newsrooms of the benefits of using social network IDs as the identifier for participants in their websites. Facebook is by far the most common choice.

The downside is that this strategy may inhibit users from contributing, as their reactions are most likely be linked to their real names, the etiquette in social networks. Some newsrooms argue that this is precisely what fosters more on-topic, civil, and fruitful discussions, as users that do not hide behind a pseudonym take more responsibility for what they say. *DallasNews.com* saw a drop of 40 percent in the number of comments after switching to social network IDing, but at the same time the reduction in uncivil content has allowed them to move from having a team of 13 moderating comments to one person who validates the few messages flagged by the users themselves (Shanahan 2013). The experience of iBrattleboro. com, a veteran hyperlocal news site driven by citizen-produced content, suggests that each case may be different, and newsrooms need to know their audience well before choosing the right registration strategy: "Using one's real name has not been an indicator of quality or civility of contributions, either. Some of the best information is supplied by those using pen names, and the sole libel case we've seen involved users using their real names" (Grotke 2013).

Moderation Strategies

There's no magic recipe for the moderation of news comments, and news websites have explored different moderation strategies over time, mostly by trial and error (Reich 2011). The choice in this case is between filtering the comments before publishing them (pre-moderation) or publishing them automatically, reviewing them later, and deleting those that are not appropriate (post-moderation). The first option is more labor intensive and users may get frustrated if there is not a quick reaction from the moderation team. Pre-moderation can kill conversations if comments take more than a few minutes to be approved. Post-moderation runs the risk of having uncivil content posted on the website temporarily, or permanently, if the supervision is not diligent enough. Newsrooms surveyed by Goodman (2013) were almost evenly split between those opting for post-moderation (42) and pre-moderation (38), with 16 others using mixed strategies. In many cases, moderators have the support of software that automatically bans messages with blacklisted words, the most sophisticated of which are artificial intelligence programs that keep learning what is acceptable and what is not based on the decisions of the human moderators (Sonderman 2012). In the US, NPR (National Public Radio) provides a good example of how moderation strategies evolve over time. In its case, it decided to add human pre-moderation to the process after surveying its users about their feelings about online conversations. NPR's Product Manager for social media, Kate Myers (2013) admitted: "We were surprised to see a full majority of our respondents actually call for more moderation throughout our comment threads." She committed to have 15 minutes maximum delay between submission and publication of contributions and hoped that this new strategy would increase the engagement and quality of the conversations.

Moderation strategies are far more flexible in social media than in news websites. That is mainly due to the fact that in spaces like Twitter, news organizations do not hold any power to actually delete inappropriate comments. On Facebook, the most popular social network globally, brand pages allow some control within that virtual presence of the newsroom in a territory that users actually perceive as an extension of their private sphere. The blurred boundaries between private and public sphere on Facebook (noted in the next chapter, by Kelly Fincham) create a delicate environment for fostering and moderating conversations. The advantage for news organizations is that users may be more eager to share their personal experiences if invited to do so at the Facebook page of their favorite news outlet, but the downside is that they may feel awkward or misled if they are not fully aware of the level of publicity that their contributions will have: unlike those on their personal wall or their friends' wall, comments on brand pages on Facebook are visible to everyone visiting that page. Another advantage is that on Facebook the number of inappropriate comments is naturally very low, due to the fact that users are in a context where social control is much more evident and anonymity is not the rule: they are conscious that their friends and colleagues will see what they publish.

The volume of uncivil comments on news websites is actually not as high as some journalists perceive. Besides extreme cases like *The Huffington Post*, the average of comments deleted by moderators is around 11 percent (Sonderman 2012). Nevertheless, no newsroom is exempt from overseeing the comments in one way or another, both on the website and in social media. In most of the surveyed newsrooms moderation was not assigned to a specific team, and it is online journalists who take on the task among their other duties. One third of the 100 surveyed had a moderation team in the newsroom, while 13 preferred to outsource the job to external companies specialized in this task, protecting their journalists from the burden. Among those outsourcing comment moderation are the BBC, *Corriere della Sera* in Italy, *The Economist*, *Le Monde*, and *Volkskrant* in The Netherlands (Goodman 2013). The problem with outsourcing is that the implicit message that the media sends to their audience is that journalists do not care about the conversations.

Generating the Virtuous Spiral

While registration and moderation strategies have been mainly designed to reduce inappropriate attitudes in comments in news, fostering quality input from audiences requires additional practices. To achieve the goal, we need to cultivate the sense of belonging to the debate community by developing the "ethics of care" that Fiona Martin explores in Chapter 7. This means granting users some responsibility for the overall quality of the conversations and focusing on a collective effort to highlight the best content as an example to be followed by other contributions. News websites that have been successful in doing this have developed strategies in three complementary directions: involving the audience in the moderation, involving the journalists in the conversation, and systematically highlighting the best UGC (Domingo 2011).

Involving the Users

Engaging the participants in the moderation does not mean letting users delete what they consider inappropriate; that would open the door to ideological wars between commentators with different points of view, warns the cofounder of iBrattleboro.com: "It's easy to say that we allow and encourage civil discourse, but *civil* means different things for different people with different ages and backgrounds. What I consider fair game may not match up with my neighbors' impressions" (Grotke 2013). Having clear participation guidelines is a must to set up the grounds for what is accepted, justify the decisions of the professional moderators, and orient the support of the users in that process. Most newsrooms limit user moderation power to "flagging" what they consider inappropriate—which will then be considered by a professional moderator. Many also ask users to signal comments they consider good, usually with the simple gesture of clicking a "recommend" or thumbs-up button. This second option is the one that is developing further in promising ways in several news websites, most times in connection with rankings of the users most valued by the community.

Voting systems allow for automatic arrangement of the flow of comments to highlight those that have most points, improving the often frustrating experience of reading through mediocre or irrelevant remarks. *Helsingin Sanomat* in Finland asks users to indicate whether a comment is well argued and showcases those that have received more votes more prominently (Goodman 2013). The introduction of a competitive factor tends to foster comments that are more elaborate and considerate, and there are proposals that the next level would be to take citizen conversations around a story into account when judging its quality for journalistic prizes (Erard 2013b). If fact, citizens tend to interpret comments this way, as an integral and essential part of the journalistic product (Barnes 2013).

We know very little about the motivations of citizens to engage in conversations in news comments. Barnes (2013) found that contributions tend to be triggered by emotional responses to a story, rather than "the Habermasian 'rational' desire to know" (2013, 12), and many readers refrained from participating because they felt that they lacked the confidence to make substantive contributions. A better understanding of the perceptions of the community of a news website about participation will help identify the best strategies to encourage them to get involved.

Involving the Journalists

The attitude of each individual journalist towards the comments associated with their news stories makes a huge difference in the tone and substance of the conversations (Bartlett 2013). Journalists who engage in conversations, showing interest in the experiences of the commenters, and responding to their doubts and queries, acknowledge that the quality of contributions tends to increase because the users feel their ideas are being heard and valued. The challenge, of course, is finding the way to integrate the involvement of journalists into their daily work routines.

The pressure of immediacy and the reluctance to enter spaces symbolically owned by the audience mean that few newsrooms systematically encourage their journalists to interact with their readers. Reporters at *USAToday.com* use the comments section of their stories to actively ask for testimonials and story ideas that they may follow up, contacting the user for an interview and creating a new article with that user as a key source (Domingo 2011). Giving directions to the comment thread can dramatically enhance the usefulness of the input. This recommendation also applies to Facebook and, especially, to Twitter, where moderation cannot be about deleting inappropriate content and therefore necessarily needs to focus on fostering topical conversations with clear invitations (questions, statements) in the official Twitter account of the news organization or, even better, through the personal account of the journalist covering that subject.

Highlighting Quality

Curating the best UGC (see also Chapter 7) involves selecting outstanding contributions, but also showcasing them prominently and embedding them into the newsflow. Involving the users and the journalists is essential for both of these strategies, but there is another key element: how is the relationship articulated between the content produced by journalists and the citizen conversations?

One of the most intriguing developments is the evolution of comment threads into annotations: allowing users to put comments within the text, or next to the specific paragraph or sentence they refer to, instead of condemning them to the bottom of the articles. *Quartz*, an online-only news site oriented to business-minded consumers, and the *Financial Times*, through its Newslines platform for the academic community, have implemented the idea of annotated news stories (O'Donovan 2013). This strategy tries to overcome the implicit message that comments are not as important as the author's text by giving them a prime spot to engage in a very fine-grained dialogue with the article (Erard 2013a). In a similar move, in 2013 *NYTimes.com* started to highlight on the side of the story text the best comments in selected sections.

Other online newspapers, like *USA Today* and *20 Minutos* in Spain, regularly use input from the comments to create new stories, acknowledging the tips of the readers for a newsworthy contribution (Domingo 2011). Another popular way to showcase selected citizen points of view is by using Storify to curate and embed social media conversations inside news articles. The most sophisticated strategy involves using design and software solutions to give more structure to the comment threads, not only to facilitate navigating them, but also to make sense of what is the overall state of opinion of citizens contributing to specific conversations. *The New York Times* and *The Washington Post* have used computerized sentiment analysis around polarizing topics such as the Defense of Marriage Act or the election of the new pope to render visual representations of the comments and enable users to access the reactions of specific profiles of commentators (Benton 2013). In a way, this allows news websites to reinvent the classic basic Yes/No polls and turn their comment sections into a more nuanced way of portraying public opinion.

Best Practices in Action: "Comment Is Free" at *The Guardian*

The Guardian is a pioneer among UK online news media in encouraging user participation. It created message boards (a forum separated from the editorial content) in 1999 and opened its journalistic blogs to comments in 2004 (Thurman 2008). In 2006, theirs became the second newsroom to allow comments on news articles (Hermida and Thurman 2008; Singer and Ashman 2009). This was seen as a natural move by journalists interviewed by researchers at different moments in the last six years. An example from an editor: "We are a liberal voice. We believe in diversity of opinion. We want lots of voices to be heard. That's precisely what we can do . . ." (quoted in Reich 2011, 102).

"Comment is free, but facts are sacred," proposed the editor of the newspaper C.P. Scott in 1921 as a key principle of *The Guardian*'s ethos. And that has set the tone of the balance that the newsroom tried to find from the beginning regarding user participation, a challenge that all newsrooms face: "journalists are struggling with how to ethically accommodate the opportunities for freedom and dialogue presented by UGC while safeguarding their credibility and sense of responsibility" (Singer and Ashman 2009, 18). And they have succeeded in creating a vibrant community that passionately discusses current events in an engaged and mostly respectful way (Richardson and Stanyer 2011; Ruiz et al., 2011; Graham 2013)

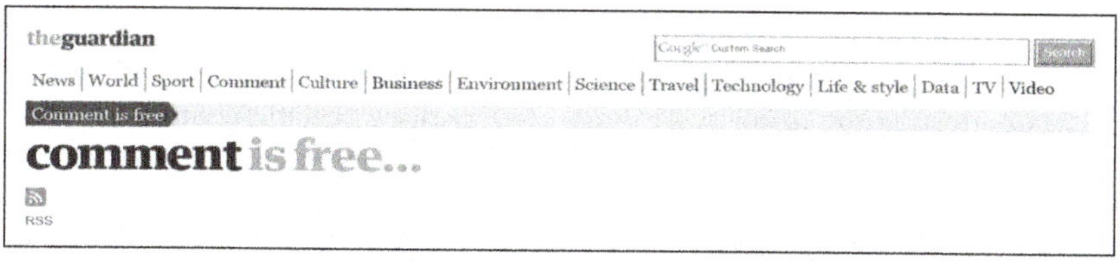

Figure 12.1 *The Guardian* fosters user involvement through its "Comment Is Free" section.

through over 9 million comments in 2013 (Epstein and Spencer 2013). Their practices are a good example of how to generate the virtuous spiral in audience participation with a combination of the strategies presented in the chapter.

Prioritizing the consolidation of a community of debate, rather than simply protecting the brand from uncivil participation, has been a key aspect of this strategy. After starting with pre-moderated comments, *The Guardian* staff soon decided that the volume they were moderating was too big to manage, and that they needed to find other moderation strategies that would actually allow for a more fluid conversation: "You can't really beat hitting 'submit' and seeing your comment there before you go away. It encourages you to come back. You feel you've engaged" (editor quoted in Reich 2011, 109). Their rules for participation consist of a brief 10-point manifesto found right under the box to submit comments. This is their own summary of best practices for users as posted on their website:

- If you act with maturity and consideration for other users, you should have no problems.
- Don't be unpleasant. Demonstrate and share the intelligence, wisdom and humour we know you possess.
- Take some responsibility for the quality of the conversations in which you're participating. Help make this an intelligent place for discussion and it will be.

(*Guardian* 2009)

The Guardian has therefore opted for post-moderation of comments, mainly based on the notifications sent by users that can click on two buttons associated to each contribution: "report," to signal a breach of the community standards, and "recommend," to indicate that they think the comment makes a relevant point. That fosters user involvement in creating a space free of abuse and where the effort to provide meaningful input is rewarded. The final decision for deleting a comment falls to community moderators, to avoid users abusing the report system against people with opposing views. While this moderation strategy is quite common, *The Guardian* is unique in that journalists are not directly involved in moderation, but it is citizens hired (and therefore paid) for the task—mainly active members of community formed around the website who apply when there are post openings (Reich 2011; Ruiz et al. 2011). Abusive behavior is minimized without affecting the majority of users' conversations: specific contributors may be switched to pre-moderation and even banned, and sensitive topics may also be pre-moderated or not open to comments. Less than 10 percent of user posts are actually deleted by the moderators (Reich 2011).

This moderation strategy does not mean that journalists are completely detached from comments in news. On the contrary, two tabs in the comment space below each article are devoted to highlight "staff responses" to user contributions and the comments "picked" by the newsroom, usually selected from those already recommended by dozens of other users. It is a collective process of curation that culminates with the showcase of UGC content on the front page of the section "Comment Is Free," side by side with the opinion columns of the newspaper, and a weekly article on the "comment of the week" (Bartlett 2013).

The strong sense of community is reinforced by a personal page for every user, where they can upload a profile picture that will show up next to each of their comments, and that also collects all their contributions, indicating those that were recommended by other users and picked by the newsroom. There is no ranking of "best" contributors, but every December users are invited to nominate the "commenter of the year." In 2013, *The Guardian* also created a weekly series of short interviews with the most active members of the community, a form of acknowledgment for their commitment to participate and to foster role models for other contributors (Bartlett 2013; Epstein and Spencer 2013).

Journalists also have clear guidelines for engagement with user contributions, which are publicly available on the website to foster transparency (*Guardian* 2010). They are encouraged to recognize "intelligent contributions" and not to "reward disruptive behaviour with attention." Actively promoting audience input on the topics they are working on is also part of the recommendations.[1] Laura Oliver, community manager at *The Guardian*, perceived the benefits of doing this: "When you prompt someone and say 'we're not just looking for your opinion, we're looking for your knowledge or your expertise or your experience', it can really help give someone the courage to say 'actually I do have a lot to say on this particular subject' " (Bartlett 2013). To reinforce this motivation, the front page of "Comment Is Free" highlights an open thread every day where a journalist is asking for input, and a story that was created thanks to information provided by users.

Discussion Questions

1. How comfortable do you feel with the idea of sharing the moderation of the conversation with the citizens contributing comments?
2. When do you read comment threads posted on news stories? What do you think they contribute to your understanding of a story or issue?

3. Do you contribute comments yourself, and if so, under what circumstances?
4. How would you integrate the interaction with the audience in your daily tasks if you were a reporter producing news stories in the field?

Note

1 In 2013, *The Guardian* also created a stand-alone website for text, video, and photo testimonials from citizens, but with no space for citizen conversations as in the main website: https://witness.theguardian.com/

References

Barnes, Renee. 2013. "Understanding the Affective Investment Produced through Commenting on Australian Alternative Journalism Website New Matilda." *New Media & Society*. doi:10.1177/1461444813511039

Bartlett, Rachel. 2013. "How to: Improve the Online Comment Experience." *Journalism.co.uk*. www.journalism.co.uk/skills/how-to-improve-the-online-comment-experience/s7/a553756/

Benton, Joshua. 2013. "With Gay Marriage Sure to Spark Emotional Responses, The Washington Post and New York Times Try Structuring Comments." *Nieman Journalism Lab*. www.niemanlab.org/2013/06/with-gay-marriage-sure-to-spark-emotional-responses-the-washington-post-and-new-york-times-try-structuring-comments/

Canter, Lily. 2012. "The Misconception of Online Comment Threads." *Journalism Practice*. doi:10.1080/17512786.2012.740172

Carmichael, Matt. 2011. "Stat of the Day: 63% of Readers Don't Care about Your Comments." *Advertising Age*. http://adage.com/article/adagestat/63-readers-care-site-comments/229341/

Domingo, David. 2008. "Interactivity in the Daily Routines of Online Newsrooms: Dealing with an Uncomfortable Myth." *Journal of Computer-Mediated Communication* 133:680–704.

Domingo, David. 2011. "Managing Audience Participation: Practices, Workflows and Strategies." In *Participatory Journalism: Guarding Open Gates at Online Newspapers*, coauthored by Jane B. Singer, Alfred Hermida, David Domingo, Thorsten Quandt, Ari Heinonen, Steve Paulussen, Zvi Reich, and Marina Vujnovic, 76–95. New York: Wiley-Blackwell.

Domingo, David, Thorsten Quandt, Ari Heinonen, Steve Paulussen, Jane B. Singer, and Marina Vujnovic. 2008. "Participatory Journalism Practices in the Media and Beyond: An International Comparative Study of Initiatives in Online Newspapers." *Journalism Practice* 23:326–42.

Epstein, Kayla, and Ruth Spencer. 2013. "Below the Line in 2013: The Year in Comments, Dust-ups and Debates." *The Guardian*. www.theguardian.com/commentisfree/2013/dec/18/below-the-line-2013-year-in-review

Erard, Michael. 2013a. "No Comments." *The New York Times Magazine*. www.nytimes.com/2013/09/22/magazine/no-comments.html

Erard, Michael. 2013b. "Four Ways to Improve the Culture of Commenting." *6th Floor Blog*. http://6thfloor.blogs.nytimes.com/2013/09/23/four-ways-to-improve-the-culture-of-commenting/

Goodman, Emma. 2013. *Online Comment Moderation: Emerging Best Practices*. WAN-IFRA.

Graham, Todd. 2013. "Talking Back, but Is Anyone Listening? Journalism and Comment Fields." In *Rethinking Journalism: Trust and Participation in a Transformed New Landscape*, edited by Chris Peters and Marcel Broersma, 114–28. London: Routledge.

Grotke, Christopher. 2013. "Lessons from a Veteran: What 10 Years of Community Journalism Has Taught iBrattleboro." *Nieman Journalism Lab*. www.niemanlab.org/2013/07/lessons-from-a-veteran-what-10-years-of-community-journalism-has-taught-ibrattleboro/

Guardian. 2009. "Community Standards and Participation Guidelines." Last modified May 7, 2009. www.theguardian.com/community-standards

Guardian. 2010. "Journalist Blogging and Commenting Guidelines: Best Practice for Journalists Blogging and/or Responding to Comments on the Guardian Website." Last modified October 19, 2010. www.theguardian.com/info/2010/oct/19/journalist-blogging-commenting-guidelines

Harrison, Jackie. 2009. "User-generated Content and Gatekeeping at the BBC Hub." *Journalism Studies* 112:243–56.

Heinonen, Ari. 2011. "The Journalist's Relationship with Users: New Dimensions to Conventional Roles." In *Participatory Journalism: Guarding Open Gates at Online Newspapers*, coauthored by Jane B. Singer, Alfred Hermida, David Domingo, Thorsten Quandt, Ari Heinonen, Steve Paulussen, Zvi Reich, and Marina Vujnovic, 34–56. New York: Wiley-Blackwell.

Hermes, Jeff. 2013. "When Comments Turn Ugly: Newspaper Websites and Anonymous Speech." *Digital Media Law Project*. www.dmlp.org/blog/2013/when-comments-turn-ugly-newspaper-websites-and-anonymous-speech

Hermida, Alfred, and Neil Thurman. 2008. "A Clash of Cultures: The Integration of User-generated Content within Professional Journalistic Frameworks at British Newspaper Websites." *Journalism Practice* 23:343–56.

Johnson, Bobbie. 2012. "Why Journalists Love Reddit for Its Brains, not Just Its Beauty." *GigaOm*. http://gigaom.com/2012/09/15/why-journalists-love-reddit-for-its-brains-not-just-its-beauty/

Jönsson, Anna Maria, and Henrik Örnebring. 2010. "User-generated Content and the News: Empowerment of Citizens or Interactive Illusion?" *Journalism Practice* 52:127–44.

Loke, Jaime. 2012. "Old Turf, New Neighbors: Journalists' Perspectives on Their New Shared Space." *Journalism Practice* 62:233–49.

Myers, Kate. 2013. "Your Questions Answered on Our New Commenting System." *Inside NPR.org*. www.npr.org/blogs/inside/2012/09/12/161019838/your-questions-answered-on-our-new-commenting-system

O'Donovan, Caroline. 2013. "Exegesis: How Early Adapters, Innovative Publishers, Legacy Media Companies and More Are Pushing toward the Annotated Web." *Nieman Journalism Lab*. www.niemanlab.org/2013/08/exegesis-how-early-adapters-innovative-publishers-legacy-media-companies-and-more-are-pushing-toward-the-annotated-web/

Pantti, Mervi, and Bakker, Piet. 2009. "Misfortunes, Memories and Sunsets: Non-professional Images in Dutch News Media." *International Journal of Cultural Studies* 125:471–89.

Reich, Zvi. 2011. "User Comments: The Transformation of Participatory Space." In *Participatory Journalism: Guarding Open Gates at Online Newspapers*, coauthored by Jane B. Singer, Alfred Hermida, David Domingo, Thorsten Quandt, Ari Heinonen, Steve Paulussen, Zvi Reich, and Marina Vujnovic, 96–118. New York: Wiley-Blackwell.

Richardson, John E., and James Stanyer. 2011. "Reader Opinion in the Digital Age: Tabloid and Broadsheet Newspaper Websites and the Exercise of Political Voice." *Journalism* 128:983–1003.

Ridderhof, Richard. 2013. "ECHR Holds News Portal Liable for Offensive User Comments in Delfi Case." *Future of Copyright.* www.futureofcopyright.com/home/blog-post/2013/10/15/echr-holds-news-portal-liable-for-offensive-user-comments-in-delfi-case.html

Ruiz, Carlos, David Domingo, Josep Lluís Micó, Javier Diaz-Noci, Koldo Meso, and Pere Masip. 2011. "Public Sphere 2.0? The Democratic Qualities of Citizen Debates in Online Newspapers." *International Journal of Press/Politics* 16:463–87.

Shanahan, Marie. 2013. "More News Organizations Try Civilizing Online Comments with the Help of Social Media." *Poynter.* www.poynter.org/latest-news/top-stories/218284/more-news-organizations-try-civilizing-online-comments-with-the-help-of-social-media/

Singer, Jane B., and Ian Ashman. 2009. " 'Comment Is Free, but Facts Are Sacred': User-generated Content and Ethical Constructs at *The Guardian.*" *Journal of Mass Media Ethics* 241:3–21.

Sonderman, Jeff. 2012. "How The Huffington Post Handles 70+ Million Comments a Year." *Poynter.org.* www.poynter.org/latest-news/top-stories/190492/how-the-huffington-post-handles-70-million-comments-a-year/

Thurman, Neil. 2008. "Forums for Citizen Journalists? Adoption of User-generated Content Initiatives by Online News Media." *New Media & Society* 101:139–57.

Vujnovic, Marina, Jane Singer, Steve Paulussen, Ari Heinonen, Zvi Reich, Thorsten Quandt, Alfred Hermida, and David Domingo. 2010. "Exploring the Political-Economical Factors of Participatory Journalism: A First Look into Self Reports by Online Journalists and Editors in Ten Countries." *Journalism Studies* 43:285–96.

Williams, Andy, Claire Wardle, and Karin Wahl-Jorgensen. 2011. " 'Have They Got News for Us?' Audience Revolution or Business as Usual at the BBC?" *Journalism Practice* 51:85–99.

13

"THESE VIEWS ARE MY OWN"

The Private and Public Self in the Digital Media Sphere

Kelly Fincham

HOFSTRA UNIVERSITY, NEW YORK, USA

> "Journalism has many 'unsend' buttons. Social networks have none."
>
> (Reuters 2013)

The role of the 21st-century journalist is being transformed by the Internet, particularly by social media, in ways that are still being negotiated. As journalism has evolved from a broadcast to a networked conversation (Boyd 2010), journalists are often the first point of "immediate, direct contact" (Sivek 2010) with the "people formerly known as the audience" (Rosen 2006).

This new participatory nature of journalism (Singer et al. 2011) means that journalists are now operating in an ecosystem that would have been unthinkable even five years ago. It is an ecosystem where the audience plays a more significant role in the production and dissemination of information (Anderson, Bell, and Shirky 2012) and the journalist acts more as a "broker" than "controller" of that information (Boyd 2010). While technology has long remade and reshaped the form of journalism (Coll 2010, 29), this is the first time that the role of the individual journalist has been transformed in such a way. Journalists are now also as public as the newsmakers they cover and journalists' personal lives are merging with their professional lives in ways not seen before.

In addition, the changing business model and challenging job market make it increasingly critical that journalists know how to "maintain and market" their social media identity. These social connections "and a body of easily accessible digital work" will help journalists seek work in the future (Sivek 2010).

However, journalists face multiple issues with the uncertain boundaries on social media platforms. And in many cases journalists, and indeed students, are operating in a space with little guidance on the ethical use of social media. As

David Craig explains in his chapter, three important emphases in digital media ethics are duty, virtue, and care. All three have implications for journalists using social media tools, as the discussion in this chapter will note. Yet the absence of commonly accepted ethical guidelines on social media means that many new and student journalists struggle with multiple issues in the workplace. Accordingly, this chapter provides a framework of best ethical practice in social media by drawing on existing best practice guidelines from international news organizations and journalism organizations. The three key questions to be explored are:

1. What factors should we consider in developing our social media identity?
2. Is it ever appropriate for journalists to express views or opinions on politics, current events, or their own personal lives?
3. Under what circumstances, if any, should journalists have separate personal and professional accounts?

There are inherent tensions in including policies from an employer's or corporate perspective (Singer 2012), particularly since these institutional guidelines don't entirely line up with the conventions of the blogging world, where many young journalists work and where more latitude is given to expression of opinion. But this framework offers useful perspectives which can serve as an evolving set of guidelines for new and student journalists internationally as well as exploring the issues and tensions that flow from the merging of professional and personal identities in digital media.

The Social Media Identity

The social media identity (or brand) is the virtual equivalent of the traditional press card. The press card functioned as a way of constructing a journalist's identity even without the official connection with a major brand employer (Knight and Cook 2013, 178). In today's networked world the social media identity does the same thing.

The digital media ethics of duty, virtue, and care must be considered when establishing a social media identity. The journalist must exercise the duty of transparency in disclosing any potential conflicts of interest (while hewing to relevant newsroom policies); exercise virtue as in pursuing a standard of excellence online; and exercise care by being respectful and mindful of the communities he or she engages with and covers on social media. New or student journalists must be mindful of these ethical considerations when building their presence on Facebook and Twitter. (We are discussing the two social media platforms for the purposes of this chapter but acknowledge that they may change over time.)

Good ethical practice has also become increasingly important at a time when a journalist's social media identity is critical to future employment (Glaser 2009).

As Smith says, once that identity or "brand" is defined it will carry over from job to job (Smith 2013). Peter Bale, general manager and vice president of digital at CNN International, says one of the biggest changes in news is the way in which the audience holds individual journalists to a higher ethical standard than the institution they work for. "It's people whom I'm choosing to follow, that I trust, not the platform" (Bartlett 2012).

This focus on the individual rather than the platform means that social media profiles are much more powerful in making—or breaking—a journalist's reputation. Online editor Wells Dunbar at NPR member station KUT in Austin, Texas, says students must pay attention to their ethical reputation on social media. "It is easy to ruin your own reputation and very difficult to repair it" (Dunbar 2013). US social media expert Kim Bui, freelance digital editor and Online News Association board member, agrees. She says journalists need to build their ethical reputation with care. "Don't post anything you wouldn't want your boss, your mom and the president to see," she says. "It's worth it to take a minute to think about how others will view what you post" (Bui 2014).

The informal nature of Twitter is no excuse for poor or questionable ethics. The British broadcast journalist Laura Kuenssberg says it is important not "to say anything that would allow your impartiality to be questioned," and "to not say anything that you wouldn't be happy having on air or in print. That means as ever you need to think about accuracy, impartiality, the law, and the impact of what you say and report" (Kuenssberg 2014). Journalists working as bloggers—and of course those who are opinion writers—may have more latitude to depart from impartiality, but their fairness in everything they communicate is still vital to their reputation.

BBC social media editor Chris Hamilton says journalists must keep ethical norms at the forefront of their social media activity. "Be aware of the need to maintain your credibility, so avoid tweeting or retweeting facts or content—like pictures purportedly from breaking news events—unless they're from trusted sources (that you attribute) or you 'know' them to be true" (Hamilton 2012). Accordingly, new users should familiarize themselves with the platform and observe its norms before participating. Many new users feel pressured to start posting or tweeting immediately but Hamilton says, "First, watch and listen" (Hamilton 2012). Australian journalism academic Julie Posetti says this listening period is essential for respectful engagement with other users (Posetti 2014).

The relevant considerations are not just ethical ones. Many journalists postpone setting up social media accounts because they fear they have nothing to say or that "no one needs to know what I had for breakfast." At the other end of the spectrum, students arrive at college with accounts featuring over 11,000 tweets, the bulk of which are in "what I had for breakfast" mode. However, both parties are missing the point. Social media provide journalists with an invaluable opportunity to develop and maintain their professional reputation. A journalist who is not actively engaged on social media will soon earn reputations as a "curmudgeon, a dinosaur or both" (Buttry 2011). And as Buttry says, while that "curmudgeon" brand may have some value, it is declining.

Journalists are advised to regularly evaluate their social media accounts and to "cull" any existing social content which may raise ethical concerns about sentiments and language (Dunbar 2013). The conventions of any particular platform also create issues for new users. For instance, Posetti cautions users to be very clear about their intentions as a journalist. "Don't assume other users understand and accept that their answers to your questions posed on a social media site are fair game for mainstream media publication. For example, when you're crowdsourcing content from social media sources be clear about your purpose (e.g., 'I'm writing an article about . . .') and indicate your publication intentions" (Posetti 2014).

In practice, Dunbar says an effective social media account should reflect the user's interests, beat, or employer and also parts of the user's personal life. Speaking at a Hofstra seminar in October 2013 funded by the AEJMC/Scripps Howard fellowship, Dunbar advised students and journalists to use what he calls the "rule of threes: One part your topic area, one part links to your work or employer links, and one part you"). Bui reiterates this: "Think about what you're interested in, and then talk to people about it. On Twitter, on Facebook, wherever. Keep doing that. Your brand is what you make of it. Mine is journalism, but has shifted over to mobile as I go into it, and always a little food and fashion. If you meet me, that's pretty much who I am. Your brand has to be true to you" (Bui 2014).

These glimpses of personal lives are essential to human interaction on social media but the big organizations are only slowly coming around to accepting them. For example, Reuters originally specifically advised journalists "not to include irrelevant material about your personal life" (see American Society of News Editors 2011). But its latest guidelines acknowledge that "journalists are people too," and says staff are free to tweet about personal matters such as "a school play, a film or a favorite recipe" (Reuters 2013). The personal touch is essential. "When you tweet be authentic, be human, be yourself. Add value. Talk about what you know and what you're doing. Share pictures, video, interesting links, and uncommon insight from others. Talk to people," says Hamilton. He says this kind of engagement is essential to building a trusted ethical identity. "Debate, but don't argue (unless you have to). Avoid giving offense, and taking it too easily" (Hamilton 2013).

Summary

- Be mindful of what you say.
- Cull potentially problematic content.
- Be clear about your intentions when crowdsourcing information.
- Use the rule of threes: One part topic area, one part work, and one part you.
- Evaluate your output regularly.

Personal Opinions

Journalism schools and newsrooms have long advised journalists to separate their private opinions from their public work. But as the lines between the personal and the professional blur, journalists face multiple ethical issues on social media with particular regard to the duties of truth-telling, fairness, avoiding conflicts of interest (acting independently), and the difficulty in addressing tensions that arise such as between transparency about viewpoints and independence from influence.

As David Craig discusses in his chapter, transparency is an important virtue for journalists working in an open network environment (though Stephen Ward's chapter emphasizes the need to consider it alongside other ethical values). Indeed, several international critics (see Jay Rosen in the US and Julie Posetti in Australia) have urged transparency about viewpoints in place of the traditional objectivity, arguing that this so-called view from nowhere serves no purpose in a networked era (Rosen 2010; Posetti 2012). Posetti has also argued that journalists should integrate community ethics rather than the other way around (Posetti 2014).

However, despite the widening transparency debate and even as social media transforms the gathering and dissemination of news, there are still major issues surrounding the expression of personal opinions on politics and current events because of the journalist's ethical duty of fairness and potential exposure to allegations of bias and prejudice. We may be in the post-industrial age of journalism (Anderson, Bell, and Shirky 2012) but so far there is little change to industrial journalism advice on the expression of personal opinions on social media.

These corporate guidelines are primarily concerned with limiting any potential damage to the brand:

- "Reuters journalists must be mindful of the impact their publicly expressed opinions can have on their work and on Reuters" (Reuters 2013).
- "Imagine what you say or write landing in an AP story or in the *Washington Post*, and imagine the damage that could cause you or NPR" (NPR 2012).
- "AP staffers must be aware that opinions they express may damage the AP's reputation as an unbiased source of news" (AP 2013).

There are some small signs that institutional opposition to transparency about viewpoints is weakening. For example, The AP says it accepts that journalists can have public opinions in less substantial areas like sports and entertainment but not politics or contentious issues (AP 2013). But overall, the guidelines warn new and student journalists to avoid making their opinions public on social media.

For example, the Australian ABC, which is a publicly funded broadcaster, says staffers should assess their own risk based on their position in the news organization. As its guidelines explain: "It would almost certainly be damaging for a political reporter to express a strong personal opinion on a contentious news story that they may ordinarily cover, or for a local radio producer to tweet something derogatory about the local mayor" (ABC 2013).

The NPR guidelines state that it expects the same level of impartiality in personal posts as professional work. "Don't express personal views on a political or other controversial issue that you could not write for the air or post on NPR. org . . . In reality anything you post online reflects both on you and on NPR" (NPR 2012). In Britain, Hamilton agrees. He says journalists should "think carefully before sounding off in a partisan way about an issue, person or company" (Hamilton 2012).

Overall, the consensus advice is that journalists should avoid making their opinions public on their social media posts. There are exceptions for columnists and pundits inside and outside large organizations who have an established brand that is overtly non-neutral and connected with their opinions. Expectations may also differ for newer journalists working as bloggers. But even in these circumstances, it is important to exercise care in any communication of opinion.

The focus so far has been on original social media postings but Twitter retweets and favorites and Facebook sharing and liking also offer cause for concern. Facebook is particularly problematic for two reasons. First, your "friends" might pass on comments that you make through their networks, so even material that you post for your own inner sanctum could easily reach a wider audience without your permission. Second, comments made in the feeds of organizations are open to everyone. Speaking in 2012, Liz Heron, then the emerging media editor at *The Wall Street Journal* said WSJ journalists were encouraged to keep it professional on all social media, even on accounts they might consider personal. "Confusing privacy settings and years of collecting Facebook friends may mean that your status updates have a wider reach than you realize" (Heron 2012).

There are other ethical concerns to consider. For example, it is now possible to track how often users share "certain kinds of views or information" on social media. So if a journalist consistently liked, shared, or retweeted material "with particular perspectives on a contentious issue, it may begin to suggest a partisan approach and compromise your credibility" (ABC 2013).

There are also legal ramifications. RTDNA, a US-based organization of broadcast and digital managers, warns that some comments could be used as part of a court action to "demonstrate a predisposition or even malicious intent in a libel action against the news organization, even for an unrelated story" (RTDNA 2013). And Reuters cautions that "everything we say can be used against us in a court of law, in the minds of subjects and sources and by people who for reasons of their own may want to cast us in a negative light" (Reuters 2013).

This also points to the need for individuals to actively monitor their social media output to ensure they are not open to those allegations of bias. In the classroom we use an exercise where students download their Twitter archive as an Excel spreadsheet and analyze it using Excel, Wordle, or ManyEyes. This exercise is often enough to help students understand the overall picture of their behavior online. In addition we use RebelMouse so students can explore ways to visualize their Facebook and Twitter social footprint.

Retweets or links can often be seen as a sympathetic recommendation despite the "retweets are not endorsements" disclaimer (AP 2013). In fact, The AP dedicates a complete section to this issue saying that the disclaimer does not do enough to protect the journalist from the appearance of bias. "Many people who see your tweets and retweets will never look at your Twitter bio (and thus the disclaimer)" (AP 2013). It recommends that reporters always add additional information to retweets, in addition to using the disclaimer, to avoid the "unadorned" retweet being seen as tacit approval. It offers some examples of problematic unadorned tweets and how to fix them.

Problematic Unadorned Tweets

1. RT @jonescampaign: Smith's policies would destroy our schools.
2. RT @dailyeuropean: At last, a euro plan that works

Better Tweets

1. Jones campaign now denouncing Smith on education. RT @jonescampaign: Smith's policies would destroy our schools.
2. Big European paper praises euro plan. RT @dailyeuropean: At last, a euro plan that works.

The extra information makes it clear that the reporter is "simply reporting" the story rather than implying any support for the content—"much as we would quote it in a story" (AP 2013). This type of tweet editing, particularly with the character constraint, clearly adds to the stress of "thinking-writing-posting in real time" (Reuters 2013), but is good practice.

Overall, the guidelines do suggest that news organizations increasingly recognize that journalists are never off the clock and that the ethics codes surrounding the public expression of personal opinions may need to change. As the Reuters policy puts it: "The issues around what we can and cannot say there are a subject of constant conversation among us, so as this is not our first word on the subject, it will not be the last."

But for the moment, journalists are advised to tread very carefully.

Summary

- Avoid posting, liking, sharing, or retweeting comments which may appear to endorse a contentious issue or topic.
- Add extra information to retweets.

- Use disclaimers in your bio.
- Monitor your social media output.
- Analyze your output using spreadsheets or visualization tools.

Personal and Public Accounts

The preceding discussion strongly suggests that there is no expectation of privacy for journalists when it comes to their identity on social media. This creates ethical tensions for journalists who want to express personal opinions and be more transparent on social media. Consequently, students and some longtime journalists instinctively lean towards creating separate accounts on social media: one for personal opinions, the other for public work.

However, given the ethics of care and the journalist's duty to the wider, networked community, it is ethically questionable for journalists to misrepresent themselves on social media by using separate, private, or anonymous accounts. Posetti, a proponent of greater transparency of viewpoints for journalists, says separate accounts are inadvisable. "It's impossible to sustain such a separation," she says. "Assume, even when operating a pseudonymous account, that you will be discovered as a journalist" (Posetti 2014).

For the most part, there is a consensus among the organizations, practitioners, and academics that social media "is about genuine engagement" (ABC, 2013) and that journalists should maintain an account that reflects their identity in and out of work. And all the guidelines now strongly advise against separate accounts. This is a fundamental change from the early days of social media. For example, the Australian ABC previously required all staff to feature references to the ABC in their account names but now describes this practice as part of "the earlier years of social media's evolution." ABC says the former practice also became confusing for viewers as it is "fundamentally important to the people who use social media to know when they are viewing an official ABC account or not" (ABC 2013).

Reuters has also retreated from its 2008 position when it recommended that journalists "set up separate profiles for professional and private activity" (see American Society of News Editors 2011). Now it advises staffers to use a single account, identify themselves as Reuters journalists, and say "we speak for ourselves, not for Thomson Reuters."

Across the board, journalists are advised to have "one account per network that you use both personally and professionally" (AP 2013). All the organizations surveyed require that journalists identify themselves as working for the organization in their bio but to refrain from using logos in the profile picture or the organization name in the user name.

Given this emphasis on the hybrid account, users should also regularly check their online friends and followers to protect against accusations of bias. For example, imagine the questions you might face in the newsroom if a Facebook friend ran for political office (RTDNA 2013). All the guidelines advise that journalists follow, friend, or subscribe to advocates and organizations on all sides of a political or contentious issue to avoid real or apparent conflicts. Both Facebook and Twitter offer Lists functions to help accomplish this, and users are accordingly advised to make sure "you're not following all Conservatives for example" (Hamilton 2012). These lists are the 21st-century equivalent of the mailing list but again, the information is public, and therefore needs to be balanced (NPR 2012). Users are also advised to be very careful about membership of social media groups because even "simple participation in some online groups could be seen to indicate that you endorse their views" (NPR 2012).

Be wary, too, of account features that might appear to keep your views away from the public gaze. Twitter, for instance, offers users a private "locked" account but this is no guarantee of privacy. Then *Washington Post* editor Raju Narisetti discovered this when tweets from his protected Twitter account were screen grabbed and widely shared after he made mildly controversial comments in 2009 about the health care bill and the failing health of Senator Robert Byrd (Alexander 2009). *The Washington Post* drew up its social media policy in response to the Narisetti affair and now warns staffers that any "comment or link we share should be considered public information, regardless of privacy settings." In a similar vein the NPR guidelines state: "Nothing on the web is truly private" (NPR 2012), and the CAJ warns that the public will connect a reporter's online identities, "no matter how hard that person might try to keep them separate" (Canadian Association of Journalists 2011).

Anonymous blogging or commenting also compromises the journalist's duty and care for the community. And, as the NPR points out, information gleaned via an account that does not mention the journalist's affiliation could not ethically be used in any subsequent reporting (NPR 2012). Posetti says this should be standard practice for all journalists. "Never quote content you've sourced via an account that doesn't indicate you're a journalist—Ethics 101" (Posetti 2014).

Summary

- Do not keep separate, private, or anonymous accounts.
- Identify yourself as an employee in your bio but don't use the organization's name as your account name or logos in your profile picture.
- Inspect friends and followers regularly to avoid real or apparent conflict.
- Follow "equal" lists of politicians, advocates, and so on.
- Regularly evaluate membership of online groups.

Best Practices in Action: Lauren McCullough on Twitter

I often recommend Hofstra grad (BA Journalism, 2004) Lauren McCullough to students looking for a good role model on Twitter. McCullough is editor of Paper at Facebook, former deputy managing editor of the NBC-owned start-up Breaking News.com and former social media manager at The AP where she trained employees how to use social media.

McCullough, who joined Twitter in February 2008, uses the same name (@lfmccullough) across every social media platform. She mentions her employer in her bio but her account name is her own. "When we trained the journalists at AP we nudged them away from using AP in their Twitter names" (McCullough 2014). She says she realized early on how important it would be to have a consistent personal brand on social media.

Her bio, like her Twitter feed, offers a glimpse of the professional and personal aspects that make up her life. "Editor, Paper at Facebook. Formerly with @breakingnews, @AP, Mom to Amelia, +1 to @Matt_Silverman. Perpetually maxing out the DVR with trashy TV." Her feed includes links to stories related to the larger industry, links to stories about social media, journalism, mobile technology, and "fun stuff." She says it's important for journalists to maintain a consistent point of view or perspective so the content you share is personally relevant to you or something that you are working on.

McCullough has averaged about six tweets per day to her more than 6,000 followers and beyond. Her tweets are a mixture of professional and personal, which is a key reason why I frequently recommend her Twitter feed.

"I definitely realized early on that the people I most enjoyed following and interacting with were people who were real and not a glorified RSS feed or people who would only chime in when they wanted links to stories they were working on or sources for stories," she says. "I am sensitive to the overshare element and I try to limit the general griping and then the things I tweet about are things that are funny and give people a better idea of who I am and what I am interested in."

McCullough, whose daughter Amelia was born in 2013, says it's important to keep a sense of perspective on Twitter. "I made a choice early on that I would not try to keep up with the people who tweet through the weekend and through the off-hours. It's just not realistic for my lifestyle to try and keep up." McCullough says Twitter is a must-be-on platform for journalists and that new journalists are uniquely positioned to benefit from the way that social media has transformed journalism. "Most employers are going to look to recent college graduates and assume that they understand the technology," she says, adding that: "There are many more opportunities for new journalists, but there is also a lot of risk."

For McCullough, the best way to prepare for those opportunities and manage risk is to actively participate. "See how other organizations and journalists use Twitter and learn from them. It is never too late to jump in and start following news organizations and public figures and journalists related to the areas you are interested in." She advises students to keep their accounts focused on the areas they want to work in. "She said that when hiring at Breaking News, they would look at applicants' Twitter accounts "because Twitter is such a big part of what Breaking News is focused on." Knowing that candidates would need to monitor social media and news in real time, it was important to know they could use Twitter well.

McCullough emphasizes that journalists should use only one account per platform. "You should focus on building a following and cultivating an audience," she says. "I have never liked the idea of separate accounts. You are one person and you as a person are multifaceted—you have other sides—you could be a mother, a father, you could be interested in bowling or gardening and all these interests provide different entry points for people to come into your account. They might come in with the gardening and then they can see other content that you are sharing."

Discussion Questions

1. Explore McCullough's Twitter account and compare it to your own. What similarities or differences can you see?
2. Compare your Twitter accounts with your classmates'. Will they help you as a potential candidate with prospective employers?
3. Find your favorite journalist on Facebook. Explore that person's account and take note of the people and lists that he or she follows. Can you detect any appearance of bias?
4. You're applying for a job with a news organization and you want to make sure your social media output is unbiased. What should you do to best achieve this?
5. Evaluate the following tweets and discuss how they can best be retweeted using the guidelines. Consider wording, tone, and character constraints.
    *   RT @dailybugle: Global warming farce as scientists stuck in ice
    *   RT @jonescampaign: Smith policies will destroy our health service
    *   RT @primeminster: No handouts for asylum seekers

References

ABC. 2013. "Social Media Policy." ABC. Accessed October 15, 2013. http://about.abc.net.au/wp-content/uploads/2013/10/PersonalUseOfSocialMediaINS1.pdf

Alexander, Andrew. 2009. "Post Editor Ends Tweets as New Guidelines Are Issued." *The Washington Post.* Accessed October 15, 2013. http://voices.washingtonpost.com/ombudsmanblog/2009/09/post_editor_ends_tweets_as_new.html

American Society of News Editors (ASNE). 2011. "10 Best Practices for Social Media." Accessed January 1, 2014. http://asne.org/Files/pdf/10_Best_Practices_for_Social_Media.pdf

Anderson, C.W., Emily Bell, and Clay Shirky. 2012. "Post-Industrial Journalism: Adapting to the Present." *Tow Center Report.* Accessed October 16, 2013. http://towcenter.org/research/post-industrial-journalism/

Associated Press (AP). 2013. "Social Media Policy." Accessed October 12, 2013. www. ap.org/Images/Social-Media-Guidelines_tcm28–9832.pdf

Bartlett, Rachel. 2012. "5 Tips for New Journalists in Digital Journalism." *Journalism. co.uk* blog. Accessed January 6, 2104. www.journalism.co.uk/news/5-tips-for-new-journalists-in-digital-journalism-world/s2/a555239/

Boyd, Danah. 2010. "Streams of Content, Limited Attention: The Flow of Information through Social Media." *Educause Online.* Accessed October 7, 2013. www.educause.edu/ero/article/streams-content-limited-attention-flow-information-through-social-media

Bui, Kim. 2014. "Interview by author." Email, January 6, 2014.

Buttry, Steve. 2011. Confessions (strategies) of a branded journalist . . . *The Buttry Diary* Blog. Accessed October 27, 2013. http://stevebuttry.wordpress.com/2011/06/28/confessions-strategies-of-a-branded-journalist-or-a-journalist-with-a-reputation-if-you-prefer/

Canadian Association of Journalists (CAJ). 2011. "Social Media Policy." CAJ. Accessed October 16, 2013. www.caj.ca/?p=1347

Coll, Steve. 2010. "A Media Policy for the Digital Age: An Open Letter to the FCC." *Columbia Journalism Review* (November/ December).

Dunbar, Wells. 2013. "Interview by author." In person, New York City, October 21, 2013.

Glaser, Mark. 2009. "Personal Branding Becomes a Necessity in Digital Age." *MediaShift.* Accessed October 18, 2013. www.pbs.org/mediashift/2009/07/personal-branding-becomes-a-necessity-in-digital-age197/

Hamilton, Chris. 2012/2013. "Interview by author." Phone, May 12, 2012; email, November 20, 2013.

Heron, Liz. 2012. "Interview by author." Email, May 12, 2012.

Knight, Meghan, and Clare Cook. 2013. *Social Media for Journalists: Principles and Practice.* London: Sage.

Kuenssberg, Laura. 2014. "Interview by author." Email, January 7, 2014.

McCullough, Lauren. 2014. "Interview by author." February 18, 2014.

NPR. 2012. "Ethics Handbook/Social Media." NPR. Accessed October 17, 2013. http://ethics.npr.org/tag/social-media/

Posetti, Julie. 2012. "Journalists, Twitter Gaffes and Freedom of Expression." *MediaShift.* Accessed October 12, 2013. www.pbs.org/mediashift/2012/11/journalists-twitter-gaffes-and-freedom-of-expression-310/

Posetti, Julie. 2014. "Interview by author." Twitter, January 8, 2014.

Reuters. 2013. "Reporting from the Internet and Using Social Media." Reuters. Accessed October 17, 2013. http://handbook.reuters.com/?title = Reporting_From_the_Internet_And_Using_Social_Media

Rosen, Jay. 2006. "The People Formerly Known as the Audience." *Pressthink* blog. Accessed October 18, 2013. http://archive.pressthink.org/2006/06/27/ppl_frmr.html

Rosen, Jay. 2010. "The View from Nowhere." *Pressthink* blog. Accessed November 9, 2013. http://pressthink.org/2010/11/the-view-from-nowhere-questions-and-answers/

RTDNA. 2013. "Social Media & Blogging Guidelines." RTDNA. Accessed October 12, 2013. www.rtdna.org/article/social_media_blogging_guidelines#.U6xYFI1dVsA

Singer, Jane. 2012. "The Ethics of Social Journalism." *Australian Journalism Review* 34(1):3–16.

Singer, Jane B., Alfred Hermida, David Domingo, Ari Heinonen, Steve Paulussen, Thorsten Quandt, Zvi Reich, and Marina Mujnovic. 2011. *Participatory Journalism, Guarding Open Gates at Online Newspapers.* Sussex, UK: Blackwell.

Sivek, S.C. 2010. "Social Media under Social Control: Regulating Social Media and the Future of Socialization." *Electronic News* 4(3):146–64.

Smith, Jennifer. 2013. "For Journalists, There's No Cookie Cutter Strategy When It Comes to Social Media." *Society of American Business Editors and Writers* blog. Accessed October 15, 2013. http://sabew.org/2013/04/for-journalists-theres-no-cookie-cutter-strategy-when-it-comes-to-social-media/

14

MULTIMEDIA JOURNALISM

Mindy McAdams

UNIVERSITY OF FLORIDA, USA

In the context of journalism, the word *multimedia* means different things to different people. Some journalists have declared the word to be past its usefulness, and yet it persists in both job advertisements and in the navigation links of major news websites, such as *The New York Times*. When different media types—such as video, text, and animated graphics—are integrated to tell a story, journalists call that a multimedia package or a multimedia feature. Some multimedia stories invite interaction with the user (who might also be called the viewer, or the reader), and others offer a mostly passive experience. Many multimedia packages provide options for navigating the story. Often they are nonlinear, unlike a print or broadcast piece. Any two users might take two entirely different pathways through the story, which raises questions about what information and context users will come away with. Yet events and situations in real life are viewed differently by the different people involved in them, and multimedia storytelling offers journalists an opportunity to show various facets of a story in parallel, rather than starting with one view and then stepping through others sequentially.

After a brief discussion of the definition of multimedia, this chapter explores emerging best practices related to several dimensions of multimedia storytelling: interactivity, simulations and animation, transmedia storytelling, completeness, and navigation. Best practices advice is summarized at the end of each section. The discussion also considers ethical implications, particularly how multimedia storytelling can contribute to telling truth in journalism, and some ethical challenges this kind of storytelling presents. The chapter concludes with two case studies to further explore what best practices look like.

Multimedia Is Dead. Multimedia Lives!

The lack of consensus about the meaning and use of the term *multimedia* makes it a challenging concept to discuss. "One of the most pressing needs mentioned by journalists in various countries was the acquisition of new multimedia skills," according to findings from a recent study that surveyed more than 29,000 journalists around the world (Willnat, Weaver, and Choi 2013, 179).

The multimedia skills listed in a job advertisement might span a range of specialties from web developer to videographer. Some ads specify "proficiency in multimedia" with no further explanation. A 2013 ad seeking a multimedia producer was more precise: "Your core duties will involve a variety of multimedia— audio, video, photos, informational graphics, and motion graphics—to support our core news content."

Despite the continuing use of *multimedia*, not every journalist thinks the term should be used anymore. Eric Maierson, a producer at MediaStorm since 2006, hates the word *multimedia* (Maierson 2013a). There is some irony in that, because until recently, MediaStorm called itself a "multimedia production studio." However, Maierson explained: "I believe 'multimedia' is the word we've come to use when describing photographers who make documentaries." Nowadays MediaStorm calls itself a "film production and interactive design studio" and produces mostly video documentaries (MediaStorm, n.d.).

Like Maierson, Robyn Tomlin said she would not use the word *multimedia* anymore. Tomlin is editor of Thunderdome, a division of Digital First Media, a New York–based company that owns 57 daily newspapers and many other media concerns. Thunderdome is the company's hub for digital content distribution, production, and training. Instead of multimedia, she said, "I would say *video* and *interactives*." She characterized "interactives" as data reporting, database applications, and other news apps "that help the reader understand the story you're trying to tell" (Tomlin 2013).

While there's no consensus about what the term *multimedia* means, or even whether to use it, it's clear that producing multimedia content is as much about mindset as skills. In multimedia storytelling, various media types are employed and interconnected, and, ideally, each one is used in a way that makes the most of its strengths. The components of the story are crafted to complement one another. Redundancy often detracts from the experience—that is, if aspects of the story are told in video and repeated in the text, users might lose interest quickly. When planning stories, journalists must decide what really *needs* to be included, and what can be cut out. Adding too many parts and pieces can make a story overly complicated.

Multimedia storytelling continues to evolve as more journalists experiment with the possibilities opened up by new digital tools and techniques. One recent high-end project that has stimulated discussion about the possibilities of multimedia is a *New York Times* digital story from 2012, "Snow Fall" (Branch 2012). This ambitious and much-praised project combined video, animated graphics, maps, audio, and photo slideshows with a 17,000-word text story divided into six parts. It employed kinetic web coding techniques—often lumped together under the term *parallax scrolling*—that emerged in 2012 (Duenes et al. 2013; McAdams 2013). Although it was not the first journalism story to employ those techniques, "Snow Fall" was seen by many as a kind of watershed in multimedia and online storytelling, and the fact that it attracted almost 3 million site visits in its first 10 days makes it an important reference point (Romenesko 2012). The project has also advanced the discussion of what best practices look like in multimedia (see, for example, Williams 2014).

The ongoing evolution of multimedia storytelling on digital journalism platforms makes it an important area to examine from the standpoint of ethics and best practices.

Interactivity

Widely seen as a defining characteristic of multimedia, interactivity can be a huge component of a story's presentation, sometimes to the point of distraction. Journalists face many decisions when they make a story interactive. They decide what the users can click or slide or change. They decide what will happen—and what will not happen—in response to each action from the user. Computer code such as JavaScript is used to turn these decisions into an app or an "interactive."

Once the code has been written, a user's options are set, like doors and hallways and stairs in a building made of concrete and steel. The user can follow more than one route, but usually there is no option to smash through a wall where no door exists. Options cannot be infinite, so the journalists must make choices. Those choices limit what a user can do.

The availability of large datasets and a growing role for programmer-journalists in newsrooms (see Stray 2011) are enhancing the possibilities of interactivity. In a 2012 data visualization, *The New York Times* represented the votes of all 50 US states in 16 presidential elections (1952–2012) on a single Web page (Bostock and Carter 2012). Using a JavaScript library called D3, data journalists enabled users to view how each state's majority had shifted between the Democratic and Republican political parties over the full 60-year span. Hovering over one state in any election year revealed that state's data. In addition to viewing one state's path across the years, users also had the option of viewing a few combinations that were selected by the journalists (all Southern states; New Jersey and California). However, users did not have the ability to view and compare two or more states of their own choice.

This example shows the two sides of the coin: (1) Because the graphic is interactive, users have access to a great quantity of information that would be overwhelming and unwieldy in traditional text, list, or chart formats; (2) Because the code limits what the users can do with the data contained in the graphic, users are not free to make every possible comparison they might like to see. In ethical terms, interactivity enhances the ability for users to seek truth and understand information, but there are still limits to which truths they can learn.

Not all multimedia packages include interactivity. If a user has no choices apart from clicking *play*, *pause*, or *stop*, that story is not interactive.

There are different views of the meaning of *interactivity*. Researcher Jennifer Stromer-Galley (2004) identified two types: social interaction between people (e.g., in online discussion forums) and interaction between people and computers (e.g., clicking and hovering on a map to see additional information). Stromer-Galley called the second type "interactivity-as-product" and specified "multimedia, click polls, hyperlinks, feedback forms" as examples of interactive "features" we use online. When discussing the presence of interactivity in multimedia journalism, in most cases only the second type is relevant.

How do journalists decide a story needs or deserves interactivity? They must not only manage the limited resources of the newsroom, but also consider whether users will get real benefits from interactive options. Researchers have found "a lack of expectation or perhaps even understanding regarding use of a variety of interactive features on online newspaper sites" (Chung and Yoo 2008, 393).

Brian Storm has been making multimedia since 1994, when interactive computer games were produced on CD-ROM. His team produced more than 2,000 web interactives at MSNBC.com, where he was director of multimedia (1995–2002). When asked about the role of interactivity in multimedia storytelling, he said, "Fundamentally, right now, people don't use it. They don't know what it is. They don't know *how* to use it" (Storm 2013). At MSNBC.com, Storm and his team used software to track and analyze every click and other actions people performed while they viewed an interactive. In spite of the time spent (which exceeded the time individuals spent on other stories, including stand-alone videos), "most people were just watching stuff," he said. "Most people just push *play*."

Why might audiences largely ignore interactive options in journalism content? After surveying users of a newspaper website to find out how and why they used interactive options, researcher Deborah S. Chung concluded that people who feel confidence in their online skills were more likely to use interactive features, and "if news organizations are truly interested in providing their audiences with various story telling options through multimedia, perhaps it is necessary for [them] to educate their audiences" (Chung 2008, 673). Similar results came from a recent study of college students in Belgium: students with a higher level of online skills were more likely to use interactive features on news media websites (Opgenhaffen and d'Haenens 2012).

Researcher Pablo J. Boczkowski found that newsroom decisions regarding the use of multimedia and interactivity "were inextricably tied to editorial issues such as who gets to tell the stories, how they are told, and to what public they are addressed" (2004, 209). In particular, the way the journalists *thought about the audience* affected their decisions about the kinds of options they made available to users. If they considered users to be technically limited, then the journalists did not produce a significant amount of multimedia content.

In a comprehensive overview of how journalists can use interactive games to engage and inform audiences, Sisi Wei, a news applications developer at ProPublica, noted that a well-designed video game *guides* a player to "learn the intricacies of complex subjects and systems" (Wei 2013). When a person feels interested in a game, she puts time into it. She learns how it works, how to maneuver, how to get what she wants from it. A player believes that the reward (enjoying the game, possibly winning, getting the highest score) will be worth the effort of learning. Many video games have a high level of complexity, yet plenty of people buy them and play them.

Interactivity puts control into the hands of the users. They can explore different options and combinations, which can provide a deeper and more thorough understanding of a story and advance the ethical goal of truth telling. This desirable result, however, depends on people actually making use of the interactive features that are provided. Simply making interactivity *available* is not sufficient. Users need to expect a reward, a fair return on their investment of time, effort, and attention. They must see a clear reason to click, slide, zoom, enter data, and so on.

Best Practices

The decision to use interactivity in storytelling must come because the interactive elements make the story more interesting or easier to understand, or they enable the journalists to include more information without overwhelming the users. Options for interactivity need to be obvious, enticing, and not hard to use. Taking a cue from video games, journalists must guide the user into an experience that quickly feels rewarding and satisfying.

Simulations and Animation

Maps have been used to illustrate news events for more than 200 years. Pop-up information adds a bit of interactivity to digital maps, such as one created by *The Boston Globe* to show the location of bomb blasts at the Boston Marathon on April 15, 2013 (Florit, Chang, and Esteban 2013). The exact location of each event must be verified before the point can be added to the map.

What about an animated path on a map? Adding motion to any graphic requires higher levels of fact checking to ensure accuracy and meet the ethical obligation to report the truth. In *The Denver Post* multimedia package "Chasing the Beast," about how three experienced storm chasers died when a tornado struck their car in Oklahoma, we see the path of the tornado's center and, separately, the path of the three men's car, with each path progressing forward until the two collide (Simpson 2013). A digital clock shows speeded-up time from 6:04 to 6:42 p.m. to provide context as the animation plays.

Adding animation requires more data, said information graphics journalist Rafael Höhr Zamora (McAdams 2005, 353). He gave the example of an animated map showing a police car chase through the streets of Madrid. Members of the public pointed out that the cars' direction was wrong in one part of the animation, because there was no way to enter a particular street as shown on the map.

If a thin moving line on a map can be in error, how much more can go wrong if journalists re-create an event with 3D computer graphics?

The Taiwan firm Next Media Animation brought this question into sharp focus in 2011 when it released a computer-generated re-enactment of the killing of Osama Bin Laden during a US military operation in Pakistan. In response to criticism of the video's poor taste as well as its questionable accuracy, NMA took down the video, including copies. Similar concerns were raised about a 2009 NMA video that showed a computer-generated confrontation between professional golfer Tiger Woods and his wife (Cohen 2009).

Video provides other opportunities for simulating real events. When Digital First Media set out to make a video that shows US Civil War re-enactors as they commemorated the 150th anniversary of the pivotal Battle of Gettysburg (Digital First Video 2013), the journalists expressed some reservations about their plan, according to Robyn Tomlin.

"In this case we really produced it. We had a story we wanted to tell before we went out. Instead of just watching them [the re-enactors], we asked them to perform certain maneuvers," Tomlin said. Some journalists asked whether this was "really journalism." They asked: "Do we need different rules for this?" Tomlin noted that on TV, re-creations or "directed documentaries" have existed for some time, but the experience is new for digital journalists.

"Then the question becomes: 'Do we need to explain to users how we put this together?' Maybe we do," Tomlin said (Tomlin 2013).

Audiences sometimes confuse reality and simulation. Documentary filmmaker Errol Morris addressed this in discussing his 1988 film, *The Thin Blue Line*, about the killing of a police officer on a lonely Texas road in 1976. He began his essay with a recollection about a reporter who asked Morris how he came to be on that road at just the right time to film the crime:

> It never occurred to me that someone might think that the re-enactments were not re-enactments at all, but honest-to-God *vérité* footage shot while the crime was happening. It's crazy for someone to think I had just happened to be out on that roadway, that night, with a 35-millimeter film crew and many, many cameras—cameras taking multiple angles, high angles from

overhead, low angles at tire-level looking under the car, even angles inside the suspect vehicle.

(Morris 2008)

Of course, Morris was *not* on that road in 1976. No cameras recorded the crime. The scene in his film is completely a re-enactment, based on research.

Best Practices

When adding animation to a depiction of a real-life event, using 3D models, or scripting and directing action in video or photography, journalists cannot take it for granted that audiences will understand how that simulation was produced. Journalists can certainly use these techniques to make a story clearer, but they should explicitly state how accuracy was ensured and whether any part of the simulation is, essentially, no more than an educated guess. Any re-enactment should be labeled as such. This can be done in the credits or separately in a "how we made this" section. This clarity of communication is important to carrying out the ethical duties of truth telling and transparency.

Transmedia Storytelling

A further aspect of multimedia journalism involves telling the story on different platforms. Just as different media types have different strengths and weaknesses, different media platforms have different capabilities. Researcher Mark Deuze described this as "the integrated (although not necessarily simultaneous) presentation of a news story package through different media, such as (but not limited to) a website, a Usenet newsgroup, e-mail, SMS, MMS, radio, television . . . newspapers and magazines . . ." (Deuze 2004, 140).

A remarkable example of a multiple-platform approach came from the National Geographic Society in August 2013, when video, photographs, and audio gathered in Tanzania over 18 months were used to produce "The Serengeti Lion" on the website of the society's magazine (Nichols and Williamson 2013). The multimedia package online includes a generous amount of full-screen video, much of it shot at very close range among the wild lions with robotic cameras (Ahearn 2013). The interface immerses the viewer in 24 chapters, each accompanied by a lush natural soundtrack. Understandably, the parallel feature in the printed magazine, "The Short Happy Life of a Serengeti Lion," differs immensely from the online package.

One might assume that the magazine's iPad app would be very similar to the web version. It is not. Comparatively little of the video exists in the app version of "The Short Happy Life of a Serengeti Lion." The app version includes two different animated maps, one with a voiceover narration, which do not appear on the website. It also includes all the text from the printed magazine, and additional photographs. Essentially, it is an enhanced version of the printed story and does not resemble the web package.

Presentation of the same story on more than one platform (television, radio, print, web) has been called multiplatform and "cross-media" (Erdal 2011; Veglis 2012) storytelling. Media scholar Henry Jenkins uses the phrase "transmedia storytelling," giving the example of *The Matrix*, a 1999 film with two sequels. The transmedia idea goes further than simply adapting the story for different platforms. *The Matrix* filmmakers collaborated with comic-book artists and writers, as well as producers of anime and video games, to *expand* the story beyond what was told in the three movies (Jenkins 2006). The comic books, games, and anime did more than retell the same story—they added new characters and subplots that never appeared in the films.

If we compare "The Serengeti Lion" and the two versions of "The Short Happy Life of a Serengeti Lion" (print and app), we find that none of the three is an abbreviated or inferior version of the story. Anyone who seeks out all three will have an expanded experience of the story.

Best Practices

Transmedia storytelling is an option for stories that have a sufficiently broad scope to justify expansions on different platforms. If a multimedia journalism project includes video, text, and interactive apps, journalists should be thinking about how to extend and expand that story on other platforms. Videos can be broken out and published on YouTube and Vimeo. An e-book can be produced for downloading and offline reading. It might be appropriate to create an app for mobile users. Transmedia does not necessarily require a big budget, but it does require a big story that will not be forgotten or irrelevant in a matter of weeks. Expanding the story can include involving readers and viewers after the initial publication. Transmedia storytelling provides a unique way to enhance the truth-telling capability of multimedia.

Completeness

Although not every story justifies transmedia treatment, it's important to consider the issue of completeness in deciding how to tell both large and small stories with multimedia. When making an online photo gallery about a single event, Tom Kennedy said he always tried to represent a full experience. "I wanted to have [a photo that served as] a scene setter, [and] some experiential moments, show some sense of reactions of the people in the event, and also the people who are observing the event," he said (Kennedy 2013). Questions often arose for him in the process of constructing a gallery. "This is an interpretation of a reality that has happened, and it's one way of experiencing that, but it's not the only way," he said. (Kennedy was managing editor for multimedia at *The Washington Post* from 1998 to 2009.)

Researcher Susan Jacobson found that many multimedia stories published by *The New York Times* from 2000 through 2008, particularly audio slideshows and videos, had a first-person point of view. She noted that those stories "represent a kind of reporting much different from what might appear in the newspaper. . . . The power of these perspectives rendered in multimedia is unmistakable" (Jacobson 2012, 877).

A visual story (video, photo narrative, audio slideshow) works well with a narrow focus: one issue, one character, or one location. The shorter the story, the more important this is, so it's not surprising that a tendency toward one-sidedness, or one viewpoint, can often be observed (see Maierson 2013b). Trying to jam too many viewpoints or ideas into a 2-minute video often makes it fail as a story (Kobré 2008). A first-person viewpoint takes the audience inside the story or behind the scenes, and it fits comfortably with a photojournalist's ethos of letting the picture speak for itself—subjects in the story do the talking, without a reporter's voiceover.

The fact that some multimedia elements work best with a narrower focus doesn't let journalists off the hook for telling complete stories. In a package about a broader topic, journalists must ensure that diverse perspectives are included, even though individual parts (such as a single video) may be one-sided. Other elements of a package, such as text or charts, can help to fill in any gaps. The multimedia journalist's job is to choose which elements work best to tell particular aspects of a story. But at the same time, producing a multimedia story doesn't require being comprehensive in every case. There is a place for stories that delve deeply into the life of one person or one aspect of a topic.

Best Practices

Because a multimedia story *package* can include numerous pieces, parts, or chapters, it can cover many different aspects of a story. Given enough time and resources, it is possible to make a multimedia package almost encyclopedic—which could be detrimental, if people feel daunted by the amount of time it would take them to explore. Each piece can be given a clear label to indicate which (or whose) perspective or topic dominates it. The audience should see obvious indicators that multiple viewpoints exist. This clarity helps to meet ethical obligations to be fair and truthfully represent a range of views. Tom Kennedy's approach to creating a photo gallery about an event serves as an example. One piece of the story is one interpretation, and multiple interpretations are possible. This requires the journalist to step back and, to some extent, let the audience draw its own conclusions.

Navigation

Choosing the pieces to include in a multimedia story is a vital part of the journalistic process. But it's also important to consider how the pieces connect and how users will find their way. Assembling a great collection of pieces will be for nothing if poor navigation prevents users from moving easily through the package. Part of best practices is ensuring that users can access all the parts of the story without feeling overwhelmed or lost. If an entry page provides too many options, people have a tendency to bookmark the story and never come back: "Too long; didn't read." People might also initially land deep inside a package, thanks to a link from social media. Then they need to be able to find their way out to the other sections. It is the nature of nonlinear narratives to allow different users to have very different experiences of the same story.

Creators of multimedia stories must consider how users will navigate and experience a story that consists of "small pieces loosely joined" (Weinberger 2002). Whether users are crossing between media platforms or exploring a digital story with linked modules, they face a range of choices about what to look at, what to ignore, and the order in which to proceed. When visitors to a news website watch a video or view an interactive graphic, do they always click the link to the corollary text article? If they watch the video and never read the text, will they take away a skewed perception of the story? In an interactive graphic, what will users choose to view and what will they miss seeing? In ethical terms, the truth that users take away (specific facts, context, breadth and depth of understanding) will depend on which pieces of a multimedia presentation they spend time with. What they take away may also be shaped by the sequence in which they navigate the elements within a package.

Journalists must take into account not only how the pieces of a multimedia story are connected but also how permanent the connections might be. The word *package* implies that all the parts of the story are bundled together, but the bundle can be broken apart and might not even appear *as a package* to the audience. In some cases, the related parts of a story will never be linked at all. In "The Serengeti Lion" package on the National Geographic website, for example, no links were included to a series of posts in the magazine's online "Field Test" section, which take readers behind the scenes of the lions project ("Assignment of a Lifetime" 2011). Even if the parts are linked at the time they are created, later archiving or changes in site structure or software might delink them. When connections between parts of a story are not clear, or the connection is lost, the potential for the story as a whole to enhance readers' understanding is diminished.

Best Practices

Multimedia packages require navigation structures that give users access to the context of the broader story and make it easy for them to understand what options exist in the story, no matter where they land. The case studies discussed in the next section illustrate a "single page" approach in which multimedia elements are embedded inline with story text, not floated alongside or linked out from it. Where links are used, journalists should consider whether links between two or more parts of a story provide a sufficiently strong connection. Will the links persist if the story is archived, if the structure of the website changes, if new software replaces the current system? Journalists cannot leave the mechanics of linking to chance. They must take responsibility for making sure parts and pieces of stories are not delinked. If newsroom systems make delinking likely (e.g., because of a story archiving process), journalists need to press the issue with management, arguing for preserving the integrity of the complete story.

Best Practices in Action: Two Examples

Now take a look at two recent examples of multimedia storytelling and consider whether best practices were employed in producing them.

"NSA Files: Decoded" (MacAskill and Dance 2013) published by *The Guardian* on November 1, 2013, presents both opinions and facts about what the documents leaked by Edward Snowden reveal about the US National Security Agency, and what it all means to the average person. *The Guardian* (and other news organizations) started publishing news stories based on the leaked documents in June 2013, but this multimedia package is different. The journalists set out to make a very complicated story not only easy to understand—but also fun (Cage and Dance 2013).

Starting with that idea, the team designed the package. This was before the writing, before shooting the videos, before deciding which information graphics would be produced. Then the journalists began to outline "all of the NSA revelations to date," breaking the large story down into topics with bullet points. Examining the outline, they next "decided where interactives/video/text/GIFs/ whatever would work best to tell that bit of the story" (Cage and Dance 2013). They chose the media type that would be used based on the nature of the information they wanted to convey.

After shooting several of the video interviews and working on several interactive graphics for the package, the journalists revised the package design (but not the outline). Originally, videos and graphics were going to be on the side, with the text making a column in the center. In the new design, the videos and graphics and text are equally central, and the reader/viewer simply moves straight down the story, consuming all media types in a line without breaks or detours. Text was written and added "when appropriate." This represents a big departure from the way many multimedia stories are constructed. The short embedded videos in "NSA Files: Decoded" do not repeat other content in the package; the information voiced in them is integral to the story and not available as text. "We want them to talk directly to our readers, because we wanted this to be like an intimate conversation between our readers and the experts," said Gabriel Dance, one of the two journalists with a byline on the package. Each video is an unedited single take (Ellis 2013).

The package was produced in about three months. The planning and design process enabled various journalists to work on different pieces of the package simultaneously, with each interactive graphic a separate unit that could be inserted into the whole when it was finished. "Ultimately, it was the workflow and the ability to treat elements as independent modules that was essential" (Cage and Dance 2013).

"Planet Money Makes a T-Shirt" (Planet Money 2013c) published by National Public Radio on December 2, 2013, tells a much more visual story than "NSA Files: Decoded," and it provides an example of a transmedia storytelling effort. In April 2013, the Planet Money team of journalists launched a Kickstarter campaign (Planet Money 2013a) to fund a reporting project about the global garment industry. People could pledge $25 to get a T-shirt, and Planet Money would report every step of that T-shirt's production, starting in the cotton fields of Mississippi. Backers put up $590,807. Ten reporters covered the story, some of them traveling to Indonesia, Bangladesh, and Colombia along with the cotton as it became cloth and, finally, 25,000 T-shirts.

Planet Money's radio segment on April 30, 2013, announced the project and the Kickstarter campaign, and the story was reported step by step in subsequent radio programs and podcasts (Planet Money 2013b). Text-only stories were also published on the Planet Money blog, and the project has its own photo-rich Tumblr (Planet Money, n.d.). The seven-month process culminated in a multimedia package combining video, text, and information graphics to tell the story of how people around the world all have a hand in producing one simple piece of clothing. Producer Alex Bumberg noted that the team "decided to be really brutal about the length. . . . [P]eople don't go to the web to watch a 20-minute documentary" (Kirkland 2013).

Best Practices

These two cases demonstrate an acknowledgment by the journalists that audiences don't have time for an encyclopedia-length story. Both cases use a fully integrated format, placing graphics and videos inline with text, that spares the users from jumping in and out of the story. In short, the stories made the readers' convenience and attention span their top priority. Stories that are smaller in scope or that allow less time for reporting can follow the same principles, integrating all media types and avoiding a mishmash of links and sidebars. Whatever the scale of the project, it is important to avoid redundant content and include only what is essential to telling the story.

Discussion Questions

1. Choose one segment from "NSA Files: Decoded" and one from "Planet Money Makes a T-Shirt" and look at how video, text, and information graphics are used in each of the two segments. How much redundancy or

repetition is there in the segment? What would be lost by removing any one of those three media types from the segment? How does the placement of the elements inline help the audience to get the full context of the story?

2. Examine the way links to previously published stories (in *The Guardian* and at the Planet Money blog) and to external sources are used in the two case studies. How does the use of links contribute to making these stories more complete?

3. Several of the information graphics in "NSA Files: Decoded" use either interactivity or animation. Examine the information graphics in "Planet Money Makes a T-Shirt," choose one, and describe how it could be made more engaging, or more fun, by using techniques you can identify in a specific graphic in "NSA Files: Decoded."

References

Ahearn, Meghan. 2013, August 21. "National Geographic Experiments with a New Form of Digital Storytelling." *Photo District News*. www.pdnonline.com/features/National-Geographic–8854.shtml

"Assignment of a Lifetime." 2011, December 1. *National Geographic*. http://ngm.national geographic.com/visions/field-test/nichols-serengeti/assignment

Boczkowski, Pablo J. 2004. "The Processes of Adopting Multimedia and Interactivity in Three Online Newsrooms." *Journal of Communication* 54(2):197–213. doi:10.1111/j.1460-;2466.2004.tb02624.x

Bostock, Mike, and Shan Carter. 2012, November 7. "Over the Decades, How States Have Shifted." *The New York Times*. www.nytimes.com/interactive/2012/10/15/us/politics/swing-history.html

Branch, John. 2012, December 20. "Snow Fall: The Avalanche at Tunnel Creek." *The New York Times*. www.nytimes.com/projects/2012/snow-fall/

Cage, Feilding, and Gabriel Dance. 2013. "How We Made 'NSA Files: Decoded.'" *Source*. http://source.opennews.org/en-US/articles/how-we-made-nsa-files-decoded/

Chung, Deborah S. 2008. "Interactive Features of Online Newspapers: Identifying Patterns and Predicting Use of Engaged Readers." *Journal of Computer-Mediated Communication* 13(3):658–79. doi:10.1111/j.1083-;6101.2008.00414.x

Chung, Deborah S., and Chan Yun Yoo. 2008. "Audience Motivations for Using Interactive Features: Distinguishing Use of Different Types of Interactivity on an Online Newspaper." *Mass Communication and Society* 11(4):375–97. doi:10.1080/15205430701791048

Cohen, Noam. 2009, December 5. "In Animated Videos, News and Guesswork Mix." *The New York Times*. www.nytimes.com/2009/12/06/business/media/06animate.html

Deuze, Mark. 2004. "What Is Multimedia Journalism?" *Journalism Studies* 5(2):139–52. doi:10.1080/1461670042000211131

Digital First Video. 2013, June 27. "How Civil War Soldiers Fought in the Battle of Gettysburg." www.youtube.com/watch?v=Gxg8fgIxm3w

Duenes, Steve, Erin Kissane, Andrew Kueneman, Jacky Myint, Graham Roberts, and Catherine Spangler. 2013. "How We Made 'Snow Fall': A Q&A with the New York Times Team." *Source*. http://source.mozillaopennews.org/en-US/articles/how-we-made-snow-fall/

Ellis, Justin. 2013. "Q&A: The Guardian's Gabriel Dance on New Tools for Story and Cultivating Interactive Journalism." *Nieman Journalism Lab*. www.niemanlab.org/2013/11/qa-the-guardians-gabriel-dance-on-new-tools-for-story-and-cultivating-interactive-journalism/

Erdal, Ivar John. 2011. "Coming to Terms with Convergence Journalism: Cross-Media as a Theoretical and Analytical Concept." *Convergence: The International Journal of Research into New Media Technologies* 17(2):213–23. doi:10.1177/1354856510397109

Florit, Gabriel, Alvin Chang, and Chiqui Esteban. 2013, April 15. "How the Boston Marathon Bombings Unfolded." *The Boston Globe*. www.bostonglobe.com/2013/04/15/explosionreports/0gpSHeDd0JDbSw6P4irqXM/story.html

Jacobson, Susan. 2012. "Transcoding the News: An Investigation into Multimedia Journalism Published on Nytimes.com 2000–2008." *New Media & Society* 14(5):867–85. doi:10.1177/1461444811431864

Jenkins, Henry. 2006. *Convergence Culture: Where Old and New Media Collide*. New York: New York University Press.

Kennedy, Tom (visual journalism consultant, Washington, DC, area). 2013. Telephone interview with the author. September 19, 2013.

Kirkland, Sam. 2013, December 3. "How NPR's Planet Money Spun an Interactive Yarn about Making T-shirts." *Poynter*. www.poynter.org/latest-news/media-lab/232069/how-nprs-planet-money-spun-an-interactive-yarn-about-making-t-shirts/

Kobré, Kenneth. 2008. *Photojournalism: The Professionals' Approach*. 6th ed. Burlington, MA: Focal Press/Elsevier.

MacAskill, Ewen, and Gabriel Dance. 2013, November 1. "NSA Files: Decoded." *The Guardian*. www.theguardian.com/world/interactive/2013/nov/01/snowden-nsa-files-surveillance-revelations-decoded

Maierson, Eric. 2013a, June 25. "I Hate 'Multimedia.'" *MediaStorm* blog. http://mediastorm.com/blog/2013/06/25/i-hate-multimedia/

Maierson, Eric. 2013b, January 8. "The Challenge of The American-Made Benny." *MediaStorm* blog. http://mediastorm.com/blog/2013/01/08/the-challenge-of-the-american-made-benny/

McAdams, Mindy. 2005. *Flash Journalism: How to Create Multimedia News Packages*. Burlington, MA: Focal Press/Elsevier.

McAdams, Mindy. 2013. "10 Examples of Bespoke Article Design and Scrolling Goodness." *Teaching Online Journalism* blog. http://mindymcadams.com/tojou/2013/10-examples-of-bespoke-article-design-and-scrolling-goodness/

MediaStorm. n.d. "We Create Cinematic Narratives." http://mediastorm.com/about

Morris, Errol. 2008, April 3. "Play It Again, Sam (Re-enactments, Part One)." *The New York Times*. http://opinionator.blogs.nytimes.com/2008/04/03/play-it-again-sam-re-enactments-part-one/

Nichols, Michael, and Nathan Williamson. 2013, August. "The Serengeti Lion." *National Geographic*. http://ngm.nationalgeographic.com/serengeti-lion/index.html

Opgenhaffen, Michael, and Leen d'Haenens. 2012. "Heterogeneity within Homogeneity: Impact of Online Skills on the Use of Online News Media and Interactive News Features." *Communications: The European Journal of Communication Research* 37(3):297–316.

Planet Money. 2013a, April 30. "Planet Money T-shirt." *Kickstarter*. www.kickstarter.com/projects/planetmoney/planet-money-t-shirt

Planet Money. 2013b, April 30. "Episode 455: The Planet Money T-Shirt Is Finally (Almost) Here." *National Public Radio*. www.npr.org/blogs/money/2013/04/30/180079862/episode-455-the-planet-money-t-shirt-is-finally-almost-here

Planet Money. 2013c, December 2. "Planet Money Makes a T-Shirt." *National Public Radio.* http://apps.npr.org/tshirt/

Planet Money. n.d. Tumblr. http://seedtoshirt.tumblr.com/

Romenesko, Jim. 2012, December 27. "More Than 3.5 Million Page Views for New York Times' 'Snow Fall' Feature." http://jimromenesko.com/2012/12/27/more-than-3–5-million-page-views-for-nyts-snow-fall/

Simpson, Kevin. 2013, October 11. "Chasing the Beast: The TWISTEX Crew's Route." *The Denver Post.* http://extras.denverpost.com/stormchaser/map.html

Storm, Brian (founder and executive producer, MediaStorm, New York). 2013. Telephone interview with the author. September 13, 2013.

Stray, Jonathan. 2011, October 5. "What's with This Programmer-Journalist Identity Crisis?" http://jonathanstray.com/whats-with-this-programmer-journalist-identity-crisis

Stromer-Galley, Jennifer. 2004. "Interactivity-as-Product and Interactivity-as-Process." *The Information Society* 20(5):391–94. doi:10.1080/01972240490508081

Tomlin, Robyn (editor, Thunderdome, Digital First Media, New York). 2013. Telephone interview with the author. September 19, 2013.

Veglis, Andreas. 2012. "From Cross Media to Transmedia Reporting in Newspaper Articles." *Publishing Research Quarterly* 28(4):313–24. doi:10.1007/s12109-;012-;9294-z

Wei, Sisi. 2013, September 25. "Your Guide to Creating Compelling Newsgames." *PBS MediaShift.* www.pbs.org/mediashift/2013/09/your-guide-to-creating-compelling-newsgames/

Weinberger, David. 2002. *Small Pieces Loosely Joined: A Unified Theory of the Web.* New York: Perseus.

Williams, Paige. 2014, January 7. "The Future of Digital Longform, Part 1: 'Snow Fall' (yep, that again—worth it) + poetry + how we read." *Nieman Storyboard.* www.niemanstoryboard.org/2014/01/07/the-future-of-digital-longform-part-1-snow-fall-yep-that-again-worth-it-poetry-how-we-read/

Willnat, Lars, David H. Weaver, and Jihyang Choi. 2013. "The Global Journalist in the Twenty-First Century." *Journalism Practice* 7(2):163–83. doi:10.1080/17512786.2012.753210

15

DATA JOURNALISM

Paul Bradshaw

BIRMINGHAM CITY UNIVERSITY AND CITY UNIVERSITY LONDON, UK

Much of data journalism practice is invisible to the news consumer. From filtering through large amounts of data to find interesting leads, to industrial-scale information gathering through techniques such as "scraping"; from the storage and leaking of large amounts of data using digital storage media, to having access to data about consumers of news and information services, new ethical questions are raised at each stage.

New forms of information as a result of increasing digitization raise further questions: the resulting range of potential sources is wide, and widening:

> Your career history, 300,000 confidential documents, who knows who in your circle of friends can all be (and are) described with just two numbers: zeroes, and ones. Photos, video and audio are all described with the same two numbers: zeroes and ones. Murders, disease, political votes, corruption and lies: zeroes and ones.
>
> (Bradshaw 2012)

More visible data journalism practices involve methods of production such as automation of processes (and the consequent loss of editorial oversight); networked and interdisciplinary modes of collaboration; global publication; an increased reliance on visual communication; and new forms of user-driven storytelling using interactivity and/or personalization.

Novel practices bring up new conflicts between ethical principles: for example, between the need to balance *proactive* principles such as seeking truth and accuracy, with *restraining* principles including privacy and protecting sources, and accountability. And it is worth noting that all of these techniques have risen to prominence in an information environment which itself raises new ethical concerns about the role of journalists when the gatekeeping role gives way to a role of reacting to a proliferation of information access and subsequent claims to "truth."

While data journalism can be defined in a variety of ways as a *process*, an *output*, or a set of *skills* (see Hirst 2013; Bradshaw 2012), the study of ethics is typically concerned with *practice*. For that reason this chapter shall focus on the new practices adopted as part of the spread of "data journalism": the decisions that we make as journalists around how we gather information, what information we choose to publish, and how.

Accuracy

Probably the most basic ethical consideration in data journalism is the need to be accurate, and provide proper context to the stories that we tell. That can influence how we analyze the data, report on data stories, or our publication of the data itself. In late 2012, for example, data journalist Nils Mulvad finally got his hands on veterinary prescriptions data that he had been fighting for seven years. But he decided not to publish the data when he realized that it was full of errors. "Publishing it directly would have meant identifying specific doctors for doing bad things which they hadn't done. So we only used the data to point us to possible bad examples from which to start the journalistic research and verify information" (Nils Mulvan, personal communication, July 2013).

Similarly, when Mulvad approached school leaders about data released by the Danish Ministry of Education, it turned out grades had been miscalculated. Getting a response on data before publishing is a vital step in checking its accuracy, and the more independent the responding party, the better.

US data journalist Dan Nguyen draws a parallel with traditional journalism processes on this:

> In traditional journalism we spend significant resources "lawyering" every name and associated assertion in a controversial story . . . and for those names that we don't lawyer, we just leave them out of the story. That's a tradeoff that probably applies in some way when it involves a bulk list of names.
> (Personal correspondence, October 2013)

Sometimes, however, the size or nature of the data makes verifying every row impossible, but there is still an ethical imperative to publish the data in order to "hold it to account." In those cases, Mulvad illustrates how he weighs up competing ethical principles:

> We need to judge if publication is more important than protecting individuals for potential errors in them by the authority which has provided them. We decided in [a story about European Union farm subsidies] that, in the absence of alternative methods, it was more important to display the

data as a way to investigate who received the money, and for what, after some general cleaning and checking. If someone then asks to be removed from the database we do it in very few cases where there is evidence that they need to hide their address or something like that.

(Personal correspondence)

Where possible errors are highlighted, Mulvad says, they contact the authorities responsible and inquire about the possibility of it being corrected.

In some cases the errors are so serious that the data should be withdrawn completely, as the *Texas Tribune* decided when it began receiving complaints about information in its prisoner database, which incorrectly showed some offenders as having been convicted of a different crime, sexually assaulting a child. "My husband couldn't understand why people were taunting him and calling him a child molester," a woman named Lori Wallace Wilson said.

[We] analyzed the information associated with other prisoners . . . and discovered that there were more than 300 inmates who, like Wilson, had been assigned [crime codes] by the agency that corresponded with aggravated sexual assault of a child—even though the description of their actual offenses included no reference to a minor. Initially, we decided simply to remove those codes from our site for those offenders. But then we learned offenders with other types of convictions were also being coded incorrectly [by the Texas Department of Criminal Justice].

(Grissom 2013)

What is important in this case is not just the principle of accuracy. Because the inaccurate data was official data, ethical principles of serving the public good in highlighting the inaccuracies need to be considered. Further investigation confirmed that the codes were not double-checked for accuracy by public officials, and as a result of reporting this, the Texas Department of Criminal Justice decided to review the records of the inmates with incorrectly entered data.

Gathering and Reporting Data

When it comes to gathering data, guidance on political polls provide a useful precedent. The BBC's guidelines, for example, specify that when commissioning polls "the methodology and the data, as well as the accuracy of the language, must stand up to the most searching public scrutiny" (BBC 2013b). In reporting polls, the importance of context is emphasized, including identifying the organization that conducted the poll, the questions, method and sample size, and the broader trend of all polls or a particular pollster. Language should "say polls 'suggest' and 'indicate', but never 'prove' or 'show' " (BBC 2013b) and "draw attention to events which may have had a significant effect on public opinion since it was done." Doubts about sources should be reflected in reporting, or in the decision to report on a poll at all.

Reporting the margin of error is particularly important: this is the range within which the "true" figures are likely to sit. The principle does not just apply to voting polls: in 2011 the BBC headlined a story "UK Unemployment Total on the Rise" (BBC 2011), but should have mentioned that the "rise" was well within the margin of error, meaning that the true figure could have actually meant no change, or even a drop in joblessness. GDP figures are similarly problematic, subject as they are to significant revision: former *New York Times* data journalist Nate Silver (2012) notes that in the US the margin of error on the initial quarterly estimate of GDP is plus or minus 4.3 percent but this is rarely reported.

Context Is King

Adding context is a vital part of the data journalism process: absolute figures must be put into the context of the size of the local population, historical patterns, and even differing demographics. Trends must be checked against changes in boundaries or data collection and classification methods. Data visualization needs to be equally clear: charts and tables, for example, should generally have a baseline of zero to avoid misrepresenting changes as being more severe than they are, and timescales should be chosen to represent long-term trends rather than misrepresenting by starting or selecting from an all-time low or high.

Clarity can also be undermined by optical illusions created by the way we interpret shapes and lines. For example: in a bubble chart or node diagram two circles which are the same size will look different if one is surrounded by smaller circles and the other by bigger ones (see Fung 2012 and Skau 2013). Journalists using data need to also be careful not to make false comparisons. Reporter Mike Stucka, for example, talks about a story where school test scores included scores from a private mental hospital (personal correspondence, July 2013).

Personalization and Interactivity

New forms of storytelling involving interactivity and personalization present a challenge for providing context: if we hand over some control to the users, how do we ensure they receive that contextual information? Does a calculator that tells the users they are better off because of the latest budget announcement lead them to believe that it is a "good budget"? The answer is that wider context must be embedded or integrated at the point when it is needed. (Mindy McAdams's chapter discusses the importance of context in multimedia storytelling.)

Personalization also raises issues around the collection of user data. In the creation of its budget calculator, for example, the BBC's Features team made sure that calculations using user-inputted data such as earnings were performed by the user's computer ("client-side"), not on BBC servers ("server-side").

Surveys and Skepticism

In data journalism surveys can be either a potential source of "easy data" or of public service fact checking. Survey-based journalism is particularly vulnerable to misrepresentation, especially when results are published without skepticism (Davies 2009; Goldacre 2009). Goldacre, for example, writes about a BBC article which reported "Six in 10 people support a new power station at Hinkley in Somerset" (BBC 2010). The story was based on a survey carried out for the energy company EDF and the question generating those results was preceded by a series of "set-up" questions on the creation of local jobs and leading statements (Goldacre 2010).

The BBC's guidance (2013b) recommends "appropriate skepticism" should be exercised when reporting the results of surveys and that "a description of the methodology used" should be included where necessary, including the numbers of respondents; "percentages should only be used with caution and when contextualized." Consequently it is important that the journalist dealing with surveys always request access to the original data, including all the questions asked. If that information is not forthcoming, then the truth of the claims cannot be established and the journalist will need to take the decision not to publish. If the survey is already in the public domain, however, the ethical decision then concerns whether the journalist should report on the resistance to publish more details or data, and criticisms about the methods used.

Skepticism is also required when gathering data yourself through surveys or "crowdsourcing" (a process of inviting public involvement in data gathering). Depending on how results might be used, your system may need a check on unusual patterns of behavior which may suggest people are "gaming" the system; or a "second check" mechanism where some submissions are vetted by other users; or even require some proof to be submitted alongside the data. One project which crowdsourced water prices, for example, asked users to also submit a scan of their bill. "While it might have put off some, it increased the credibility of the data," notes Nicolas KayserBril (2012).

More broadly, journalists should adhere to the ethical principle of transparency in attributing sources (Friend and Singer 2007) and linking to the full data where possible, with the exceptions detailed above and in the section on protecting sources below.

Predictions

Predictions are one type of data where the conflict between the principle of accuracy and minimizing harm comes to the fore. Silver, in his book *The Signal and the Noise* (2012), explains how the publication of predictions can be both self-fulfilling or self-cancelling, as well as dangerous to publicize:

> If you can't make a good prediction, it is very often harmful to pretend that you can. I suspect that epidemiologists, and others in the medical community, understand this because of their adherence to the Hippocratic oath. *Primum non nocere*: First, do no harm.
>
> (Silver 2012, 230).

Journalists should be especially wary when other predictions do not indicate the same thing, as can happen in political voting intention polls (Silver implies that Rick Santorum's lead in a single poll in the 2012 US primaries may have led voters to switch allegiance).

Hacks/Hackers: Collaboration and the Clash of Codes

Journalism's increasingly collaborative and global nature in a networked environment has raised a number of ethical issues as contributors from different countries and from professions outside of journalism with different codes of ethics come together. This collaborative spirit is most visible in the "Hacks/Hackers" movement, where journalists meet with web developers to exchange tips and ideas, and work on joint projects. Data journalists also often take part in and organize "hack days" or "hackathons" aimed at opening up and linking data and creating apps, or work with external agencies to analyze data gathered by either party.

This can lead to culture clashes around differing ethical principles. In his seminal volume *Hackers: Heroes of the Computer Revolution* (1984), for example, Steven Levy outlines normative values that hackers should adhere to, most relevantly: sharing, openness, decentralization, and improving the world. Journalists not adhering to these values, for example, those who do not share their data or who are not open about the processes involved in acquiring or analyzing it could find themselves accused of unethical behavior by their collaborators.

In these cases it is important to be aware of different parties' ethical assumptions and clear about the journalist's role. For example, in the collaborations between Wikileaks and various news organizations, *The Guardian*, along with *The New York Times* and *Der Spiegel*, wanted to retain a gatekeeping role and "wanted to make sure that we didn't reveal the names of informants or unnecessarily endanger NATO troops" (Rogers 2012). However, the very structured nature of the data still allowed them to make most of it available by simply removing the fields that could identify individuals:

> We wanted to make it simpler to access key information, out there in the real world—as clear and open as we could make it . . . we [allowed] our users

to download a spreadsheet containing the records of every incident where somebody died, nearly 60,000 in all [but] removed the summary field so it was just the basic data: the military heading, numbers of deaths and the geographic breakdown . . . we couldn't be sure the summary field didn't contain confidential details of informants and so on.

(Rogers 2012)

In the end, however, a journalist did perform a role in leaking the complete data that served as a lesson in protecting sources. In his book on Wikileaks (Leigh and Harding 2011), *Guardian* journalist David Leigh included a password of Assange's which turned out to be "the full pass-phrase to WikiLeaks' copy of the encrypted, unredacted cables."

To Leigh, the PGP password might have seemed like a harmless historical detail . . . He later said that Assange had told him the password was defunct [but to Assange] and any other hacker, revealing a password represented a glaring security breach. Those familiar with PGP know that when a file is encrypted to a particular key, the key will always open a copy of that encrypted file and thus can never be revealed. Secret keys remain secret for life.

(Greenberg 2012)

Privacy

Another example where ethical codes sometimes differ between occupations and countries is in privacy. The Farm Subsidy investigation into recipients of EU farm subsidies is a particularly good example of this. The investigation was a collaboration between journalists in different countries with differing concepts of "personal data." They used those countries' access to information laws to identify individuals receiving multimillion-euro subsidies (Vaglenov and Balabanova 2010), before a judgment of the Court of Justice of the European Union limited publication on the basis of protecting personal privacy (Zijlstra 2011). The judgment is illustrative of the ethical tensions involved:

The Council and the Commission had to look for methods of publishing information that might also obtain the objective of transparency, but not have the same impact on the privacy of the beneficiaries involved. This could include limiting the publication by name of the beneficiaries according to the periods for which they received aid rather than maintaining it for 2 years. As the Council and the Commission did not consider such measures, the provisions . . . were considered invalid insofar as they imposed an obligation to publish personal data relating to each beneficiary without drawing a distinction based on relevant criteria such as the periods during which those persons have received such aid, the frequency of such aid or the nature and amount thereof.

In the UK there already exists guidance on when a similarly "private" piece of data—salaries—should be disclosed (Department of Finance and Personnel 2014). The guidance identifies "a legitimate public interest" in general pay bands of "more senior staff who are responsible for major policy and financial initiatives" but not junior staff with little power or influence. It acknowledges: "There could be factors that weigh in favour of greater disclosure, such as legitimate concerns about corruption or mismanagement, or situations in which senior staff set their own or others' pay." That seems a sensible guideline to adopt in publishing (more recent judgments have also recommended disclosing specific remuneration).

In the US personal data is more accessible, but that does not mean its publication does not create ethical issues. Following a mass shooting in Connecticut, the *Journal News* in New York decided to publish an interactive map of pistol permit holders in the area, based on Freedom of Information requests. The map led to a backlash from readers and calls for a boycott of the paper (Culver 2013).

Kathleen Culver notes that the publication could have considered the ethical issues more carefully. The ethical principle of "minimizing harm," for example, was not served by making it easy for criminals to identify which homes did not have a pistol (or at least a license for one) and were therefore less well defended or conversely, which ones had a gun they might steal. The principle of accuracy may have been ignored by publishing data which was out of date, and the principle of context was overlooked in not comparing the license ownership to anything else (such as gun use, or patterns of ownership). Culver suggests the map should not have identified individuals but rather aggregated totals, allowing the map to still serve the public interest while avoiding the attendant risks (Culver 2013).

A similar example is *Tampa Bay Mug Shots*, which pulls a feed from police websites of people charged with a crime. Nora Paul, the director of the Institute for New Media Studies at the University of Minnesota, felt the site's lack of context meant it "borders on journalistic malpractice" (Milian, 2009), although some precautions were taken "so that the data do not haunt the alleged criminals forever." "Every listing is hidden after 60 days from booking, and the developers have taken technical precautions to ensure that Google's search engine won't crawl and index the pages." Lower on the page it also clarifies that "Those appearing here have not been convicted of the arrest charge and are presumed innocent. Do not rely on this site to determine any person's actual criminal record."

Even anonymized data can reveal private information. When the *Kansas City Star* analyzed a health care practitioner's database and combined it with other records, it found 21 doctors with multiple malpractice payments that had never been disciplined. "[The reporter] had performed broad research of courts, state agencies and hospital actions, 'allowing them to connect the dots' to individual doctors. But he said the federal database itself did not reveal identities" (Wilson 2011). Once again, the judgment is between public interest and individual privacy. In this case there was a clear case, in the absence of action, for disclosure.

Sophie Hood describes the change brought about by the digitization of public records as

> The difference between the practical obscurity of a paper record versus the ubiquity of an electronic record . . . The information is the same, but it is radically altered by the novel ways in which it flows. When documents are published online, there is more access but there is also more susceptibility for error . . . what is at stake is different—dramatically so.
>
> (Kinstler 2013)

In a paper with Helen Nissenbaum, she returns to the importance of context:

> Instead of characterizing privacy as control over personal information, or as the limitation of access to information, [contextual integrity] characterizes privacy as conformance with appropriate flows of information, in turn modeled by the theoretical construct of context-relative (or context-specific) informational norms. When information is captured or disseminated in ways that violate informational norms, privacy as contextual integrity is violated.
>
> (Kinstler 2013)

Identification does not always take place in the published data. A story in the UK's *Birmingham Mail* based on spending data headlined "City Council Spends Nearly £1m on Bed and Breakfast Rooms for Birmingham's Homeless" (Gibbons 2013) not only named Smithy's Hotel as one recipient, but also led the story with prominent photographs of two hotels identified by the data, even though the data itself was not published.

Given the vulnerability of groups staying in these hotels, it might be asked whether the impact of publishing such details was justified. In this case, although the identities of recipients added concrete detail, it was not essential to the story, which was about the body spending the money. Having an internal list of groups considered to be vulnerable might assist in making quick decisions in the newsroom in similar situations.

A similar example comes from an investigation into Olympic torchbearers. The author received an anonymous tip-off that two daughters of one sponsor's chief executive had been given Olympic torchbearer places. This did indeed turn out to be the case, but as one of the daughters was under 16, the decision was taken not to name the executive because it would identify his daughter.

User Data

Journalists sometimes look for stories in data on the users of their site. In one particularly high-profile example, a journalist at the financial news service Bloomberg noticed that one of the users of the service had not logged in for some time. He picked up the phone and asked the person's employer Goldman Sachs if the person had left the company. The question led to a complaint from Goldman Sachs and a growing scandal about journalists' use of data on 300,000 users of Bloomberg services.

"Bloomberg staffers could determine not only which of its employees had logged into Bloomberg's proprietary terminals but how many times they had used particular functions," reported the *New York Post* (DeCambre, 2013). Spokesperson Ty Trippet pointed out that the data did not include "security-level data, position data, trading data or messages," but it did include the behavior of fellow workers and bosses (Seward 2013), and the controversy was significant enough to lead the company to announce that journalists would no longer have access to client login activity, and to review its internal standards.

Mass Data Gathering—Scraping, FOI, Deception, and Harm

The data journalism practice of "scraping"—getting a computer to capture information from online sources—raises some ethical issues around deception and minimization of harm. Some scrapers, for example, "pretend" to be a particular web browser, or pace their scraping activity more slowly to avoid detection. But the deception is practiced on another computer, not a human, so is it deception at all? And if the "victim" is a computer, is there harm?

The tension here is between the ethics of virtue ("I do not deceive") and teleological ethics (good or bad impact of actions). A scraper might include a small element of deception, but the act of scraping (as distinct from publishing the resulting information) harms no human. Most journalists can live with that. The exception is where a scraper makes such excessive demands on a site that it impairs that site's performance (because it is repetitively requesting so many pages in a small space of time). This not only negatively impacts on the experience of users of the site, but consequently the site's publishers too (in many cases sites will block sources of heavy demand, breaking the scraper anyway).

Although the harm may be justified against a wider "public good," it is unnecessary: a well-designed scraper should not make such excessive demands, nor should it draw attention to itself by doing so. The person writing such a scraper should ensure that it does not run more often than is necessary, or that it runs more slowly to spread the demands on the site being scraped. Notably in this regard, *ProPublica*'s scraping project, Upton, "helps you be a good citizen [by avoiding] hitting the site you're scraping with requests that are unnecessary because you've already downloaded a certain page" (Merrill 2013).

Attempts to minimize that load can itself generate ethical concerns. The creator of seminal data journalism projects ChicagoCrime.org and Everyblock, Adrian Holovaty, addresses some of these in his series on "Sane Data Updates" and urges being upfront about

> which parts of the data might be out of date, how often it's updated, which bits of the data are updated . . . and any other peculiarities about your process . . . Any application that repurposes data from another source has an obligation to explain how it gets the data . . . The more transparent you are about it, the better.
>
> (Holovaty 2013)

Publishing scraped data in full does raise legal issues around the copyright and database rights surrounding that information. The journalist should decide whether the story can be told accurately without publishing the full data.

Issues raised by scraping can also be applied to analogous methods using simple email technology, such as the mass generation of Freedom of Information requests. Sending the same FOI request to dozens or hundreds of authorities results in a significant pressure on, and cost to, public authorities, so the public interest of the question must justify that, rather than its value as a story alone. Journalists must also check the information is not accessible through other means before embarking on a mass email.

Protection of Sources

Many news organizations' professional guidelines include sections on protecting sources. In some countries this is also enshrined in law. Many journalists, however, are not aware of how they can betray sources' identity by publishing original files online. Metadata stored in those files, information about the date and location of access, the computers and accounts used, and other data, can be used to identify a leaker. Even photocopied or printed materials can bear invisible digital watermarks which describe what machines were used to produce them, and when (Reimer 2005; PicMarkr 2008).

Journalists should, therefore, avoid publishing original source material online where the identity of the source is not known. For the same reason, journalists should avoid providing such material to public authorities, and exercise caution around storing such files online in cloud-based services which may be subject to interception by security services or legal pressure.

In some cases lack of cooperation with public authorities may also represent a form of virtue ethics in asserting the independence of the journalist or news organization. The International Consortium of Investigative Journalists (ICIJ), for example, resisted sharing the results of its investigation into offshore banking with government agencies (Ryle 2013; Guevara 2013) because: "The ICIJ is not an arm of law enforcement and is not an agent of the government. We are an independent reporting organization, served by and serving our members, the global investigative journalism community and the public." This is particularly interesting given the international nature of the organization, where local claims on duty (deontological ethics) might be weaker than in a national or local news organization (see, for example, White 2008).

Leaks and "War"

"Most people would accept restrictions on war reporting to prevent information reaching the enemy which would endanger military operations," writes Karen Sanders in *Ethics & Journalism* (2003). The ethical principle in play here is of minimizing harm, but, as Sandler points out: "Avoiding harm to UK nationals may involve causing harm to Afghan citizens."

Dealing with "mega leaks" that relate to the military or national security raises similar issues. When war is constant and the enemy ill-defined, as is the case in the "war on terror," balancing "public interest" against possible harm is particularly difficult. Intelligence strategist George Friedman notes of Edward Snowden, for example, that: "[He] is charged with aiding an enemy that has never been legally designated. Anyone who might contemplate terrorism is therefore an enemy" (Friedman 2013).

Publishers might ask whether "warlogs" containing historical about deaths in Iraq and Afghanistan weakened the security of US, UK, or German military operations. But there is an equal consideration to be given to the ethics of not publishing, as Sandler adds:

> The difficulty arises when *failure* to report something would cause unjust harm to someone else and at the same time its publication would prejudice others. [In] cases where harm to the national interest cannot be proven, there must be a strong presumption in favour of openness and transparency to safeguard honest and effective government.

This, of course, is the discussion taking place around Edward Snowden's leaks about the surveillance of internet traffic by US, UK, and other government agencies. Australian academic Ben O'Neill's assessment of Snowden's actions quotes legal scholar George Strong on the enforceability of contracts that: ". . . an illegal contract is one that is unenforceable as a matter of policy because enforcement would be injurious to the best interest of the public" (O'Neill 2013a). On the matter of database property rights he adds:

When a private firm commits a crime using its own property as an instrument of wrongdoing it loses the right to claim ownership as a safeguard against investigation . . . The same applies to documentary evidence of a crime—it may legitimately be taken by an investigator as a means of proving criminal wrongdoing . . .

Government claims to ownership have no special status in this regard, and do not override these ordinary principles of property rights. In fact, the situation for government claims of ownership is even weaker than for a private enterprise, since the latter will generally have acquired the tools of its criminal dealings with its own money.

(O'Neill 2013b)

Automation and Feeds

Since Adrian Holovaty built ChicagoCrime.org in 2005 to automatically update a map with police crime statistics, automation has been an important element of data journalism. Few news organizations have guidelines on automation, but the BBC's guidelines (2013a) on *video* feeds do provide a framework. The guidelines state that a senior editorial figure must approve the feed first, and that he or she "should aim to maintain editorial control." The stated objective is to protect "editorial independence and reduce the risk of intrusive, harmful, offensive or unduly promotional images appearing on our site" and in line with that the guidance recommends monitoring the output of the feed. "The level of monitoring should be appropriate for the content of the camera. A producer should normally be in a position to cut the feed from a live webcam if it becomes necessary."

In the same sense, then, it might be argued that re-publishers of data feeds should be in a position to halt them if it also becomes necessary.

The New Information Environment

Perhaps the final ethical dilemma facing journalists in dealing with data is its sheer volume and public availability. In this new context, where journalists no longer act as gatekeepers, there may be a new ethical claim to increase the time devoted to fact-checking and increasing public literacy around data. Predictions, for example, can be retrospectively tested, as *The New York Times* did with "Budget Forecasts, Compared with Reality" (Cox 2010). Editorial space in print, online, or on air can be devoted to unpicking statistical spin, opening up datasets to public scrutiny, and publicizing key changes affecting context, such as decisions to reclassify terms such as *poverty*, or to change an authority's boundaries.

Data itself is increasingly the "power" to be held to account, with journalists investigating its flaws, uses and abuses, and giving a voice to the data which is "voiceless." In fashioning guidelines for your own data journalism practice, then, consider the following checklist:

1. How do we ensure that reporting on data is accurate? What processes should be routine in seeking clarification?
2. How do we put data into context? Is data always reported in relative terms (i.e., per person), and alongside historical trends? Do we check how the data was gathered?
3. What are the considerations to be made when publishing data in full, or when automating publication of data?
4. What are the considerations to be made when obtaining data?
5. In collaborative projects do we ensure that all parties are clear on shared ethics, values, and roles?
6. And finally: how do we ensure we choose the most important data which may require more work to obtain rather than simply the most available?

Best Practices in Action: Paying for Data

While many US guidelines say that journalists should "never" pay for source material (*The New York Times* 2005; Reuters 2012, 15), in other countries more judgment is exercised. In the UK, for example, MPs' expenses data was offered for sale to a number of newspapers before being bought by the *Telegraph* newspaper. In this case the arguments in favor of payment were as follows:

*   Unlike the US, there is no financial compensation for "whistleblowers" in the UK. The source had been advised that it needed to protect against possible loss of livelihood as a result of leaking the information.
*   The material was not available through other means. In fact, the "unredacted" data was being leaked precisely because the source believed that the level of redaction meant that the public version of the data would lack key information which was in the public interest.

In this case the ethical decision involved balancing the public interest of disclosure against the principle of not paying sources (Winnet and Rayner 2009). Other ethical considerations included (financial) protection of sources or "minimizing harm."

The principle of not paying sources exists for a number of reasons. *The New York Times'* guidelines (2005), for example, explain that paying for source material "would create an incentive for sources to falsify material and would cast into doubt the genuineness of much that we publish." Similarly, Bob Steele, former director of the ethics program at the Poynter Institute for Media Studies, told one reporter that: "The standard line is news organizations don't pay for information. The public perceives that the information is tainted by financial motives . . . They will discount the value of the information" (quoted in Heyboer 1999).

But data is a different type of information to the potentially embellished first-person tale. Steele admits that it is "a hard line to draw" between paying for tip-offs, images, and video, "a time-honored tradition," and exclusive interviews. "One of the distinctions is who is giving you the information, and are they a party to the story . . . or a casual observer?" (Heyboer 1999).

It might be argued that data is more akin to a tip-off than a story, which can be verified and indeed in this case was verified before payment was made. Does that then negate the objections around falsification and credibility? As is the case with many ethical dilemmas, different principles may conflict with each other.

Discussion Questions

Identify a case of paying sources for data and list the principles in play. For example:

- What are the "virtue ethics": the principles of behavior that you live out as a journalist? (e.g., independence, honesty)
- What are the "deontological ethics": the duties that might be upheld or violated, for example, privacy?
- What are the "teleological ethics": the harm caused, balanced against the resulting good?

Acknowledgments

The author would like to thank Katy Culver, Chris Keller, Maria del Mar Cabra Valero, Nils Mulvad, Dan Nguyen, Francis Irving, Yemisi Ogunleye, Iain Overton, Martin Rosenbaum, Martin Stabe, Mike Stucka, Julian Todd, and the NICARL community for their suggestions regarding this chapter.

References

BBC. 2010. "EDF Survey Shows Support for Hinkley Power Station." *BBC News: Somerset*, October 12, 2010. Accessed March 20, 2014. www.bbc.co.uk/news/uk-england-somerset-11521839

BBC. 2011. "UK Unemployment Total on the Rise." *BBC News—Business*, August 17, 20011. Accessed March 20, 2014. www.bbc.co.uk/news/business-14555264

BBC. 2013a. "Editorial Guidelines." Accessed July 16, 2013. www.bbc.co.uk/editorial guidelines/guidelines/

BBC. 2013b. "Guidelines: Section 10: Politics, Public Policy and Polls: Opinion Polls, Surveys and Votes." Accessed February 20, 2014. www.bbc.co.uk/editorialguidelines/page/guidelines-politics-practices-opinion/

Bradshaw, Paul. 2012. "What Is Data Journalism?" In *The Data Journalism Handbook*, edited by Jonathan Gray, Liliana Bounegru, and Lucy Chambers. Sebastopol, CA: O'Reilly Media. http://datajournalismhandbook.org/

Cox, Amanda. 2010. "Budget Forecasts, Compared with Reality." *The New York Times*, February 2, 2010. Accessed July 16, 2013. www.nytimes.com/interactive/2010/02/02/us/politics/20100201budgetporcupinegraphic.html?_r=0

Culver, Kathleen B. 2013. "Where the Journal News Went Wrong in Mapping Gun Owners." *MediaShift*, February 22, 2013. Accessed July 13, 2013. www.pbs.org/mediashift/2013/02/wherethejournalnewswentwronginmappinggunowners053

Davies, Nick. 2009. *Flat Earth News: An Award-winning Reporter Exposes Falsehood, Distortion and Propaganda in the Global Media*. London: Vintage Books.

DeCambre, Mark. 2013. "Goldman Outs Bloomberg Snoops." *New York Post*, May 9, 2013. Accessed July 12, 2013. http://m.nypost.com/p/news/business/goldman_outs_bloomberg_snoops_ed7SopzVLaO02p9foS7ncM

Department of Finance and Personnel (UK Government). 2014. "When Should Salaries Be Disclosed?" Accessed March 20, 2014. www.dfpni.gov.uk/_section_13_when_should_salaries_be_disclosed.pdf

Friedman, George. 2013. "Keeping the NSA in Perspective." *Stratfor Global Intelligence*, July 16, 2013. Accessed July 24, 2013. www.stratfor.com/weekly/keepingnsaperspective

Friend, Cecilia, and Jane B. Singer. 2007. *Online Journalism Ethics*. Armonk, NY: ME Sharpe.

Fung, Kaiser. 2012. "Insufficiency and Illusions." *Junk Charts*, September 12, 2012. Accessed July 16, 2012. http://junkcharts.typepad.com/junk_charts/2012/09/insufficiencyandillusions.html

Gibbons, Brett. 2013. "City Council Spends Nearly £1m on Bed and Breakfast Rooms for Birmingham's Homeless." *Birmingham Mail*, February 20, 2013. Accessed July 16, 2013. www.birminghammail.co.uk/news/localnews/citycouncilspendsnearly1m1330817

Goldacre, Ben. 2009. Bad Science. New York: Harper Perennial.

Goldacre, Ben. 2010. "Hello Madam, Would You Like Your Children to Be Unemployed." *Bad Science*, November 20, 2010. Accessed July 16, 2013. http://www.badscience.net/2010/11/hello-madam-would-you-like-your-children-to-be-unemployed/

Greenberg, Andy. 2012. *This Machine Kills Secrets*. New York: Dutton Adult.

Grissom, Brandi. 2013. "T-Squared: Why We Unpublished Our Prisoner Database." *Texas Tribune*, July 22, 2013. Accessed March 15, 2014. www.texastribune.org/2013/07/22/tdcj-data-errors/

Guevara, Marina W. 2013. "Council of the European Union Requests ICIJ Offshore Data." *ICIJ*, June 20, 2013. Accessed July 16, 2013. www.icij.org/blog/2013/06/councileuropeanunionrequestsicijoffshoredata

Heyboer, Kelly. 1999. "Paying for It." *American Journalism Review*, April 1999. Accessed July 24, 2013. www.ajr.org/Article.asp?id=461

Hirst, Tony. 2013. "Several Takes on Defining Data Journalism." *School of Data*, June 11, 2013. Accessed July 16, 2013. http://schoolofdata.org/2013/06/11/severaltakesondefiningdatajournalism/

Holovaty, Adrian. 2013. "Sane Data Updates Are Harder Than You Think." *Source*, March 2013. Accessed July 16, 2013. http://source.mozillaopennews.org/enUS/learning/sanedataupdatesareharderyouthink/

KayserBril, Nicolas. 2012. "Crowdsourcing the Price of Water." In *The Data Journalism Handbook*, edited by Jonathan Gray, Liliana Bounegru, and Lucy Chambers. Sebastopol, CA: O'Reilly Media. http://datajournalismhandbook.org/

Kinstler, Linda. 2013. "When Openness Backfires: Is There Room for More Gray Area in How Court Records Are Made Public?" *Nieman Journalism Lab*, July 19, 2013. Accessed August 2, 2013. www.niemanlab.org/2013/07/whenopennessbackfiresisthereroomfor moregrayareai nhowcourtrecordsaremadepublic/

Leigh, David, and Luke Harding. 2011. *Wikileaks: Inside Julian Assange's War on Secrecy*. New York: Guardian Books.

Levy, Steven. 1984. *Hackers: Heroes of the Computer Revolution*. Garden City, New York: Anchor Press/Doubleday.

Merrill, Jeremy B. 2013. "Upton: A Web Scraping Framework." *The ProPublica Nerd Blog*, July 22, 2013. Accessed July 24, 2013. www.propublica.org/nerds/item/uptonaweb scrapingframework

Milian, Mark. 2009. "Tampa Bay Mug Shot Site Draws Ethical Questions." *Los Angeles Times*, April 10, 2009. Accessed July 17, 2013. http://latimesblogs.latimes.com/technology/ 2009/04/mugshots.html

New York Times. 2005. "The New York Times Company Policy on Ethics in Journalism." Accessed July 24, 2013. www.nytco.com/companypropertiestimescoe.html

O'Neill, Ben. 2013a. "The Ethics of Whistleblowing." *Ludwig von Mises Institute*, July 8, 2013. Accessed July 16, 2013. http://mises.org/daily/6474/TheEthicsofWhistleblowing

O'Neill, Ben. 2013b. "The Ethics of State Secrecy." *Ludwig von Mises Institute*, July 9, 2013. Accessed July 22, 2013. http://mises.org/daily/6475/TheEthicsofStateSecrecy

PicMarkr. 2008. "What Is Digital Watermarking?" Accessed July 14, 2013. http:// picmarkrpro.com/watermarking/

Reimer, Jeremy. 2005. "EFF Decodes Secret Color Laser Printer Spy Markings." *Ars Technica*, October 18, 2005. Accessed July 14, 2013. http://arstechnica.com/uncategorized/ 2005/10/54472/

Reuters. 2012. *Handbook of Journalism*. February 16, 2012. Accessed July 24, 2013. http:// handbook.reuters.com/extensions/docs/pdf/handbookofjournalism.pdf

Rogers, Simon. 2012. "Wikileaks in the News." In *The Data Journalism Handbook*, edited by Jonathan Gray, Liliana Bounegru, and Lucy Chambers. Sebastopol, CA: O'Reilly Media. http://datajournalismhandbook.org/

Ryle, Gerard. 2013. "Why We Are Not Turning over the Offshore Files to Government Agencies." *ICIJ*, April 5, 2013. Accessed July 13, 2013. www.icij.org/blog/2013/04/ whywewillnotturnoveroffshorefilesgovernmentagencies

Sanders, Karen. 2003. *Ethics & Journalism*. Los Angeles: Sage.

Seward, Zachary M. 2013. "Bloomberg's Culture Is All about Omniscience, Down to the Last Keystroke." *Quartz*. Accessed July 13, 2013. http://qz.com/83862/bloom bergcultureisallaboutomnisciencedowntothelastkeystroke/

Silver, Nate. 2012. *The Signal and the Noise: Why So Many Predictions Fail—but Some Don't*. New York: Penguin.

Skau, Drew. 2013. "Illusions in Data Visualization." *Visual.ly*, March 2013. Accessed July 15, 2013. http://blog.visual.ly/illusionsindatavisualization/

Vaglenov, Stanimir, and Tsvetana Balabanova. 2010. "A Family Affair—Transparency in Farm Subsidies Triggers Criminal Investigation." *EU Transparency.org*, September 16, 2010. Accessed July 16, 2013. http://eutransparency.org/afamilyaffair/

White, Aidan. 2008. *To Tell You the Truth*. The Ethical Journalism Initiative. Accessed July 24, 2013. http://ethicaljournalisminitiative.org/pdfs/EJI_book_en.pdf

Wilson, Duff. 2011. "Withdrawal of Database on Doctors Is Protested." *The New York Times*, September 15, 2011. Accessed July 19, 2013. www.nytimes.com/2011/09/16/health/16doctor.html?_r=1&

Winnet, Robert, and Gordon Rayner. 2009. *No Expenses Spared*. London: Bantam Press.

Zijlstra, Ton. 2011. "ECJ Rules on Farm Subsidy Case: Privacy." *European Public Sector Information Platform*, July 16, 2011. Accessed July 16, 2013. http://epsiplatform.eu/content/ecjrulesfarmsubsidycaseprivacy

CONTRIBUTORS

Paul Bradshaw runs the MA program in Online Journalism at Birmingham City University and is a Visiting Professor in Online Journalism at City University London. He also runs Help Me Investigate, an award-winning platform for collaborative investigative journalism. He is an author of a number of books and book chapters about online journalism and the Internet, including *The Online Journalism Handbook* and *Scraping for Journalists*.

Lily Canter is a journalist, lecturer, and journalism studies researcher at Sheffield Hallam University in the United Kingdom, and also works freelance as a print and online journalist. She is festival chair and co-founder of the short film festival Film Northants.

David Craig is a Professor and Associate Dean at the Gaylord College of Journalism and Mass Communication at the University of Oklahoma in the United States. He is the author of *Excellence in Online Journalism: Exploring Current Practices in an Evolving Environment* and *The Ethics of the Story: Using Narrative Techniques Responsibly in Journalism*.

Tim Currie is a Professor of Journalism at University of King's College in Halifax, Canada, where he teaches online journalism, digital media skills, and reporting techniques. He is co-editor of *The New Journalist: Roles, Skills, and Critical Thinking* (2010), and has authored social media guidelines for the Canadian Association of Journalists.

Juliette De Maeyer is an Assistant Professor in the Department of Communications at the Université de Montréal in Canada. In 2013 she was awarded her PhD from the Université Libre de Bruxelles focused on how the hyperlink shapes the dynamics of online news production.

David Domingo is Chair of Journalism at the Department of Information and Communication Sciences at Université Libre de Bruxelles (Brussels). Previously, he was Visiting Assistant Professor at University of Iowa and Senior Lecturer at Universitat Rovira i Virgili. His research focuses on the evolution of the professional identity and practices of journalism. He is a co-author of *Participatory Journalism: Guarding Open Gates at Online Newspapers* and a co-editor of *Making Online News*.

Kelly Fincham is an Assistant Professor in the Department of Journalism, Media Studies and Public Relations at Hofstra University in New York, where she teaches advanced online journalism in the undergraduate and graduate programs. Her research explores the intersection of social media in journalism practice and curriculum.

Ansgard Heinrich is an Assistant Professor of Journalism Studies and Media at the University of Groningen in The Netherlands. Before commencing her academic career, she worked as a freelance journalist in her native Germany. She received her PhD from the University of Otago, New Zealand, in 2008 and is the author of *Network Journalism: Journalistic Practice in Interactive Spheres*.

Alfred Hermida is an Associate Professor of Journalism at the Graduate School of Journalism of the University of British Columbia in Vancouver, Canada. He is a 16-year veteran of the BBC, where he was a foreign correspondent and the founding news editor of the BBC News website in 1997. He is the author of *Tell Everyone: How the Stories We Share Shape What We Know and Why It Matters*, which is published by Doubleday Canada.

Jonathan Hewett is a Senior Lecturer in International Journalism at City University in London. He has extensive experience both as a journalist and as a journalism educator, having led and taught on courses since 1997.

Fiona Martin is an Australian Research Council Discovery Early Career Research Award fellow and a Senior Lecturer in Convergent and Online Media at the University of Sydney in Australia. She has been a media educator for 15 years, following extensive experience as a radio producer and journalist with the Australian Broadcasting Corporation, as well as work in print, online, and cross-media journalism.

Mindy McAdams is a Professor of Journalism at the University of Florida, where she teaches courses about digital journalism. Her book *Flash Journalism: How to*

Create Multimedia News Packages was published by Focal Press/Elsevier in 2005. She has trained more than 200 journalists in multimedia skills, and has worked for a number of print outlets, including *The Washington Post* and *Time* magazine.

Neil Thurman is Senior Lecturer in Journalism at City University in London. He has worked professionally with interactive media since the early 1990s and has published extensively about online journalism.

Stephen J. A. Ward is Professor and Director of the George S. Turnbull Center in Portland, of the University of Oregon. He is the author of the award-winning *The Invention of Journalism Ethics*, *Ethics and the Media*, and *Global Journalism Ethics*. He is founding chair of the Ethics Advisory Committee of the Canadian Association of Journalists. He was a reporter, war correspondent, and newsroom manager for 14 years.

Lawrie Zion is an Associate Professor of Journalism at La Trobe University in Melbourne, Australia. He has worked as a broadcaster with the Australian Broadcasting Corporation and as a film journalist for a range of print publications. He wrote, researched, and co-produced the 2007 documentary *The Sounds of Aus*, which tells the story of the Australian accent.

INDEX

DATE DUE

PRINTED IN U.S.A.

CPSIA information can be obtain
Printed in the USA
BVOW08s0158050615

403301BV00007B/65/P

9 780415 858854